SantoSaint

SantoSaint

God and the Devil's Playground

Santos J. Hernandez Jr.

RESOURCE *Publications* · Eugene, Oregon

SANTOSAINT
God and the Devil's Playground

Resource Publications
An Imprint of Wipf and Stock Publishers
199 W. 8th Ave., Suite 3
Eugene, OR 97401

www.wipfandstock.com

PAPERBACK ISBN: 978-1-6667-7242-5
HARDCOVER ISBN: 978-1-6667-7243-2
EBOOK ISBN: 978-1-6667-7244-9

VERSION NUMBER 10/09/23

God always be praised, because without Him there is nothing.

Obedience is the fruit of love, and our actions
are the choices between good and evil.

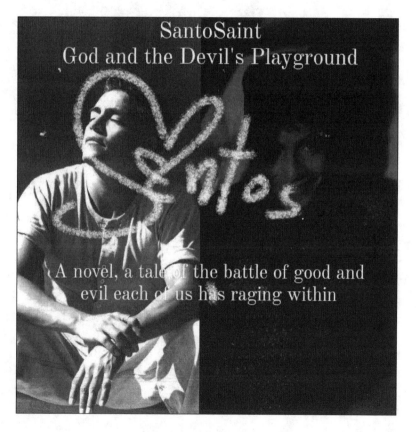

Photographer: Warren Mark Casler

Lost in a Label

A label for you
A label for me

A label for anyone
A label for anybody

A label for everyone
A label for everybody

A label for someone
A label for somebody

A label for this
A label for that

Another label
Hoarding many a label

Because one label
Is not enough

To label
The Self

In our own
Personal fable

Chapter 1

The grogginess is wearing off, and I hear someone in the room. I can't move and I feel like I just got hit by a Mack truck right in the chest from inside and outside my body. Everything suddenly rushed back to me, but I'm still not completely aware of where I am and what happened. There is someone next to me but doesn't seem concerned that I am here and waking up. I can't move, and I can feel that my mouth is open and something, something shoved deep into me that is preventing me from swallowing. My skin feels tight and hot. I can't open my eyes. I'm trying to remember the last thing I was doing, or where I was last, it was foggy but clearing up. It smells like stale sweat and dried blood; I'm in a daze like a dream you can't wake up from, while you try with all your might. I can sense a body right next to me as I lay there immobile. What is the person up to? What does this person want? I try with all my might and my eyes start to flutter, I can see light and something coming into view.

Everything hurts, my body aches with a pain I've never felt before. What is this, where am I? I try to swallow again, and I realize that I can't, and I start to gag as I feel I'm drowning with my saliva. My throat screams with pain and I can feel whatever is in my mouth slithering all the way down, passing my larynx, all the way down, and feeling like it goes into my stomach. I try so hard to remember, but I've been drugged, and it is no drug I've ever taken on my own. It doesn't feel like any trip or bad trip I've ever been on with any drugs I've used before. My eyelids start to open finally, just a slit and even that is painful. As my vision starts to sharpen, I notice the bright light and I start to see some things come into focus. I try with all my might to open them a little wider, but I can't, so I concentrate all my efforts focusing on what is in my view.

I see windows with blinds open and people working on the other side as they sit at computers. I notice the room where I am laying is dark and I'm in a bed lying flat on my back and I see things coming into focus. As everything becomes clearer, I instantly realize what happened before I ended up here in this dark room, smelling of some type of sanitizer or disinfectant, as well as dried blood and stale sweat so pungent before. Things were coming back to me. Mixed with the pungent, tequila or vodka-like smell. Oh, that brings back memories, but I digress. There was also the crisp clean air rushing into my nostrils with such a force that it seemed to hit the dark corners of my sinus cavity. There was nothing I could do about it because I felt so heavy, and I could not move. I was in extreme pain as I lay there trying to get my wits about me, was I in danger? Is this a dream, I wondered. Suddenly it all hit me like someone flipped a switch and I instantly became aware. I became frightened, somewhat indignant but calm and reassured. Immediately I thought, 'Shit! I'm still here.'

I lost track of time and did not know how long I had been in this room. The last thing I remember was talking to Dr. Oszczakiewicz, yep, I thought the same thing the first time I heard his name 'I'm not going to be able to pronounce that' but luckily, he shortened it to Dr. Oz when he introduced himself. I met him in a bright white, extremely clean, and cold operating room, but not my operating room. I was in happy land because I was still feeling the drugs they used earlier when they struggled to stabilize me. "Don't worry, you will have new plumbing when this is all over and you will feel like new again" he said after introducing himself. He had a very comforting voice and had a handsome, kind face. You could tell that he was in his element and was comfortable as well as confident. I guess you must be getting to do what he was about to do to me. His pleasurable demeanor and confidence put me at ease, which I was thankful for since I recently suffered a bad anxiety attack prior to the procedure that perpetuated the situation I currently found myself in. The drugs helped but I was very aware and coherent as to what was happening, and all the people that were standing around us and I lay there wondering if I would ever see the cover of my first published book, one of my greatest achievements so far at this point. That is saying a lot since I have had many unique experiences in my short life. I didn't start living until I was about 21 when I joined the Army just because my best friend joined, and I needed money for college. I said 'Doc, if you can, do whatever you have to so that I can live because my very first book has been published and will be released in a few weeks and I would like to go on a book tour". He let out a good-hearted laugh and everyone else in that room laughed as well. That made me feel good, that under such trying circumstances, I was still able to make people laugh. I enjoy making people laugh and it brought a smile to my heart that I could make light of a situation where I was facing death in the face and daring it to take me because I knew it did not have a stake on my soul. That belongs to God. That's when he told me about the new plumbing, and he returned the favor and made me laugh as well as everyone else. We would get along just fine, I thought.

As my vision came into focus and everything came back to me, I realized at once that I was still alive. I was just coming out of anesthesia and coming out too slowly, but I knew this was not a dream because I never felt pain in any dream I had ever dreamt. I had felt sadness, fear, panic, love, joy, peace, but never pain. The new plumbing Dr. Oz was talking about were the new veins being taken from my leg and attaching them to my heart to bypass those that had built up so much plaque as to deprive my heart of essential blood and oxygen. They could no longer keep my organs supplied sufficiently to keep me alive. I started to panic after realizing that I had survived surgery and then remembered what one of the nurses told me just as they started wheeling me out of the bright white room, "If you don't remember anything else, remember not to pull out the tube in your throat when you wake up". I remembered, but I was still starting to freak out and then I remembered that someone was in the room with me. Right next to me, I sensed someone there so I mustered up all the strength I could and without moving anything but my arm I tapped this person standing right next to my bed. I felt my forearm connect with the person's leg, and as this person started to speak, I realized that it was a man. He said "Mr. Hernandez your surgery went well, and you are in ICU, my name is Madison, and I will be taking care of you tonight. I am changing your IV right now, I'm almost finished." I tried to speak, and all I felt was the abrasiveness of the tube rubbing the inside of my throat like someone rubbing sandpaper against my tonsils. My mind knew exactly what I wanted to tell him, but all I heard was a gargling, raspy noise almost like the sound a vacuum makes when sucking up water. "Mr. Hernandez do not try to talk," said Madison. "You cannot talk with that tube, so don't try to talk." I was freaking out; my anxiety was about possessing me in a way that I would not be able to control it. I knew that I must find a way to communicate with him, otherwise, I may not survive the recovery. I tapped Madison's leg again with a little more urgency and pointed to my mouth. He must have known exactly what I was motioning for, because he said, "Do you need me to suction the saliva out of your mouth?" I gave him an enthusiastic thumbs up. I had tried to swallow but I had never had something forced into my mouth before and remained there without me having some type of control over it, so this was very foreign and extremely uncomfortable. Madison grabbed something and started suctioning out all the saliva that had been building up. I instantly felt relieved, and a strange thought entered my mind, 'How did this saliva not build up the entire time that I had been lying here before I woke up?' This made me realize that the body, when relaxed, was able to swallow some way so this encouraged me to think this through. I started to concentrate on letting my throat relax and swallow with the back of my throat while knowing that I had something in it. I really don't know how else to explain the technique I was using but it was working for me, and this helped calm my anxiety. Still on the verge of a full-blown anxiety attack but holding it at bay for now, buying me some time to figure out rather quickly how to communicate better with Madison. After he suctioned all the saliva out, I slowly raised my left arm as far as I could above my chest with the open palm of my hand facing toward the ceiling, and then with my right hand, I pointed with just my index finger to the open palm of my left hand and made looping motions like I was writing in cursive. Madison understood the motion at once and said, "Do you want something to write with?" Again, I gave him an enthusiastic thumbs up and I knew that I would be able to communicate with him soon. "I'll be right back Mr. Hernandez. I'm going to get you a tablet and something to write with."

The movement of raising my hands above my chest as far as I could and patting Madison's leg to get his attention had taken a lot of energy and I was exhausted. As I lay there in pain and feeling that an elephant was sitting on top of me, I reflected on my first thought when I realized I survived the open-heart surgery and was still alive, 'Shit, I'm still here." Even though that is the first thing that came to mind when I made that realization, I also was thankful to God. There was no pause after I had that thought of disappointment to what I said next, 'I'm sorry God, I didn't mean it the way I just said that (even though all this was happening in my mind) because I know that you have other plans. You know what is in my heart and you know that I was ready to go be with you, this world is getting really crazy." I continued with this apology. I told Him that I thought that I was in a particularly good place, and I didn't want to screw things up so much that it could prevent me from joining my parents with Him in heaven. I knew that I had a book hitting the market soon and that those who would grieve my death would be left with a piece of my heart to console them in their sadness at my abrupt departure from this world. I had put all my affairs in order and had just the month before written my will. Texas had locked down because of Covid-19, a pandemic with no cure and that was taking lives like a thief steals as much as they can, whenever they can, no matter who is involved. It was May 14, 2020, before any vaccine, or medication to combat it. The world was going crazy, and it seemed like the end of the world, the entire world was shutting down and so many were dying alone and laying in ICU with tubes down their throats just like me, except that I had survived because it was just clogged plumbing and Dr. Oz had taken care of that problem. Now, with a new lease on life, I thanked and praised God. 'Since you kept me alive, God,

I know that you have plans for me and that you have not called me home. Please give me the strength, the courage, and the wisdom to figure out what Your will be for my life, and let me be open to receiving the direction of the Holy Spirit to find the path you want me to take. You know what is in my heart and You know that I didn't mean it the way it came out, but I was ready because like I said before . . . this world is going crazy.

Just as I was finishing up Madison came back with a writing pad and a pen, a Sharpie marker. I knew he was good because he knew that my entire body was swollen. My finger sausages needed the fatness of the marker, and it would be very difficult to write legibly. 'He is good,' I thought. I worked up some energy and I raised the tablet and since I couldn't lift my head, I had to situate the pad where I could somewhat make out the tablet. It was no use; I was going to have to write mostly blind to what I was writing because my vision wasn't 100%. My eyelids were still swollen, and I was looking through two slits like when I was standing in a foxhole in MOPP 4 when I was in the Army. For those who have never been in the military, MOPP 4 was full protective gear including a full-face mask when fighting on the battlefield where chemicals had been released. It was cumbersome, claustrophobic, with limited vision especially since I had lens inserts to be able to see far (nearsightedness).

Well, this felt like that and even worse because I was healthy back in my military days so there was no pain nor was, I swollen and felt like I was in a permanent bear hug from a giant bear. I really concentrated, 'I can do this' I thought, and I was determined to communicate, otherwise, I may not survive recovery and God had plans for me. So, I lifted the pad, and as best as I could I made sure the first letter was big and clear. It was an easy letter to write in three lines, I thought. I started with the first line, I wrote it at an angle like a slash from bottom to top, and without lifting the Sharpie, once I reached the top I came back down the other side at the opposite angle. After this, I angled the pad towards my face to make sure I got the third line right. I still couldn't see very clearly but I saw the pyramid shape of my two lines and then I took the Sharpie and connected the two lines with a horizontal line about the midpoint of the triangle. The first letter was done, it was an 'A'. I started on the second letter and then I had to rest my arms and put my arms down. Madison waited patiently. I wrote the third letter, just two lines crossing each other to make an 'X'. I wrote the fourth letter, a line with a dot at the top. I rested again. Madison was waiting patiently. Then I started hurrying so that Madison would not get impatient and leave because I was sure that he had more important things to do than waiting around for me to write one word. What I would learn later is that people like Madison who work in the ICU take a certain type of person with a real desire to help people. Since I didn't know this when I was writing, since Madison and I had just met, I hurried. The 5th, 6th, and 7th letters were written faster and I'm pretty certain a lot messier than the first letters with almost all my energy spent, I gave it all I had and finished it with an exclamation point and dropped my arms in complete exhaustion. Madison took the tablet and the Sharpie and read the word, "Anxiety!", he asked. I mustered just enough energy to give him a thumbs up without raising my hand too far just because I didn't have it in me. "I will be right back!", and I could tell the urgency in his voice. As I waited for him to come back, I concentrated on swallowing calmly, working on staying calm which was easy since I was exhausted. It didn't take long before Madison returned and I could sense him at my side again, "I am giving you something for the anxiety through your IV, you should feel it very soon.". Again, I gave him a thumbs up and as I drifted off to sleep, I was joyful that I was able to communicate with Madison and that I couldn't wait to find out what God had in store for me.

The desire and wanting to leave this hospital were all I could focus on, I was strong in the capable hands of some of the bravest people on the planet, those who care for us when we are sick and/or when we can't take care of ourselves. I overworked myself on this day and gave myself a fever with the hot, hot water I used to shower for the first time all by myself. It was one of the goals to get released. I was thrilled, everything was going well, thanks be to God, I thought, as I was distracted by the repairs to my house. Juan told me that he had reached out to Pasqual, the guy that did an awesome job at Juan's house and Gus had already started to tear out the old shower. That job was major, and I was put at ease with the way we were all focused on getting a loved one back on their feet after some major surprise like this one. This family has been through its share of hardships, but my mother and father were heroes, and angels, to us. Sure, there are times when after being punished for something (I knew better anyway, every single time, so the punishment was always just) . . . we all turned out alright. I told my mom one time, that for better or worse, they had raised leaders; this is why we don't really prefer to work together (although this always made my parents proud and happy) because no one wants to take orders from any of the others. We do, of course, and as we get older and wiser, we start to step around our brother's or sister's buttons.

As I was saying, they released me after I cooled off from that hot, hot shower. I even registered a temperature of 101. I was breathing heavily, and it's because I didn't figure out how to use the water faucet. I thought it was broken, and I wanted to complete this goal. It was after this that they told me I was released, they just had to let me get back to normal and finish up the paperwork. I asked for something for anxiety and pain, I don't like this type of medication, but I just had my chest cracked open (yeah, I know, but true) and my heart stopped while they worked on it. I'm assuming now, by what people told me. When Cynthia from respiratory at Baptist Hospital accompanied me on my walks down the hallways of that hospital wing, we sat as I rested, and this is when she mentioned that part of the procedure was to stop my heart while they worked on me. This is the reason I had those wires protruding out of lmy sternum, so they could jump-start my heart. That's funny but seriously crazy!

My sister Alicia drove up to give me a ride to Gus' house, where I was told that I would recuperate and that I had no choice in the matter. I was relieved that someone loved me so much as to take control in such a loving, but stern way. Plus, they were smart, they had started the much-needed work on my house. It was under construction. As the nurse rolled me down to the patient pick-up, I saw Alicia, this was the first time and first family member to see since I couldn't remember when, thanks to the pandemic. Yes sir, this emergency open heart surgery happens on May 13, 2020, right smack dab in the middle of a world shutdown where Covid-19 ran rampant throughout the world and the ICUs, even at Baptist, were full of Covid-19 patients. No one was allowed to visit or go with any pa-tients into the hospital. My only communication with everyone was by cell phone, social media, and telephone in the room. I wasn't alone, because of the nurses and everyone else who contributed to my recovery from the people that cleaned, to the phlebotomist, minister, doctors, x-ray techs, and everyone else. Still crazy how quiet the hospital was, not that I spent a lot of time in hospitals but towards the end with my mom, I am familiar with how noisy hospitals can be.

That night, when I met Gus and Toni in front of their house, I remem-ber getting anxious because all they gave me was Motrin 800mg, but this has never done anything for me. I remember when I twisted my ankle when I was in the Army, testing for my expert infantry badge, on the second to last task, a 12-mile road march, with a full rucksack. In the beginning mile of the walk, another soldier was coming up from behind on my right, so I naturally (because of the way I was raised) moved over to my left to make it easier for him, but what I didn't pay attention too, was the washed-out asphalt. Next thing I knew, I twisted my ankle, my rucksack shifted weight and instead of taking the load off that ankle, I twisted it again! Ah, the pain! I feel it right now . . . anyway, it swelled up so much I couldn't get my shoe on for the Military Ball at Fort Polk in Louisiana to honor those of us who be-came expert infantrymen. A handful of soldiers, during a generally peaceful time, earned the right to wear this rifle on their chest to live up to the call of the Infantry, 'Follow Me'. All they prescribed me then was Motrin and it didn't do jack for me, and I understand we are all different and drugs affect us differently at times. I get that. So, since I was used to the pain meds I was getting in the hospital and someone who knew what I meant about I need something because this doesn't work for me, something only a fellow soldier can understand, she understood and prescribed I don't even remember what. I just know that it allowed the pain to subside enough to allow me to go to sleep because there was a lot of pain but not unbearable. Only when I coughed, laughed, and sneezed, that I would hug my heart pillow against my chest and over my heart. Keep everything together, you know? No, most of you don't know, consider yourself fortunate.

On the seventh day of this life-changing event, I was released from the hospital. My brother Gus, short for Gustavo and named after a Mexican President, along with the eldest of the bunch . . . Alicia, they made certain that I could not stay at my house, what was my Mother's house, built after hurricane Harvey after our old house was extensively damaged and through a FEMA grant my father decided to have a new house built. My best friend Juan contacted Pasqual, the contractor that had repaired his house, to begin repairing my mom's house. This prevented me from moving back in, which sounds crazy that I would even consider it. Gus gave me no choice, as he said, "Jr. I'm not asking you to stay with us, I'm telling you that you are staying with us." There was no arguing, I was deeply moved and grateful for his brotherly concern and love for me. He is the baby of the family and was the one who expressed his love physically and verbally when he was young and was the conduit God used to help our family express the love, we felt for each other both physically and verbally. He would hug and kiss Mom and Dad goodnight, and I would follow suit. We would race to take Dad's boots off when he came home from work, which only love would do because Dad's socks were soaking wet with sweat, but I don't remember a repugnant odor. Dad was a welder at Bethlehem Steel in Beaumont, TX. He became a welder in his early 40's because he was wise and knew that he could provide a better life for his family being a welder. He was born and raised in Asherton, TX, just like Mom. They had been migrant farmers, following the crop yield up north to places like Hereford, TX, and around Victoria, TX to the south. This is when they weren't working in the fields in Asherton. My father, Santos, was well-known for his speed in sewing the costales (sacks) they would pack the onions in. Asherton, or that area of Texas is said to have been, at one time, the yellow onion capital of the world. I guess because there once was a railway and it became one of the largest shipping points of that Yellow Bermuda onion. The town was so small but hit 2000 but never grew any bigger especially when the railway was re-diverted due to political give and take. My mom would tell me stories of how they would be so sleepy in the early morning hours that they would eat chili peppers to stay awake. The land is so flat there that the wind can get to running pretty fast, whipping itself through every crook and cranny of what is there, but it will not be stopped. Hehe, I'm just thinking about the Holy Spirit and why Jesus used the wind as an example.

Right down the street from Asherton, about a 20-minute drive East on US-83 for 16.75 miles you run into the big bag of the fastest growing and viable 3rd political party: La Raza Unida established on January 10, 1970. Asherton or those only that have roots in Asherton identify better with its nickname (or official for those who have a stake in it, and roots) Cheto. There was a white side and the barrio de San Luis, the Plazita, the cemetery, a little gem of a farming community raising their kids and dealing with the hardships and treasures as they came. Like in every small rural town, it was three thousand strong and once even hit four thousand. Lately, it has been a hotspot now of the oil and gas industry. I remember a dream Pop shared with me about standing on the edge of the bank of an expanse like an ocean, but it was pitch black, he told me this as he and I were driving around Cheto, as everyone likes to do when you visit the town you come from. I loved those drives and visiting my mom and dad's friends and our relatives. Gus, was always 'El que nació allá.' Meaning he was the only one of all of us children who was born in Beaumont, TX, the city Pop settled in with the family. The climate was quite different between the two, but Pop knew that education would bring a better and higher standard of living. Both were ridiculously hot; one was just wetter than the other. Beaumont was and still is greener than Cheto, but Beaumont didn't have the watermelons that grew around Cheto. The watermelon capital, Dilly TX, where the watermelon grew just fine in the 100° dry heat and was one of our stops going to and coming from Cheto. When we were kids and went back to visit, usually in the summer and Christmas, I remember we would come back with onions, carrots, and watermelon plus some great memories. Also, some stories, stories of the family secrets behind closed doors and those stories of old memories and some old and true gossip that never hides or shouts, just whispers and motions and starts conversation with 'You know what?' or a demure 'Did you know?' but by far my favorite, 'What had happened was . . . '

The night skies in Cheto were blankets of twinkling stars that filled the universe as it lay on top of you as it descended to meet the aromatic scents of fresh dew on the sunbaked dirt. The sky is big, and no buildings or light destroys the beauty of a night sky. This was my favorite part of going back to Cheto, besides the family and trips around town, especially to Raul's where we always gave him one of our school pictures that he would display in the candy case. It was one of the very first adventures me and Gus would try to get into. Oh, I remember the smell was like nothing I've ever smelled since.

The smell of love, hope, and freedom. It was only about two blocks, but it was different to be grown enough to walk a couple of blocks in a tiny town as familiar but with distant family and friends. I would save my allowance because in Beaumont, I go to the little store to buy a Coke, or Crush soda and a candy bar, like a Hershey Bar to dip into peanut butter when I would get home. I would try to save up even if we went to Quick Check too many times, but I also knew that 'Buelo would give us a couple of dollars, I just found out a few years ago that he would give Gus and my favorite cousin (yep, I said it, but I love you all) Aricelda a fortune $5.00. But like I said there were stories behind the stories, behind the curtain, and buried in the cemetery. That was another stop, every time we visited. Mom and Pop would always pay their respects to our ancestors and recently departed family and friends because life happens. Both Mom's dad, Gregorio Ramon, and Pop's dad, Julian Hernandez, died at 35 and 36. Mom's twin, who I think was a stillborn, was buried there as well but we had long lost the location of her gravesite. Mom told me once that at first someone would take her to visit the grave of her twin sister but she couldn't remember when the visits stopped or where, only that it was at the base of a big tree. Mom also had a small brother who lived until the age of 3, Jesus Ramon, but he got sick and passed away. When I asked Mom one time, she told me that all she remembered was that they were away following the crops, and 'Buela and 'Buelo went into the hospital with her little brother and when they returned, they left, and Jesus wasn't with them. No one ever talked about it again.

Pop would tell stories, maybe not to everybody as I am beginning to understand. This may come as some big news to some, but hopefully, it awakens a memory long buried that one of my siblings, aunts, or uncles will remember. This also goes to the story I'm trying to tell. A love story. There are so many love stories by so many people, places, or things. I'm not trying to rehash a love story, or even create the best story of all. I simply want to tell you a love story about how someone can get things so wrong but that one love, that one everything, that one who you would give your life for, that one that you want to be a better person for, that one that fills you with so much joy and love that no matter if they hurt you, you would still do it all over again with them together forever. That one, who knows you better than you know yourself, that one that can put a smile on your face even when life had just closed-fist punched you right in the middle of your face. That one! In my dad's life that was God, Mom, and us, the kids. Alicia, the oldest, Julian, Cruz, Veronica (Betty), me, and Gus. Pop would tell me stories about the prayers he would pray to God when Mom came close to dying because of a gallbladder infection when Julian had meningitis and many others. He told all his kids and grandkids pretty much the same stories, even though I do this nowadays and some of my friends are starting to call me on it. Anyway, Pop told me one time that he had heard some stories about his dad, that he had a black book. He said this black book had names in it and that he may have been part of the black mafia. Just like the mafia they also dabbled in black magic. I remember after telling me this that he commented that he was afraid that he would have to pay for the sins of his father. He never spoke about it again, and I don't know if he only told me once or twice, but it stuck with me. I was probably around 12 or 13. Both my mom and dad lost their parents incredibly young so I'm sure they could comfort each other knowing they had someone in this world that they could completely trust and lean on through anything. Julio told me that they had an altar up towards the middle of the wall in a corner. I guess my need for some type of alter comes from my mom. I can't remember, but Pop told me a little more than this when he spoke about it, but I can't remember any more than he didn't know what the names were for, and how he came to find out about the book. There were also stories about 'Luchusas' those with bodies of owls and heads of a human who whistle through the night waiting for someone to whistle back, and they consider this an invitation.

The Notion of Life

At the end of the tunnel, I see a light, instead of walking straight for it, I climb the walls. A more difficult feat, unnecessary, and a waste of time, but I climb anyway.

The light breaking through this suffocating darkness tingles and beckons me to run into it. I choose to keep climbing the walls, inching my way forward . . . backward, sideways, up, and down. I kept my eyes on that prize, that light on the other side.

It's getting darker and harder to breathe, and the light is fading and further than I first thought. I'm stuck upside-down and clowning around with bad luck.

I steal a breath of fresh air from the secret lair of my heart, and I hear the light's voice. It is singing to me melodies of hope and encouragement with a chorus of come to me, and a series of notes saying I love you.

My heart pulls me upright and off the walls; I stand upright and reach for the light. I still have a long way to go, but it is darker and harder to breathe. I listen to joke after joke, and they are all about me.

I run in place and am unable to keep this pace, so I sit down and weep. Black shadows break through the walls, and they are grabbing for me, trying to rip me apart. It is the start of fear breaking my heart.

My nightmare ensures that I lose my place in the light as I start to crawl backward, and away from the light. Wrapped in uncertainty, I stop and start sinking into the darkness suffocating me. A thought enters . . . you will never be free.

My heart screams for help, but I hear nothing. I go silent. I detect a whisper I cannot hear. I listen. The whisper raises its voice and becomes thunder in my heart. I tiptoe towards the start of something new that I already knew.

The light, once too far, is now touching my heart and lifting me. Filling me up with a new start. It creates a map of a straight path leading me to it, and I can start to feel it, live it, and believe it.

All warm and tingly, shiny and new, my heart jumps with joy. Skipping to the beat the light has planted in my heart; I ignore the darkness all around me wanting to steal my heart. Once more I am floating towards the light now shining bright, like a new star.

This is the cycle I am destined to repeat until one day I reach that light at the end of my life or when I decide that strife is only the distraction and destruction of the notion of life.

Chapter 2

This tale begins in my 1976 school year when I was only ten years old. It starts here because this is where the Holy Spirit made me aware that this is when satan first seized on the opportunity to lead me down a path of self-destruction, while disguising his attack as a coming-of-age rite of passage. At this time, I would like to offer a disclaimer, because I feel it is necessary to first make the bold statement that there is a devil who goes by plenty of names and has been given plenty of names. There are also Angels and demons, and this is not only my belief, but they can be found throughout Scripture. It amazes me to this day that even those who speak of Christ Jesus and God will be completely uncomfortable in believing that demons exist or that even satan exists. I guess people will continue to pick and choose what they desire to believe even while being completely aware and even students of Scripture. Nonetheless, this story will include all of it. To make this story more interesting, I have given characters names that do not necessarily reflect their real names or any names that have been given to them in Scripture. While this is a tale of God's love story, it is the tale I am telling that will hopefully get beyond the argument of 'Do they exist' to one of 'Damn, I know this character' and the tale will undoubtedly take on a life of its own.

Up until this day in my 1976 school year, I was a happy-go-lucky, shy, little boy. Scrawny and smart, cute, and loveable. I was mindful and respectful, caring, and carefree. This would all eventually change, but as we tend to find out late in life if we are so fortunate, the decisions we make around this tender age will be the basis or foundation of the hardships to come. Depending on what you read or what you study, there are many stages of life. This tale begins in my childhood and smack dab in the middle of puberty except that I was a late bloomer when it came to dating but an early discoverer of the little pleasures that come with exploring one's own body. In my spiritual life, I was conflicted and confused about what I was learning in the Church, and even with some of the more erotic stories in the Bible . . . it didn't make my learning of what God expected of me any easier. My family was no help in the matter because we did not speak of such things, much less share stories with my friends. I was too shy, and too introverted, so I internalized everything. I was reared in a traditional Catholic home, where my father worked, and my mother cared for the children and the home. I knew nothing of brokenness or scandals, abuse, or being a victim. I was just a happy kid with the world ahead of me. As you will come to know in the next few chapters, Mel (my guardian Angel) is assigned to be my protector in the spiritual sense, and I am experiencing my first temptation of pride. I'm not doing so well at resisting it because I'm only ten years old and I am being tempted by Charo who has been around since the dawn of Creation—not a fair fight at all but don't worry about the ten-year-old, he is pretty resilient, but what happens in the next couple of decades would almost destroy him.

Kids are everywhere, and I know most of them because we have been going to the same school since first grade. All of us tried to get to our classrooms before the tardy bell started ringing while trying to say hi to our friends but no time to stop because Mr. Busby was not a class you wanted to arrive late. I hurried passed all the kids, giving a smile and a tilt of the chin to those friends not close enough to hear the hello. I climbed up the large staircase to the second floor and slid into my seat with no time to chat with those around me. I did not like to talk in class, I was a kid who followed all the rules and while not by choice became some teacher's pet. I did not know what it was about me that attracted attention and drew people towards me, but I felt invisible anyway like I was just visiting. I guess, looking back, I have always felt this way. Like, I am just visiting, and I do not have a home. This would help me later in life, but I was unaware of this in the fifth grade; I was just ten in 1976. What a time to be alive, my father had bought a brand-new white Dodge D100 with the shift on the column. My Dad would teach me how to drive in the parking lot of Parkdale Mall on Sundays when stores are closed. Yep, Sundays were holy days, and no stores were open except the 7-11. My Mom started dropping me and my brother off at school after lining us up in the morning at the kitchen sink to comb our hair. She would run the comb under the stream of cold running water and grab my chin and comb my hair and off to school we would go and even though our elementary school was only about four blocks away, I enjoyed the ride to school.

At home, my mom would play rancheras, basically Mexican country songs, in the kitchen with the occasional Elvis. My Mom loved him so much that she kept a photo album filled with Elvis newspaper and magazine clippings. One day as I came home from school my Mom was crying, and I only saw my Mom cry like twice as a kid, I was really scared but when I found my Dad and asked him in a whisper why Mom was crying, he said "Es que murio Elvis", yes, we spoke Spanish at my home when we spoke to Mom and Dad. He told me that she was crying because Elvis had died. I felt sad for my mom because I never saw her cry, I did not understand why you could cry so much for someone you did not really know except through their music, but I respected her feelings and kept quiet and out of the way so that she could grieve properly. My dad, on the other hand, just chuckled when he told me why she was crying, I guess he did not understand either. Outside of the home and in my room, I was listening to ABBA, Elton John, KC, and the Sunshine band had released Shake, Shake, Shake and I remember how some songs like that could hit the airways because it said the word 'booty' in it. Shows like Charlie's Angels were amazing because it was three badass girls fighting and shooting guns and catching bad guys, all the while intrigued at how they could keep Charlie a secret from them and us. Some of my favorite shows on TV were more like Walton's Mountain where a serene life in a small mountain town always ended with everyone saying goodnight to each other from their corner of the house, and it really showed how a family sticks together and worked out problems together even while sometimes you thought you were on your own to figure things out.

As my mom pulled up to Fletcher Elementary School, I was excited about the day because I loved school. Not the social aspect of school, but the learning. I loved the learning, the reading, the math problems, the writing, the homework assignments, the tests, the lectures, I loved all of it. I was not much of a reader but for some reason, one of my favorite places was the library. Maybe because I loved the silence and was surrounded by adventure and history. The day was like all others except that I was more excited about the recess and the metal uneven climbing bars next to the swing set and monkey bars where we could play. Earlier this year I stumbled upon a secret so secret and sweet that I never told anyone about it and kept it a secret well into adulthood. I was like a drug addict, and it became something I enjoyed, I knew in my heart that there was something not right about this, something bad but I was paying no attention to that, it was only like something nagging me in the back of my mind or heart. I walked with a new spring in my step and waited for that recess break, the longer one after lunch where I could take my time. But right now, I had to go to class, and before the tardy bell rang throughout the school; trapping you in a moment in time. Our first real conformity to a standard and reinforced by a variety of punishments from those authorized to enforce conformity. It was after homeroom, first or second class that I realized that I had forgotten my homework for my English class which was right after lunch and fear gripped me for the first time I could remember in school. I never had a bad moment in school, but this was a disaster. I remember completing my homework last night, as I always did, my parents never had to tell me to do my homework because I loved schoolwork. How could I have forgotten my homework and it was not a class where I was the teacher's pet, it was Mr. Busby's class, and he was an enforcer with a paddle ritual. He would start the class by calling the role and he expected you to speak up loud enough so he could hear you and did not have to look up, just a quick way to get the roll call out of the way, I guess. After the roll call, he would collect homework, and then he would check to make sure everyone turned in their homework. He would start calling the names of those who did not turn in their homework one by one, and he would proceed to paddle those who did not turn in their homework. This was a terrible nightmare.

As soon as the bell rang, I hurried as fast as I could to the school office and explained my desperate situation and they allowed me to call home. My mom answered the phone and as I was trying to explain but made no sense my sister had stopped by to have lunch at the house. She worked a few blocks away in downtown Beaumont at the county courthouse so she would stop by my parent's house often and luckily this day was one of those days. She told me that she would drop off my homework after lunch and this was perfect because I did not have English class until after lunch and she always took an early lunch from 11 to 12. I was so relieved, and I forgot all about the unfortunate event and turned my attention to lunch and especially the playground which had all my attention now that I had resolved my homework problem. I don't remember much about my childhood, only bits and pieces and really no rhyme or reason for why some memories lingered while others disappeared. As I climbed the stairs to my English class, I was a carefree young boy with a full stomach and content that I spent time with my friends on the playground. So much to do, some of us played kickball, others showed their skills at marbles, tether ball, swing set, playing chase and there were always monkey bars and uneven bars. It was the uneven bars that I had an affinity to which also became a doorway to hell, not in any portal to different dimensions type, but what I did with them was the portal of which Charo and Riggs-G were able to convince me of an alternate universe of pleasure, excitement, and intrigue. My mood quickly changed the minute I crossed the doorway into my English class. My homework, oh yeah, my homework. Shit, I forgot about it until now, but I solved that problem so why am I so nervous and frightened, unsure? I sat down and my nerves took over, I felt myself trembling and it was summer, and I don't remember the school being air-conditioned like they are now. The sun was beaming through the windows, The classroom was on the second floor so you could catch a glimpse of the treetops and mostly the sky. I noticed Mr. Busby getting his black attendance record to call roll and simultaneously checking us as present or absent and whether we had turned in our homework. When I first walked into Mr. B's classroom, I didn't make eye contact as I was accustomed to doing because of my not handing him my homework. We had to put our homework on his desk as we entered the classroom but this day, I had nothing to place on his desk, so I just hurried past his desk and took my seat. We had tables with chairs around them, not individual desks, so we sat across from each other and there were four rectangular tables with about six students on a table. I didn't even say hi to anyone around me, I just took my seat and I think I started sweating a little or at least I know my palms were getting wet from the uncertainty that my sister had dropped off my homework since I didn't ask, and Mr. Busby did not mention it.

Mr. Busby started calling roll and I heard my classmates answer here, present and there was always the kid that tried to get attention or just their way of saying I'm different answer in a manner that always perturbed Mr. B, like answering 'yep' which always came with a reprimand and sometimes a lecture but today nothing was delaying the inevitable. As Mr. Busby came to the end of marking off who was in his classroom today, things seemed to slow down, and everything seemed to be moving in slow motion. Even the dust lingered in the rays of the sun as it beamed through the windows. I caught a whiff of fear rising from underneath my shirt, or was this just from playing chase outside with my friends during our lunch break? Even in an era where things ran at a slower pace, today it seems to pass all the slower and more deliberately. Now, came the time to start calling out the names of those who did not turn in their homework and in alphabetical order, so I had time to sweat because I was about halfway down this list. Mr. Busby called out the first name, which didn't surprise any of us because he rarely turned in homework, 'Marcus, make your way up here' and just like that it started . . . something which never mattered to me, and I often wondered how someone would not complete their homework. I always completed my homework and followed all the rules, this is just the kind of boy I was growing up to be. A kid that, I found out later, my parents would throw in my siblings' faces whenever they did something really bad like not telling my parents where they were or coming home late without asking permission. I always did the right thing, except on those uneven bars.

Marcus was a serial breaker of the rules, chatted in class, and gave the teachers a tough time. To me, it seemed as though Marcus lived in a home with no rules, no supervision or accountability. I didn't know him well; we just shared a couple of classes, and he wasn't in my homeroom class. Later, I would miss starting the day with homeroom. Homeroom was where we started the school day, heard announcements from our homeroom teacher and I couldn't tell you to this day why it was necessary, but I guess eventually someone figured out that homeroom class was a big waste of time. The only important thing I remember about homeroom is that this is when we exchanged Valentine's Day messages with our homeroom classmates and when we took school year photos, we would take our pictures and then a homeroom class picture. Marcus always looked as if his mother never ironed his clothes and never fitted him well so I just thought he must be poor, and this is why he was always in trouble. Being ten comes with not knowing anything but I was about to learn a whole lot in a short while. As Marcus made his way up to the front of the classroom, I had a thought which never occurred to me before because I had never been in this position where I was wondering about my homework and if my name would be called. I thought how degrading this whole show was, almost like a public shaming but before I always thought that whoever didn't do their homework deserved to get paddled in front of the class so that everyone would know how wrong it was to not do what was required of you. Today was different of course and I started to look at this daily regimen that Mr. Busby performed as a waste of time and so humiliating to the person suffering this punishment. The other teachers always took the kids right outside the classroom and paddled them in the halls where there were no witnesses, no prying eyes, and no public condemnation.

When Mr. Busby asked Marcus why he didn't do his homework again, Marcus just grinned and bent over, assuming the position. I started to admire Marcus because he didn't seem afraid of anything, and he never cried when he was paddled, Mr. Busby was not the only teacher I witnessed paddling Marcus. He just didn't seem to like or have time to do any homework. Mr. Busby grabbed his paddle from the corner of his desk, always proudly displayed so that it was one of the first things you saw when entering his classroom as you placed your homework on the desk. Mr. Busby in one graceful motion lifted the paddle above and slightly behind his ear and like a masterful axe man cutting down a tree, brought it down and as the paddle connected with Marcus' butt you could hear the slapping noise. You could feel the sting and imagine the pain, but Marcus didn't flinch. Mr. Busby repeated this three times, Marcus straightened up and walked nonchalantly back to his place at the table as everyone stared, except Kim who was the smartest in the class. She seemed as uninterested as I used to be, never paying attention because that could never be me, and had better things to do than to waste any time thinking or even watching what the bad kids were doing just to get attention. She just kept reading our English textbook and like me every day in English class when this ritual played out, getting ready for the day's lesson. One right after another, today it seemed that more classmates didn't turn in their homework, I didn't think that the homework assignment was any more difficult than any other assignment we had to this point. These were things that never crossed my mind before because I was one of the good kids who always did what he was told, always completed my assignments, and turned them in on time. I was always quiet and answered the teachers with respect. Today was going to be different, way different.

As I was sitting there, for the first time, I was watching each of my classmates get paddled. After watching them I noticed that not all were like Marcus, there was the kid who cried even before he received his licks, and other kids who couldn't stay still and Mr. Busby had to be very careful with these kids because he could have easily hit their hands or another part of their body. They wiggled and squirmed, and some giggled out of nervousness and fear. I thought how brave Marcus was in showing no emotion or pain, he took it like a man I thought. The next thing I know as I'm lounging in my thoughts, Mr. Busby calls my name! It was like a nightmare; my name being called but not for recognition like so many other moments in my school career thus far. No, today my name was called because I was suddenly thrust into a world, I was unfamiliar with. I was a bad kid, just like that, my name was called because I didn't turn in my homework. All my classmates turned their gaze towards me, even Kim looked up from her textbook to look at me. These are kids that I grew up with, that I started the first grade with, they all know me as a teacher's pet, a kid that always did what he was told and was always respectful and who never was mean to anyone, not even Becky who everyone made fun of because she was different. I never thought she was different, I thought she was just special, and I felt bad that other kids teased her, even some of my close friends but I was never brave enough to say anything to them. I just never took part in their foolishness, as I perceived it to be. Things slowed way down, and I think I had my first out-of-body experience that day. I could feel myself moving upward, standing up seemed like an effortless action this day almost not noticing what I was doing. I could feel everyone's eyes on me, I started to feel ashamed and tormented by my fall from grace. What could I say, beg that he not paddle me? No, I would not be that kid, the kid that can't be brave. Be like Marcus, no emotion, no pain, no begging for anything. I looked at Mr. Busby and made eye contact and I could see the surprised expression on his face, and I recalled what sounded like confusion and disbelief when he said my name, almost like he was asking a question. We stared at each other for what seemed like an hour but were only seconds, and when neither of us said anything, I assumed the position Mr. Busby repeated that graceful motion, and the paddle rose and fell smacking my butt three times. It stung so badly that I wanted to cry out, I had never experienced anything like this! This was my first paddling, Yes, my mom spanked me and whipped me when I would fight with my brother, but a wooden paddle designed to inflict as much pain as possible and without moderation the forceful swing of the teacher inflicting this punishment was meant to be harsh so that it would teach a lesson to the guilty and the innocent as a form of deterrent.

Although the whole thing was over in no more than a minute or two, it seemed everything slowed down, and it took as long as it takes a turtle to cross the street. I kept thinking to myself, 'Don't cry, don't cry' as I walked to my desk, all eyes still on me except Kim's because she had lost interest long ago. Initially surprised that my name was called she just as quickly lost interest, grouped me into the bad kid category, and continued to be one of the good kids, preparing for today's lesson. As I sat down, the minute my butt brushed the seat as I slid into it, I winced but I did not cry and I do not think that I showed any emotion because I was concentrating to be like Marcus, strong and brave. As I was sitting there in shame wondering where everything had gone wrong and thinking my life was ruined, yes this is how this ten-year-old processed this whole ordeal. Nothing changed around me, except for the dust that was lingering in the sunbeams penetrating the windowpanes, now they were dancing all about as Mr. Busby's swings of the paddle dispersed them with the whoosh of air as he swung the paddle up and down, kid after bad kid. This horrible ordeal was not over, Mr. Busby called my name again! This never happened, a kid's name called twice, and right as I sat down and tried to make sense of this whole spectacle. I felt the sting of tears welling up and I fought them back with all my might because I did not want to break, I wanted to be one of the brave and strong. I didn't experience crying all that much except when I got whooped by my mom for fighting with my brothers, especially when I would get extra licks 'because I was older and should know better' according to my mother as she did what she had to do to keep six kids in line. We didn't cry much in our family; it was rare to see any crying not even happy tears. Although similar, the whooping, the punishment at home for fighting with my brother, and the punishment in school for not turning in homework were both meant to enforce conformity to a certain character or behavior that was more in line with civil order and society. On the one hand, one discouraged violence and the other encouraged responsibility.

Mr. Busby was looking at me, as were all eyes in the classroom because his calling a student's name twice was unheard of. I couldn't speak but everyone was waiting for an answer, but before anything could come out of my mouth Mr. Busby exclaimed 'Your homework is right here, your sister dropped it off. She told me you forgot it at home and that you called her to ask her to drop it off to me.' All I felt was relief, my anxiety faded away slowly because he wasn't calling me for further embarrassment. He was

vindicating my status as a good kid, restoring me to the student privileged
. . . a good kid, just as everyone knew who had other classes with me and
who had grown up right beside me in school. I was relieved but Mr. Busby
asked me a question, 'Why did you not say anything? You should have said
something because now you made me paddle you for no reason.' HA, there
he said it, I was a good kid, and I did my homework he also mentioned my
resourcefulness by calling home when I realized I forgot my homework and
coordinated with my sister to drop my homework off with him. Mr. Busby
did not look pleased though and was waiting for an answer from me and
so were the other kids, except for Marcus and Kim, they had lost interest
when Mr. Busby said he had my homework so for them the show was over
and everything was back to normal; there had just been a slight hiccup with
the course of events for this day so they went back to what they normally
do and there were still other kids to punish for not completing their assignment . . . the bad kids. While this show was over, there were all kinds of
things stirring in my heart and mind, just like the stirring of the chalk dust
whirling around the room and dancing in the sunlight, but for me, at ten
years old in fifth grade English class and in the span of only a few minutes
I learned about cause and effect. I forgot my homework, I relied on others
for my responsibilities, I did not speak up, I caused Mr. Busby to delve out
an unnecessary punishment and now he stumbled with a couple of words
in wondering aloud why I would not speak up and allow him to inflict harm
on an innocent child. In all the dynamics of that tortured ordeal, I also was
keener on my surroundings and noticed that everyone has their own story,
that each person whether young or old has a story that sometimes is lived
in the public eye and a story that is written in the privacy of their own heart
and mind which is never shared or revealed to the public. That day in my
elementary English class I learned a great deal about life and that is that I
have responsibilities and decisions to make that will affect me and those
around me. At ten years old, in 1976, I was keenly aware that this was the
way of the world and that my life before this moment I had been living in
a state of childishness, which was okay because I was a child. At ten years
old I started to put away childish things because I had a new understanding
of the responsibility and decisions I make, which have an impact on easy
living or living with self-inflicted hardships. I was growing up, but I didn't
know how much . . . not even as Charo enticed me to play on the uneven
bars at recess. I first met Charo as he whispered a question into my spirit
as I tried to climb up to the top of the uneven bars, I didn't know him back
then, but I didn't tell him to stop whispering in my ear either. That was
before 'Stranger Danger'. 'This feels good, doesn't it?' And my, oh my did
it feel good, I wondered how I had never felt this feeling before but at this

moment I did not want it to stop and Charo kept encouraging my spirit to keep it up because it was only going to feel better and that I would know it when it happened because what I was feeling in this moment was nothing compared to what I would feel when I reached that glorious moment when pleasure is excited in every cell of your body. A climax of everything wonderful, tantalizing, and exciting that made my toes curl and my heart race with passion as I squeezed my legs tightly around the pole and against my groin to get every last bit out of that moment. Everything Charo said was true, but he never revealed to me how much it would cost me later after Riggs G had his way with me. My life was about to see a silent upheaval that would ensnare me for decades before I realized that my spirit had become what seemed to be a playground for God and the devil. Good thing Mel was walking with me even before I knew what was going on.

Little did I know that this was the start of a battle, a secret and not-so-secret battle that would haunt me the rest of my life and take me down dark and deep rabbit holes. I sometimes wish I could remember the exact day but what does that matter now? There are certain things you ponder, and it is best to ponder them at a distance or get sucked back in, but I must recount the story because it matters, even if it only matters for my own salvation but I hope that maybe others will understand how easily it can be to become a pawn in a game of lies and shenanigans.

temptation

i wink at the moon
as it moons the heavens
i bend into its glow and swoon
its mystery speaks of impressions
and of a romantic honeymoon
while imprisoned like prideful felons
a far cry from opportune
and as the vengeful moonlight beckons
we make love in a cocoon
with a tidal wave of concessions
i stare and wink again at the moon
and speak of greedy possessions
while we gyrate in tune
through recollections
from a pornographic cartoon
and a slew of broken intentions
it is too late while too soon
for apologetic transgressions
the sun screams "Get a room!"
while i buy more sessions
and seal my doom

Chapter 3

T his kid is clueless, and while he thinks this feeling between his legs is an innocent tickle, I saw it as my way to entice him. Saccharo is my name, but you can call me Charo, not quite as vivacious as the sexy character María Rosario Pilar Martínez Molina Baeza's Charo, but with the same aim, to give you that cucchi coo, that tickle your fancy, fun time. Making light of life and shaking what God gave you to giggle your way into hell. Around the same time as her talent was crossing America in the 1970's I have been around since before man was created. I am one, among many, that believe in Riggs G. He d'man! As you weak souls would say. I've been with Riggs since he first started grumbling about Elohim and His divine plan. Didn't make sense to Riggs and I thought it pretty weak and disturbing myself. We will talk about that more later but for now, let me get back to this juicy ten-year-old's soul feeling that tickle otherwise I lose my opportunity to infect him with sin, leaving it open to more sin.

Such a striking young boy, just starting to grow and understand how the world works. Most of us at this tender age are so naive and innocent and this adorable boy is very green. He is a golden ticket, shy and innocent but curious and open. He goes to church with his family every Sunday and Sunday school but has yet to understand why it is important and clueless about the war going on. I have been watching and waiting. Checking in occasionally, since he was born, as we do with all children new to this world (our playground).

He loves to climb on the uneven bars during his breaks from school, preferring these to the swings and tether ball. He likes to play marbles but at school, there are some good marble players, and they play for keeps so he doesn't play as much because he loves the mysterious way they can place a design inside the clear glass, these are his favorite. Some kids play kickball, but this is mainly during PE where the coach uses this game to try to instill a sense of teamwork while adhering to rules. I love the way these worthless spirits try to build individuality through team-building exercises not realizing that it is all futile because of the real war taking place and they are too weak-minded to realize this oxymoron approach will only instill competition and greed. Thanks to Riggs, this was his idea, we did this long ago, and we still reap the rewards without really any effort at all. We build systemic flaws, and they work for us while we go on to the more challenging trophies like this little saint I am about to corrupt. Otherwise, if we didn't do things like this, Elohim would have us beat down here because they don't remember their source of power and this makes them exceptionally weak, vulnerable, and tasty. Yes, we eat children, in our own way, just like that tale of Hansel and Gretel but there are very few children that escape our tale of treachery because we have been at this since Riggs started his show in Eden. It works, planting these seeds of fear, lust, greed, envy, gluttony, and slothfulness in their children and as adults they arrive on their own (sometimes with a little tap from me) to pride and wrath. When they grow up and reproduce their weak spirits this cycle continues on its own without them being at all aware of what's going on. Clueless and blaming everyone and everything and we get a pass, unobstructed to continue to entice these little saints to be. They give off this little aura of cheer and joy when in their company, it is maddening and sickening. Such innocence, such humility, such a sickness to the power they really have. Any one of these could destroy our whole mission, just like that one virgin that, if not for her, we could have won the war and reaped the spoils of war.

Riggs' plan is ingenious, we get into their heads with lies and temptations; we dress them up like their favorite loves and give them sweet flavors and glamorous beauty and then we let is fester, grow, and destroy itself. Marvelous to watch and even more glorious to plant, which is my forte, this is why I was chosen by Riggs. I make it taste as fake as sugar but without giving the secret away and before they know it, they are in a battle that they keep losing, and after losing battle after battle the majority die without ever knowing what happened because their focus is on this material world, this fake world, this land of milk and honey or so you think. From the beginning, it was meant to be a paradise for eternity, no death, no sadness, no pain, just a blissful existence. Riggs had other plans and I marveled at the ease of how he planted that seed with lies and manipulation, speaking in the voice of free will he was able to bring the house down! It fell like cards but so did we, but it was worth it to see these weaklings fall from their tower of grace. Fell flat on their faces, we had a party that night once we got our bearings and lost the war in the Heavens, but we had this whole world as a gameboard and all these little puny humans as pieces on a gameboard increasing our army.

I locked on this kid's spirit when he forgot his homework at home and then he panicked, it set off like a siren because in that panic there was a hint of pride at being seen as a bad kid. Pride is our gold standard, so we are especially tuned into the sound it makes. Like a train blowing its horn at 2AM and the conductor, one of our creations and angry about everyone sleeping while he works, blows so many times it wakes you up and stirs your wrath and messes with your ability to sleep. This little boy wasn't there yet but this is how we get notice of some kids' potential, and his horn sounded at ten years old. So I wrapped up some business around the world like my meeting with Hua, promoting the smashing of people's faces with fists, tying up the loose ends on what will become one of the most lucrative of Riggs' ideas and glorifying the very fruit of these weaklings demise and of course I had to assist Isabel flee a coup since we approved of her handling of the mantle of leadership we helped her acquire. Great stuff, but this one really needed my urgent attention because it was too good to ignore, the potential was just enormous for our cause, and we are always looking for great soldiers. I caught up to him as his horn grew louder and shriller, just as his pride increased. This was a dazzling display, almost as good as the opening artillery barrage of the Battle of the Seelow Heights in my favorite war that would result in our grandest of achievements. Ten years old and from the time of the first sound of his pride song to the full-blown barrage of proud pride was only a span of about one- and one-half hours; this was an impressive display utterly unnoticed by anyone who should have known. Except for Mel, which was trying to put the genie back in the bottle, but the kid was too distracted and didn't know what was happening and to think all those preachers' stories and religious classes that again, did not prepare these kids for the real battle, the one that matters. Mel caught a break and the kid's sister listened to Mel and helped the kid out but the kid, never knowing what hit him, was too scared to say anything, what a dope. With one question, I would have no business here but pride is a blinding thing and he fell hard, always trying to be the nice kid but trying too hard to please and never focused on what matters, and who their spirit is tied to . . . only the most perfect being with perfect love, but if they don't have people to guide them to understand their fundamental responsibility in this world, well they are easy pickings and low hanging fruit. His parents did a good job of taking him to church on Sunday, Sunday school and regular school but our systems have been in place soon after the first trial run and after the first murder, now that was fantastic!

Here goes nothing, I thought, as I placed my hands on his thighs and made his crotch press hard against the cold steel while I placed my hands over his and didn't allow him to pull his body up the uneven bars. The bell was ringing, and his classmates were climbing down and scurrying to the line forming on the sidewalk while the teachers scanned the playground to make sure every kid was heading their way to get in line. He pressed his waist against the steel bar, and I could see and smell the excitement. I could feel his pulse racing and his breathing heavier. I'm sure the excitement of being watched and the fear of being caught was intoxicating to this kid that never felt anything like this in his ten years of life. I was taking full advantage and then I just stepped back and watched. He looked around in a daze, I knew this look when I was introduced to lust, looking as though he could see nothing but pleasure like when you see carnival lights for the first time and smell all the good treats at the same time. He kept moving his crotch up and down pressing himself tighter and harder and using his legs to ride that steel bar until he reached that sensation that is something between ecstasy and fantasy, and by this time one of his friends that had been fooled by his silly attempts to act as though he couldn't climb up the bar took off to get in line. When he hit this state of ecstasy, he held the bar close as though he was hugging his favorite blanket and sucking every inch of pleasure from this experience. One of the teachers yelled out to him and a few other stragglers who didn't run because they were already mine and I was slowly teaching them insubordination with a hint of rebuke of authority. Amazed and in a state of pleasurable shock, he jogged as best he could to get in line with the rest of the kids, but everyone was too busy falling in line and facing to the front. The whole display that comes with me planting this seed went unnoticed by everyone but those who count, Riggs G, Mel, and Elohim. The battle was on, and I was winning this round. He became our playground until we can turn him into a game piece, I would have my fun. I checked on him often and sometimes I came to visit just to see my trophy when he would fake climb those uneven bars until his pride song rang out again. My work had started on this one, and it would not be long before the seed started to grow.

A beautiful child, a teacher's pet, a parent's dream sitting in the expansive room in his elementary school. There were four classrooms in this huge room, one in each corner. Teachers instruct their students and hands go up to answer, so orderly. This saintly kid, now bruised with the seed I planted, was uncomfortably ornery this day just sitting there and no one paying any attention to him. He watched as the teacher called out students that were ill tempered and wrote their names on the top right corner of the chalkboard. His pride song wrang out, but this time it was more like a heavy metal band playing in your living room on a weekday morning, so I was interested in what was about to happen. He didn't disappoint, this kid raises his hand to get the teacher's attention and she calls on him. He tells her that he wants his name on the board with the other kids and she reminds him that only kids that will be in trouble and disciplined later had their names written on the board and he slyly and somewhat mockingly tells his teacher that he knows why she writes kids names on the board and insists that his name be written on the board with the others. Some of the other kids around him look on in disbelief, others dismissive because it has nothing to do with them and the ones with their names on the board have what appears to be an evil grin like a partner in crime that is getting away with the piece of candy they just stole and only they know what happened. His teacher, knowing the kid is a good kid and wonderful student, knowing he did absolutely nothing wrong asks him why he wants his name on the board and the kid, gotta love him, says three words that clocks some points in my book . . . he tells his teacher because he wants his name up there on the board. Being challenged like that by a ten-year-old, the teacher stares in disbelief for what seemed like hours but was only a few seconds turns around, picks up the chalk and writes his name on the board. This kid is gleaming, he sits up straighter and pushes his chest out like this was some amazing accomplishment and I was leaping for joy. This kid is great! I am going to have a lot of fun with this one, I visited him more often, but Riggs had new plans for the moment and since he is the boss, I had to wait but it all made since later as the years passed.

Forbidden Fruit

'Twas the dawn before arrogance,

And all throughout; Love's sustenance.

A mere whisper from resistance,

Beckoned her to come witness.

Eat and be filled with eternal alertness,

Paternal warning, only a happenstance.

This fruit is ripe with delightfulness.

Why do you obey a selfishness?

I do not lie to you, my sweetness.

Pick, bite, eat and swallow His richness.

Be a god and absorb your uniqueness.

Pass it along and increase your fullness.

Your spouse will be raised in boldness,

Erasing any form of cowardice.

Whispering to her love, there is no bitterness.

It told me this fruit enriches us.

He bites and partakes of the indulgence,

Instantly, an awkwardness,

A sadness.

A forbidden foreboding, a messiness.

The great fall from graciousness,

To lay with a lie only stokes bitterness

To create the lie rains resentfulness

Emptying oneself of all righteousness.

Absorbing the lie, you inherit weakness.

Promoting evil's mischievous playfulness.

There is only one hopefulness,

Donning the air of meekness,

And doling out forgiveness

In truthfulness

Only then receiving an awareness

Of your evil rudeness

You are filled with kindness,

And your heart, a witness.

Love in all its greatness!

Chapter 4

Allow me to introduce myself, I am the satan in all of us. I am the evil that festers and lurks in the deep recesses of your heart and mind. I wait and scheme of the ways to infiltrate your decisions to lead you to nowhere places and to a dead end. An end of everything you know and hold dear, the mind suck that destroys your morality because you have lost track of your humanity. I am the satan of old, the one who stole the angels from heaven as they were loosed on this world where humanity roams in misery while pursuing delectable delights with their sex, pride, greed, and violence. I lead them to themselves and into those dark crevices filled with want and preservation of power and influence. A world that me, the satan, has been portrayed as a beauty worth indulging and the demon worth exorcising. Come listen as I whisper sweet, intoxicating banter of delusion and despair, but selling it as sinful pleasures too wonderful to hold in a lifelong fast. Worse yet, I indulge your every evil inclination and applaud your lustful indifference.

I am the evil you cannot escape. I would even bet that I am the evil you do not want to escape, most just want the ride without having to pay the price of a ticket to nowhere places. Some of you even sell your soul (if you have one) and sell it cheap. Others ask for a higher price I am willing to pay if the soul is right and not already corrupted. Either way, it is up for sale, and I want it, I need it, I desire it. I cannot live without you. I long to absorb your fear and resentment as part of the deposit I require, while I wait excitedly for my recurring payments. The darker the soul the sweeter the taste of all that I crave, to dominate your life and make you do whatever I say. Without ever asking me why, you just carry out my lie. With some remorse at first, until we become one and then you do it because you need it as much as I do.

When you are born, I am there when your mom and dad mate, especially when it is in bad taste or better still, when I take center stage and the mating is unwanted and resisted. I have a special hold on this type of creation, not because I have dibs on you, but because someone will always remind you where you came from. The world is this cynical and predict-able. I carry on undisturbed in my mission with so many fighting for the chance to pal around with me and my kind. Evil and fun, fun and evil. This is my idea of a good time and I wait for you to come around but when you do, I latch on, and you can't get me out of your mind. I build cobwebs in your mind and place obstacles in your heart so that I daze and confuse. If you make attempts to clear it all out, I have also laid emotional mines that were set in a time that was especially painful and reckless so that when you hit one, you're blinded and stumble long enough for me to come to the rescue to save the evil I've planted.

While you at times detest me, you learn to live with me because you know that this world is unkind, dangerous, and unpredictable. You long for the day that I can be unleashed against all those who you perceive as a threat, or you just don't like their politics, their religion, or their pious hypocrisy. I am a necessity, you think, and that is all I need and expect. Your fear is what quenches my thirst and fills me to the brim with the bile of in-gratitude which is my fine wine. I am your saving grace when you fall from grace, ready to take the blame for what you think to be insane and vengeful. What you do not realize is that I don't make you do anything, it is impos-sible for me to, I can only entice, encourage, trick, or lie to get you to agree or react, with me leading the charge. You find comfort in this, thinking I have your back while all I am planning to do is stab you in the back with the corruption and evil that you hide inside your heart and mind.

I am the satan inside everyone, even those you admire and follow their every word. Blind as water and clueless as mud, you wallow in my misery because it was meant only for me. You came along for the ride because some of you love the ride, others out of fear and some out of per-ceived necessity. Even those who think they are saints, that pride is what you hide even from yourself and think it is all absolved when someone tells you your forgiven, but you never really confessed to how much you really care about having me close to do your bidding or hide you from your crimes. Not just those crimes in the book of man but the book of life. All the while I'm trying to erase you from the one that counts or have you locked up like an animal. To what do I owe this pleasure of mine, to be king of lies? To be the father of the lie? I owe it all to your pride to be like me, a deceiver opposing truth and love.

Riggatha Gevah at your service, Aramaic for lust and pride and I think it has a nice ring to it. Everyone calls me Riggs or Riggs-G, but I want all of you to call me Master. That's my day, and my night job, all around job really. Don't sleep, so I got what you things call 24/7 shift. I never stop working at murdering souls. Even if you don't sit at my table, I have the answer to all your desires, your wishes, and your prayers. Call me Riggs for short, and some call me G. Whatever you desire to call me, I can be that for you. I share you with my partner, Saccharo but I call him Charo for short. Together we desire your attention and praise your every move so much that we lift you high enough to touch the stars while you ride right past the moon. That chill in the air is our love connection, like electricity that hits a tree. Something spectacular! That is our attraction, but it comes at a small price. So small that you will not even notice your contribution, just trust us, we have been around a while. The very first fib I told was only to lift the spirits of a bored young girl, as innocent as a glance but that was enough to pique the interest of the queen of paradise, I didn't know yet that pride would be her interest. Like me, she decided that she wanted to have a little fun, but knowing that it was only to make her feel beautiful again, like when she was first made aware of her beauty, or was it just her recollection of the desire for love that maybe Adam had neglected to satisfy with his love? So, not knowing the difference between spite vs. lust, she decided to mimic the glance I stole from her and that was enough to entice the king of the eternal garden of paradise where everything is perfect, even the way the light shines on my beauty. And this is the beginning of our love story . . . I love to hate you, that is the title. How do you like it? I will make sure I dress it up and change the taste so that you believe in the lie I'm about to live with your life.

There comes a time when you must take a stand! Otherwise, you go through life without excitement, or any semblance of sanity or eventful-ness in the whole of things, in life there is but strife and often people just dwell in it, which for Charo and me, we gorged and continue our gorging. Like two fat pigs hungry for slops. Addicted and well versed in Creation, you have no chance against my temptations like white is white and black is black until someone like me comes along to convince you otherwise. For those that don't give in to Charo's charm and wit, that's when I come along and close the deal. Like a fast-talking used car salesman or a courteous Maître d' at a fancy hotel, or anything in between. I promise you every-thing and by the time you realize that I have control of the steering wheel you are already hanging on by your fingernails. While I'm LMAO, you only begin to understand what is happening to you. Clueless, and scared as a cat in the dog pound, you make choices with eternal tornado consequences. You are lifted, shaken, forcefully tossed all about, slammed into objects, in a tailspin of wind, water, and dirt. You cling onto hope for something that you can easily be distracted from and do not understand. I can help you with all this. Just have a seat with Charo and me; we will make all things better while we make you understand.

Oh, so back to that little price, well maybe not so little but more insignificant than anything else. I must convince you to love yourself just a little bit too much while you think that you are getting the short end of the stick and that you are entitled to whatever you desire because, and we agree with you, you deserve everything and everything first, not last or when someone else decides but now. Why you don't even care about the one who created you enough to love a stranger who decides they want to kill a baby, but you still like to call out to some Lord who lets this happen. You never see the whole picture because you live life wanting and desiring the wrong things, but you have the choice to live life loving and serving those who decide to give up on life and live in the streets but when they ask you for a little of the extra that your Lord has given you, you mock and call them names. Just like some school children did to you. I appeal to the bully and the bullied alike because they all want the same things, attention, and praise; they just have different ways to go about it, or some are even so in love with themselves that all they want to do is be alone with themselves and their own devices.

Remember folks, this is all about choice, Charo and I just present you with the best of options to cope and have fun. Welcome to the circus! Who doesn't like a good Circus, especially when there is a carnival all around it with all the goodies, games and carnival rides and freak show attractions your heart could desire. While my intoxication is as buttery as the carnival popcorn you smell in the air or that sensual feeling in between your legs when the ride spins and drops really fast. As you drink in the amusement of it all and ready to reach your climax the conductor calls out to you . . . I will get your ticket now, is it just one or do you have friends you are treating? I will do all of you for the same price, go ahead and pass through because I trust you can pay me when you're done. Do everything you want to do, your credit is good with me, Charo will assure you it's not that painful while he is lifting you past the clouds. I take over and I will fill you with that warm delight and pleasurable desire that races you passed the moon and both of us will whisper into your mind the notion that your finger is fondling a star; leave it to the masterfully magical Riggs G . . . at your service. Shit, we can even work out a payment plan if free isn't good enough or too expensive for some. All we really desire from you is a 'Yes' and a please, well, that would be mighty swell. Remember you have that credit baby . . . all that credit, until your bill comes due. Right now, all we want you to do is come out and play with us.

My Crown

My crown is heavy,
too heavy for just anyone,
made just for me . . .
one of hate, the other of eternity.
I left my throne for you,
clouded in mystery
in the open to see
but hidden from everybody.
Only a few would know,
but know for sure?
I was baptized at thirty
so, they soon would choose.
I spoke of Truth and Love,
revealing secrets from the Almighty.
Power shook with fear,
religion followed suit,
and with a whiff of savagery
committed to a lie.
I knew of their plan
to end their misery
and disguise their hate.
Loving and forgiving them,
as they nailed me with profanity
and laughed at My crown.

Chapter 5

B lah, blah, blah, there the satan goes rambling on and on about how great, awful, and beautiful he is. Another big lie to cover the lie he tells with every lie. Hello, I am the good in all of us. Peaceful is my name and love is my game while truth is what I plant in your heart. I do have to shack up with this darkness in your heart and mind, I am by no means subject to it, nor do we co-mingle. I am the independent good in you, the one assigned to you from your first existence when, in love, God created you to be who you are. There were many of us that jumped at the chance to be your romance when God showed us your soul and we rejoiced to be near it. I was the one that was picked from so many to be with you always until you returned home to heaven, if this was your choice, but we will talk about this later. Right now, I just want you to know how special you are. When God blessed your soul and sent you into your mother as the biological procreation took place, you had a choice, and you took it. To try your hand at saving souls that God already knew would have a tough time with the free will He gifted to us. You jumped at the chance, even if we forget why we were sent, this is our whole existence. To serve, love and save by sharing the things God whispered into your heart and shared with me so that I could keep you on track if you let me help.

I can help you navigate the darkness like a lantern on a dark night, I can help you see the narrow road it takes to travel in this dark world. Especially when you have someone trying to mislead you and lying to you all the time. I will remain true, because I love you and this love comes from the source of love so it has no measure, it is infinite and there is nothing you can do to dissolve it or lose it. As long as you live, I am here. No matter what you walk into, I am here. Nothing you say or curse can shake me loose, I am here. You can't pray me away, you can't wish me away, you can't even order me away. I am here to stay, until the very end of your days here in this material world. I am the hope you feel that everything will be ok and the excitement in loving someone so much that you weep either for joy or out of sadness for them. I am the expectation of something real, something fantastical, something incredible, all things wonderful and beautiful, I am the good in each one of you. I cannot be sad or mad. I cannot hold a grudge, and I cannot be jealous because I love you. I can only love, that is more than enough to help you get through this life.

We exist together in love, the source of love who created everything and now he has created you. Specifically for this time and age because He believes in you and that you will choose Him over your own ego and against the ramblings of the other that clings to you to destroy you. I am that small voice, that feeling, that notion, or that insight that warns you and leads you out of danger or mishap. I am at your bedside when you are sick, I am with you as you sleep, I am with you at work, school, at play. My sole purpose is to accompany you on your journey in this world with love and in truth. I cannot lie to you or guide you into mischief because I am the pure love of our Father that he has bestowed upon you. Sometimes when you feel that warmth of love all over, it is when I pass through you just to let you know that I am with you and because I long to embrace you. You are my special someone and I am yours alone, but you can ask me to talk to others like me when you are having trouble with someone. In love, we can usually work things out and influence both of you with love and understanding so that the encounter is experienced in love.

It is a longing pain I feel when you ignore me or don't acknowledge that I exist. I can't leave you so I have to witness as you are misled into the darkness and all I can do is weep because you refused my comfort, my advice, my direction, my love. I am so excited and joyful when you turn back to me or refuse the temptations of the satan in you. I cheer you on and applaud your return as you rebuke the evil all around you. I jump for joy when you turn my way and ask for my help because I know you love me and want to love God. From the moment I was chosen to be with you, I have cheered you on and have defended you in love with the Creator's Son. They smile when I tell them all the love you have in your heart or when you chose Him over your pride, hate, or other sin. I give Him a true account because we cannot lie, so when I have some bothersome news to report about how you gave into evil temptation I also explain and rejoice in how quickly you recovered and how reverently you turned back to Him in love and obedience. I love you and together we will get through this life and together we will stand before our Lord and plead your case for eternal life in Paradise.

Now that you have met the satan and me, and because I have been matched with a human soul, this tale regards my charge. Before I introduce you to my special soul, I want to make it easy for you to identify who is speaking to you and since we do not have a gender, I have chosen names that are neutral. From now on you can call me Mel and you can call the satan Riggs. With these formalities out of the way, let me introduce you to the soul who won my heart who I almost lost to Riggs who works every day to steal him away from the Lord.

My poor sweet boy, I tried to hide your existence from Charo and Riggs, but I knew when I met your soul and when I volunteered that you would be a target. I should have let another guide and protector guide you, but it wasn't really my choice. Elohim asked me to do it, even though it was not an order but a request, and I accepted because I trust in His plan for you. Your innocence I protected for ten years, and we did so well together. The joy you showed when your father would come home from work where he spent hot suffocating days in the hulls of ships with his welding machine and gear sweating away his life to provide a life for you and your family that he didn't have but wanted it for his wife and children. He had such a great relationship with Elohim, even after losing his father at such a tender age that he never knew him and remembered so little about him. He gained great blessings by taking care of his grandfather as he grew older and less able to care for himself. His son, my charge, was a lot like his father and his father's father. There was talk that his father was aligning himself with Riggs, but this is not his story, I will just say that this boy was not going to give himself to Riggs if I had anything to say about it and I have a lot to say.

Free will and all, a controversial concept that struck a bad chord with a third of us and Riggs was at the forefront of the rebellion. Unimaginable since he was the son of the morning but his actions on earth were called out and eventually his plan to turn on Mankind rather than serve him, drew the wrath of Elohim, and was cast out of the heavenly realm after their war with their fellow guardians and protectors. He meant to convince Elohim that his plan was flawed and drew on something no one else had entertained . . . pride. Once the son of the morning, now he found himself slithering on his belly on the very dirt that Elohim used to mold and create Mankind in His image. This is where the saying that pride comes before the fall comes from, once the most powerful and beautiful creation brought into being from nothing to serve as Elohim's most entrusted of guarding protectors would thwart Elohim's plan for Mankind. Riggs used their free will to choose love and obedience to instead choose pride and lust.

Riggs and I have battled for hundreds of thousands of years, so we know each other well, I knew this kid would catch Riggs' interest the minute he knew I was back on earth as the kid's guardian protector. I was not expecting that Charo would get his claws into him at the tender age of ten, this was too soon. I heard the song of pride, sounding like the wailing horn of a train, softly at first but within the span of an hour or so the song sounded like the screaming of a cicada sitting next to your ear. This was attached to pride when Mankind fell so that we would all know to pay closer attention but there was no way to hide this sound from Riggs and his gang of dirt dwellers, as they are known now. I came to Santos as soon as he realized he had forgotten his homework at home and started to have doubts and fears. I moved him to call home, a simple fix, just go to the school office and ask to call home. It worked, and Santos calmed down and the pride song, only a whisper then, had all but disappeared. In the back of his mind, I could hear and feel his fear that things would not work out with his sister, and his homework that she promised to drop off would not ever make it to Mr. Busby's English room class on time but for now, it didn't seem loud enough to catch the attention of Charo. I kept my sensors out for Charo because Santos' initial fear may have been discovered if Charo was not too busy at that particular second, we may have averted a bad situation.

I didn't leave Santos' side because I needed to make sure that Charo and Riggs would not come around and make things worse for him. I helped him focus on other things like playing with his friends and what they were serving for lunch, things kids should be doing at this age in 1976. These were definitely not the things kids were doing back in 30 A.D. when Msheekha was walking the earth. In this day and age kids like Santos were safe to be kids in the Avenues of Beaumont, people left their front doors unlocked and windows open and they slept soundly and in relative peace and safety. He was chosen for this time just like all of Elohim's children were chosen for their time, their souls are each created with something to contribute to Elohim's master plan. It is our job as guardian protectors to make sure we guide them in a way where they can choose to realize their full potential and Elohim's plan for them along with their skill set and gifts that they are given. Like a piece of an intricate puzzle, he was created for this era and for this particular place in the world. No one really knows why, only Elohim, because only He knows the final outcome because there is no sense of timing for Him. In Him exists the past, the present, and the future all combined into one, which is beyond any of our comprehension. We have a glimpse of it, but we exist from age to age without a time span. The only thing that is certain is that Santos is relatively safe in this age, but no one is ever safe from Charo and Riggs. Never, no matter what age you are born in because a war rages on in the spirit world where many, many souls dismiss this as either a mystery so difficult to understand that they tire of the concept, or rebuke it all together as impossible, and even worse . . . consider it foolishness.

I felt it the moment Santos' pride song started playing again as he walked into Mr. Busby's class, and I tried to distract him by encouraging the guardian protectors of his close classmates to talk to him and take his mind off it. At the moment Santos walked into the classroom I nudged him over to Mr. Busby's desk so that he could ask him if his sister brought his homework and turned it in, but Charo was able to distract Mr. Busby with Marcus, who was easily manipulated by Charo. I don't know why Santos was so worried about how other students would view him. I have noticed that this generation, unlike prior generations, and particularly this society in America in 1976 was moving in the direction of Riggs and his attitude about life in general. Sure, their music mentioned love, but at the same time they were experimenting with some pretty harsh drugs that made them sexually immoral and the attitude towards sex seemed to allow free expression of nudity, voyeurism and self-gratification through fornication and masturbation. A conflict of free love and war in the 1960's while a race war was being led by Riggs. You also have those mental health experts, at Riggs' encouragement, teaching and espousing how messed up someone would become emotionally if they were to suppress this sexual exploration. It was a different kind of problem in past generations, with little regard for human dignity other generations engaged in immorality as a necessity, abuse, or because people were treated like property to do with what they wanted. These times were confusing children, through various forms of media, society was sending conflicting messages that children without reasoning skills could not possibly understand without their guardian protectors working to keep them safe and by exposing them to truth within their hearts and most of their minds followed. With multimedia sending both messages of love in the 1960's and violence on the rise in the 1970's made guardian protectors busier and the rapid pace of expansion in all forms of communication gave Riggs an edge since he has no rules in this war.

There my little soul sat, as I caressed his hand trying to reassure him, but the rules say he must decide within his own mind and heart to choose his emotions and reactions. I cannot interfere with this, but Riggs has no rules and can prod and tempt, provoke, and torture. This is the price of a free will, that it be tested to do the right thing. This makes one's faith stronger and more resilient to future attacks and displays the depth of love in someone's heart. Their devotion to Elohim, their love for Him, must be chosen and can never be forced. This is at the heart of the war, this is why Riggs abandoned his position as the morning light because he refused to accept that mankind should have a free will and that they would only resort to the nastiest and most gruesome of choices without their absolute surrender and governance by Elohim and if Elohim couldn't see this, Riggs believed it was he that would save God from such a disastrous mistake to Creation. This is when pride was born.

Time is Ticking

Time keeps ticking,

Tick-tock, tick-tock.

What happens when it stops?

Tick-tock, tick-tock

Do we enter into another life?

Tick-tock, tick-tock

Do we cease to exist?

Tick-tock, tick-tock

Do we become part of a fantasy?

Tick-tock, tick-tock

Is it nothingness we will see?

Tick-tock, tick-tock

What does science tell thee?

Tick-tock, tick-tock

Did not Love tell us already?

Tick-tock, tick-tock

But do we really listen?

Tick-tock, tick-tock

I love my Jesus, don't we say?

Tick-tock, tick-tock

Ain't I saved this way?

Tick-tock, tick-tock

Didn't He pay my way?

Tick-tock, tick-tock

What about Love's parables?

Tick-tock, tick-tock

The rich man threading a needle?

Tick-tock, tick-tock

The weeds growing with the wheat?

Tick-tock, tick-tock

The way of the seeds?

Tick-tock, tick-tock

The fruit, is it sweet or stale?

Tick-tock, tick-tock

What guarantees do we have?

Tick-tock, tick-tock

Would you rather the nothingness?

Tick-tock, tick-tock

What about blissfulness?

Tick-tock, tick-tock

So, what is the secret to all this?

Tick-tock, tick-tock

What does Love tell you?

Tick-tock, tick-tock

Different than what the world tells you?

Tick-tock, tick-tock

Is there paradise, hell, and nothing?

Tick-tock, tick-tock

What does Love say?

Tick-tock, tick-tock

Can you hear?

Tick-tock, tick-tock

Do you listen?

Tick-tock, tick-tock

What does Love say?

Tick-tock, tick-tock

Do you live in Love?

Tick-tock, tick-tock

Or do you live some other way?

Tick-tock, tick-tock

Do you wink to love, and say later?

Tick-tock, tick-tock

Or do you glorify the hater?

Tick-tock, tick-tock

STOP

Now, you will have your answer.

Chapter 6

It is 5:15AM on August 3, 1966, and just like that another of God's miracles. The same way Jesus came to Earth. Fascinating as much as it is nerve racking. But for this couple, Santos and Lupe, Jr. was their fifth child. Santos first met Lupe in the plazita in Asherton, a wonderful city of Texas full of its mysteries, secrets, and simple laid-back living with dirt roads. Why it only installed its first, and only, traffic light in 2015. One day, leaving the movie theater in Carrizo Springs on a date, Lupe saw her stepfather drive by the front of the theater and saw her with Santos. Lupe was terrified, in 1954 a young lady from a respected family with a tendency towards violence and abuse, was not a good thing. Santos, being in love and having found his princess bride, knew that destiny was being played out in the front of the movie theater that night. Santos and Lupe were married in 1955 and 1956. Initially by the Justice of the Peace and then a Catholic wedding at the beautiful Immaculate Conception Church in Asherton.

Asherton has been a special place for Jr, he enjoys the sounds of nature, the wind blowing through the mesquite while watching a roadrunner making his way through the vast wilderness of prickly pear and mesquite trees. The night sky is an infinite blanket of stars with the sweet smell of dew sprinkled dirt roads. While the days can be treacherously sun baked, the nights were when the small community of about 1,300 starts coming out of the shade and neighbors visit, stroll to the tiendita for a nice cold drink. Back in the day, you could get a raspa with nieve from Sabino's. Jr spent his first few months with his grandmother, a strong woman who overcame life's hardships with her marriage to Gregorio, though ending abruptly. Knowing she had to support Lupe and her little brother, Jesus, she remarried. Natividad had four children with Ignacio, but tragedy struck and shortly after they were married, Lupe's little brother went into a hospital and never came out and that was the last memory Lupe had of her little brother. Lupe was only six years old when she lost her father, Gregorio. She also had a twin, but her sister died at childbirth.

Santos also had his own hardships, especially not fully accepting the racism of the day he dropped out of school and only made it to the third grade but was the wisest man that Jr would have growing up, to guide him, and keep him safe. Santos lost his father when he was around the same age when Lupe lost hers. Both Ramon and Julian died at 35 & 36 years old. Both had stepfathers and both Guadalupe and Natividad remarried and had more children, but Jr did not have as close family ties with his father's family, not like he had with his mother's side of the family. Mainly because of the distance that divided them, lives, choices, and life because things have a clock ticking in this world, the material world.

Santos and Lupe were both born in Asherton and grew up there, and when they were old enough, they started working in the fields picking yellow onion, cotton, carrots, cabbage, and no telling what else because they would follow the crop seasons. It was on one of these work trips up in the lower panhandle of Texas in a small town named Dimmit, Jr was on his way to breathing the air of earth for the first time. There was no time to reach a hospital, like his other siblings were born in. Jr would be born in a two-room small town Doctor's clinic. Only a couple of hours after delivering, Lupe and Santos were told to take the baby home, because the Doctor needed the room. Lupe told Jr one day, when he was asking questions about when he was a baby, that she remembered being in a dark room in the small housing units that the large farmers would provide for the farm workers. There was a small window but covered, contributed to Lupe becoming very anxious. Lupe had gone through so much already, but Santos and Lupe were going to have many more headaches, heartaches, and challenges along with all the happy, joyful, and memorable.

My charge was born as the fifth child of two beautiful souls who first set their hearts on one another in their small hometown of Asherton, TX. Asherton natives call it Cheto. In the barrio side of the town which is separated by S. Highway 83 there is a plazita where many fiestas and important events take place. More often in the past than today but it has a lot of history. The town's population peaked when his parents met around 1953-54 and included 2,425 souls. It was during a fiesta that Santos Navarro Hernandez first laid eyes upon Guadalupe Ramon. It would be about 12 years later that my loving charge would be born into their lives and as a blessing to the world, just as all souls are meant to be a blessing to this world. It is only free will making individual choices that hinder or obstruct the blessing they can be. From now on I will call him by the name he took when he welcomed the Holy Spirit into his heart at the age of 15, may I introduce you to Santos Juan, Saint John in English and for this book we will refer to him as Jr.

Jr moved with his family to Beaumont, TX in 1967 about eight hours from Asherton, TX and with a population around 119,000 (at the time was the sixth largest city in Texas). His father had gone to welding school in Eagle Pass, TX and upon graduation he was hired at Bethlehem Steel, this meant more people and more opportunity for Riggs to negatively affect his life and manipulate his decisions. For Jr it was not going to be an easy going of it. Riggs, knowing how special he is to God, the good intentions of his heart, and his prayerful family, he was going to work extra hard to dig into him early and ruin his life. I had my work cut out for me, but I loved him so much that I was ready and prepared for this challenge.

This all began back in Junior's fifth grade class with Mr. Busby. I could not prevent what Riggs G was able to inflict on him physically. In that same year I heard Jr cry out and fall to the floor on the second-floor landing at his school, Fletcher Elementary. Some kids walk by in a hurry to get to class and are not used to caring for others. Many of the kids just looked and kept going but those people who are just full of love, kindness, and peace are traits God blesses them with, so we have them in our lives. Anyway, the staircase was busy, and he was in tears, sobbing. He couldn't bend his knee without excruciating pain. I did all I could to try to get him help and comfort him because he was so scared. I knew Riggs and Charo were behind this, I could smell their decaying spirits. The stench lingers, like sin, it always lingers. I pray to the Holy Spirit towards him, so to protect but Jr is not only experiencing his first bites of pride, but there is also lust. Not just experimentation, I know and understand the levels of demons, and this was no junior demon, this had the markings of Riggs G.

I filed a concern grievance with 'The Arch' (Elohim does not like it when we cut names short . . . I'm trying to stop), I mean the Archangel's Grievance and Assistance Procedure Service for Support. It is when I need to bring in the big guns in combating something that is verified to be of significant urgency and its evil burdens. I know Jr is ignoring the support I'm providing because he just learned what pleasing himself physically is all about, and now he has also found his older brother's collection of porn magazines in their hiding place in our bathroom. He took one look, and I knew it would be hard in getting through to him because you should've seen those big, beautiful innocent (well, before this anyway) eyes, just beaming with excitement, intrigue, curiosity, and lust.

Bursitis in the knee was the diagnosis and was hospitalized. This would be the first in a series of illnesses and physical problems that would move Jr towards a path of darkness and treachery, where all despair roams about in a fog of enchantment and confusion. That same year he developed pneumonia where he again was hospitalized and under a tent, the poor little child can only remember how cold it was under that plastic tent, where they periodically but regularly dumped a whole bunch of ice in a container to keep the tent cold. It is very difficult for me to understand how all of that physical world works, especially how one little thing (out of the millions of things) goes out of whack in the human body, it could spell disaster and even death. How some people can't except just that one simple fact as proof that Elohim is for real, I just don't get it, but that is neither here nor there and I digress . . .

Jr. is a sickly child right now, but still messing with all those porn magazines and playing up down on the door of the bathroom, the poles in the lassos, the ground and a kid in the neighborhood. He was out of control and getting worse, and for all the power that I have to protect him with, no can do, if he don't listen! Ooooh, what an a-n-g-e-l of a child. He does have a heart for justice and that heart that wants to help people. Such a passion in his little spirit that moves towards hope, no wonder I fell in love with it as soon as God created it. I was so happy to be protecting it in this world, but ooooh, he can be difficult and hardheaded. His best friend Juan said it best (I laughed and laughed), "Don't try to figure him out Cruz, he is a walking contradiction!" Jr laughed and agreed. It all started right here, listen up parents!

As the physical attacks would continue, Riggs was now directing Charo to inflict him with the desire for depression which would be easy as he became sicklier and in and out of hospitals. You could tell it was weighing on him as he lashed out one time at Dr. Fernandez when he made a house call, and while he could not render a diagnosis for Jr's chest pain, he made the mistake of telling his parents that it was all in Jr's head. I immediately enveloped him with love to soften the reaction to this baseless judgement by Dr. Fernandez just because his medical training lacked the knowledge to diagnose Jr's chest pain. It wasn't enough, Jr (now mind you, he is only about 11 or 12 in the 1970's) who is usually shy and quiet, spoke up loudly and declared, "You can't tell me it's all in my head just because you don't know what's wrong with me. I can feel the pain, and it is NOT in my head." This little boy was going to be a great advocate for the voiceless if he made it past this dark and treacherous period of his existence.

I prayed every free moment, but Jr was troubled and laid in bed awake worrying about loneliness into the wee hours of the night and early morning. Sometime my poor little spirit child only got an hour or two of sleep a night, it was not because I didn't lavish him with enough love, it sometimes left me very weak. I would show up to the Love Regeneration and Charging Realm almost on empty because he needed so much just to keep him from going crazy and becoming lost to his lustful passions and fear of loneliness.

Riggs and Charo have not let up, relentless in their attempts to sway him towards sin, for every hour spent with Elohim, sometimes double and triple was the time spent on desire, lust, and fear. What he does when he is on the right path, is something short of amazing with all the skills and talents that God blessed him with are just roaring to get to work to glorify God. He started altar serving at the church across the street from their house, Cristo Rey. He also loves his Sunday School classes, and he enjoyed going to church with his mom. They always sat in the back pew for 11:30AM Mass on Sundays, his dad always attended the 9:00AM Spanish Mass so I don't think he ever went to that Mass unless he had to alter serve. I can attest to the fact that my little spirit child is not a morning person and never will be, even after all this time. Not even after his emergency open heart surgery, and yes, I was there and I'm still here as he is writing this book.

Santos and Lupe, the day after Jr. were born connected in a way that only a mother and father can with a son. No different a love than any of the other four children they have raised so far. For a moment in time, a few days before this day and the day after, their emotions and the stress of providing and caring for a family of seven now with Jr was a challenge already but at least Alicia, the first born, can help. I remember that there were a good many of us in this sector of God's creation who were excitedly awaiting the arrival of a newborn angel, that's what becomes of a soul that uses their free will be gone card to serve for the glory of God in heaven and in complete love choose to stay with God. It is a bittersweet moment from how I see the pain it causes you all. I can only imaging because Jesus was the only one who experienced it the way God chose to redeem his human creation. Jr was their fifth and something had to be done, while Santos was getting an education in welding, through a work program between the Texas Workforce Commission and Bethlehem Steel in Beaumont, TX were educating and training the welders so that Bethlehem Steel could then hire on to their workforce. Again, Charo was a bother, he would stir up hate, fear, and uncertainty when change occurs for the good, Riggs G catches wind of something and dispatches his able bodied devoted mini riggs. After getting the whites all stirred up a few of those men would spit towards them or sling racial slurs around the shipyard, but none of those men with Santos didn't scare easy because they had the gift of faith, and they were embarking on a new and hopeful existence that no one up to this point in both of their families, or in their town of Cheto had done before, re-train in a skill like welding move eight hours away to the southeast side of the state of Texas with a family of seven, with my little spirit Jr only a little over a year old.

The welcome they received from Cristo Rey was very warm, after they arrived all the families went to an event put on by the Texas Workforce

Commission and Bethlehem Steel where they took pictures of all the men. They were invited to Cristo Rey where they were given a housewarming gift of items they thought a family would need when they moved all the way from the westside of the state and this was so warming to our hearts, and righteousness was triumphing in their lives and in their experience and journey with God. Santos would speak of this often, the experiences and the stories of the discrimination and childishness of men. Santos would never, ever call them childish but he had a way of loving you and comforting one even as you knew that you were getting the affection that a child would acting more childish than their age, emotional age that is, but he was gentle and kind with everyone. There were dark times in his life as well and Doci would have his work cut out for him when Santos suffered a heart attack and five bypass surgery, which forced his retirement at the age of 56, Jr's age right now (yea, he is still my little one . . . everyone is, I was created a long, long, long time ago if you are keeping human time. You know, while I have your attention, I would like to point out that having to keep our eyes on human time while existing in no time gets a lot more difficult as humans, throughout generations, get more complex about subjecting themselves to living and noting time, and you all feel there is never enough of it. It kills me, but I can't die).

Perhaps, if Santos and all those men had not worked harder, fought harder, endured worse, and struggled to put food on the table and a roof over their heads they would have fallen for Charo's tricks and traits, those sweet whisper I see them concocting amongst themselves to make their interference sound like the singer Annie Lennox when she was with the band the Eurythmics in the song 'Love is a Stranger' Sounds great, but sells you on the material and that you should be wary of love, it is a stranger for those who oppose the truth, Love itself. Riggs G is the father of lies, it hurt all of our hearts when this was no longer between the top but was made known to the entirety of eternity. Lucifer lied, was the two words that destroyed him along with one third of all the Angels who went along with the Big Lie. That Big Lie, Riggatha Gevah invented that brought on the destruction of life itself, exists unto this generation, permeating the individual, the family, the community, states, provinces, regions, countries, nations, both spiritual and material are lathered in it and the only thing that wipes you clean is the blood of the Lamb of God, the One, the only One, that could break that seventh seal. Washed them with His blood, and mercy, forgiving all of their sins. How our God is the Almighty and we praise Him forever and ever. That was what Doci took advantage of and gained protection for Santos' decision to drive to Vidor, TX to watch the KKK gather and burn a cross in an open field. Doci was able to steer Santos to stay his distance. Santos would tell Jr that story and then say, "Yo solo quize verlos." Jr would ask him, curious but shy, even with his family except for Gus, they had a unique relationship. Gus reminded me of how Pop would take us on a drive, and we would go over the Memorial Bridge towards Rose city, a small place right before you reach Vidor, TX where they would burn the crosses and when there was a rally or march, he would go just because he wanted them to know that he was not scared of them. I knew Gus would be the one to plant that seed of will to live in his brother's heart, because I got to help out with him also. We often get to double up and triple up, depending on the unity of the family or friends or whomever God brings together.

They were a great example to Jr and all those that experienced them in only ways you all can do. You comfort, you kiss, you hold hands, you rub backs, long hugs, short hugs, just so many ways to show your love and kindness. I know that Elohim is flowing through, inspiring, and inviting, so many experience this but just like Jesus was saying, that day that the disciples were being taught about the parable of the Sower. There was a community surrounded and welcomed by the Church, the people of Cristo Rey Parish, and they moved a few years after arriving at a house that was once owned by Rojas, at 1378 Forsythe Street, right across the street from Cristo Rey. God was moving things, He was designing the lives of Santos' entire family, we had our knowledge and wisdom sessions where we covered human reality and spiritual ingenuity. There were also shorter meetings where we covered rapid response to free will choices gone awry, and if none were present, we would cover things like accommodations for goodwill deeds, actions, and behaviors. When obedience is rewarded with God's grace, and mercy, there is a totally different and wonderful chorus of us that I can't wait for you all to experience.

Charo was just getting started and my little spirit was not even putting up a fight. So secretive, so quiet, so charming, and he was a beautiful boy. On the verge of his teens, smart, skilled, and gifted, both shy and well behaved. He loved God and I was busy delivering prayers and relaying good actions and countermeasures to sin, boy did this boy keep me busy! I'm not complaining, because this is what you do in Love, since I exist in Love I do not really know anything else except when I get to watch and observe all of humanity, you start to pick up on certain things and how the human experience itself, not the human, only the experience, can be very much different but the same. Right now, Jr is feeling this, and it sits heavy on his heart, his prayers have focused more on duplicity (dupi) vs. duality (dua). I'm helping him navigate this arena, I plan to seek counsel from the principatus if he keeps contemplating and expanding his understanding of how there is unity and chaos in dupi-dua as I've decided to call it. I don't know how long Jr will hold his interest, he is a restless little spirit and keeps me on my toes. I do imagine I have plenty of time since I have not been enlightened to the complete plan, only the Trinity knows and can handle what all that entails. Imagine knowing everything, all things, all the time, and knowing tomorrow because you created it. No, of course, we can't imagine such a thing. Trust me, you guys tried! Eden was a beautiful disaster, but God, existence itself, has no limits our boundaries, highs or lows, He is constant. Only you wonderfully created humans can enjoy such an existence, His most precious creation committing high treason! Oh, the stars wept and the sun ashamed to shine while the moon retreated into darkness. The Angels and Celestial Beings, all held their breath for God's Justice, and always and forever praising and glorifying Him, did it softly, and with the solemnity only we can offer to God.

Y'all did that, you, the most precious of God's creation! I've tried to open Jr's heart to the things of Heaven, and a lot of it has been seeded and just waiting for him to nurture them and let them bear fruit, but first he has to recognize Elohim in him and poor lad, has no direction and is too shy to ask anyone but God. My little spirit has always had this special relationship with God from a little, tiny boy. He surprises me sometimes, well, not for those twenty years or so that I'll let him tell you about, he will tell you about how he didn't recognize me working in his life, but he felt it all his life. He has been speaking with God, and for a large part of his life, especially during his darkest hours of battle with Riggs and Charo and a slew of others they invited at various stages of my little boy's spiritual journey with God. Asking all the wrong questions, which is pretty common, it comes up all the time in the Attempt to Encounter logs we keep for consideration to be entered into the Book of Life. No cry out to God, no matter how small or seemingly non-substantial the shout out, we record it and submit them. We don't do this for like, a weight and scale system of sin vs. good deeds, it's nothing like that but many of you human spirits have been deceived to think so.

The Attempt to Encounter Logs our record of the evidence to offer the true attempts to Encounter God, and we record it for when Riggs G tries to distort the truth when he records things from his point of view, which he always distorts. Unlike the Order of Order of Heavenly Things, where order reigns, Riggs G runs his house divided, and since I can't imagine anything like that because, those that are with God, cannot experience such things. You can imagine it, because in your current existence in a fleshy fallen world, living amongst the demons, like David in the Lion's Den, you can imagine this chaos, full of confusion and doubt, fear and a disdain for order while feasting on lies being hand fed by Charo under the guidance of Riggs and all the others, even those that choose their side.

The side that believes in the lies they tell. The side that believes that you all should never have been created, or at the very least don't put them above all else in God's creation. Which is exactly what they petitioned for from God's Justice Jurisprudence Commission on Human dignity after Riggs was unsuccessful at the Petition for Peace Tribunal.

You all are the one creation that God breathed into and gave you life. Wow! If you were only fully aware of the plan God has for each of you, our work would not be as critical because you can actually feel more than we can. After all, we've never known anything else, and this is because at the Petition for Peace Tribunal Riggatha Gevah made his case against your free will blessing. He argued that you could not handle such power of God's creation, that because of your humanness, you would destroy each other and then turn your vengeance towards God. He knew of a better way, Riggs said, and proceeded to make his case. I'm sure he will brag about this himself, his pride will not allow anything else so I'm not going to bore you with the details, just know that he lost, pride was born in him, he lied and convinced others, the war ensued, God won and that's the truth that Riggs tries to distort and blaspheme through your hearts, minds, and mouths. He knows he has been defeated because the Lamb of God was sacrificed for you and has repaired the chasm that was ordered to be put in place. Oh, the sadness and estrangement that we all felt that day so many of God's creatures instantly started on their path to death, both death of flesh and spirit.

Jr was starting to become aware of the ways of the world and his first brush with both lust and pride at the tender age of 10 in the fifth grade because he was born August 3rd, so he started 1st grade at Fletcher Elementary at the age of five. Santos and Lupe were moved by their guardians to register my little charge into kindergarten at St. Michael's in downtown Beaumont, TX. I remember how his eyes would light up when they served fresh rolls with the browned tops glistening with butter. I wouldn't know what that experience feels like, but throughout the generations that has always been a delectable delight to the great many of you. Your noses go up trying to catch and breathe in the aroma rising from this bread stuff. Yea, we do not eat, breathe, or sneeze, or anything like that remember that those are things only a human can experience, apart from the animals, they breathe and stuff, but I don't think I always have to point this out. I will tell you that, in case many of you have overlooked this in Scripture, it was man that gave all the animals their names but none of them were sufficient partners for man. Oh, what a day, or I should say night, because man was in a deep sleep while God created woman, and man was pleased. All of Heaven erupted in a celestial song of thanksgiving and praise that God had satisfied man's loneliness and longing for someone like him to accompany him all the days and nights enjoying God's Garden of Eden where right before sunset and with a slight movement in the air, a whisper of a wind, to alert that God was passing through to visit His creation and converse with man and woman in the dusk, almost like the tucking in you all do for your children. God tucked in His creation with a simple visit, in all his almighty glory He would visit you and you screwed that all up . . . sorry, that was uncalled for, and I detest that it is the truth of what transpired but we are not there anymore, God has made all things new, through His Son, our Lord.

It was the same battle then as it is today, and Rigg's tactics have only become simpler, more direct, and forcefully enticing, lying about truth, and making it so humanity redefines truth to satisfy his need to be gods above God. For my little spirit, it was just beginning, his eyes were open to pride, with the very first bloom of 'I'm ashamedly naked', this was like a high pitched dog whistle to Charo, who in turn alerted Riggs G and together they pounced into action, unashamedly two entities older than dirt against my young newly created spirit, crawling and stumbling through a world of endless fantasies of perpetual sin available at the high cost of one's redemption and everlasting life. "Here they come", I remember thinking and starting to move those humble and gently spirits to surround and guide Jr to a place far away from pride, but they had gotten a jump and Jr was too eager to experience the lustful demon now taking up a place in his heart, and making himself comfortable while planning a reunion party with other shedims to overtake this innocent soul. A cancer of evil, torturing my little spirit for years, and this, the first to invade his heart. Starting to rip his innocence away from him before he even knows that there is a battle. I can feel and see the goodness in his spirit, that of God, and he is extremely troubled at what he is experiencing but at the same time, in this generation (early to mid-seventies) was entranced with the freedom to mimic sexual intercourse through dance and expression, while words and respect started to wain towards family, community, and a devotion to God. Riggs G and Charo were flying high right now and increasing in their numbers to include humans, which is the only way they can grow their ranks, they recruit them as humans and when they fail their final journeys and their spirit chooses disobedience and pride, they join forces with Riggs and he gains another Charo, another mini riggs. I was not going to go down without a fight for this little spirit, so I strapped in and started calling in some reinforcements. Even with all this, we only managed to ward off the worst for Jr but not before Riggs left a powerful demon in charge to manipulate him away from God's love and lied to him about God not caring, not paying attention, making him something he didn't want to be, choking the life out of any future is how my little Jr felt and as much as I guided him and whispered God's love to his heart on his way to Church on Sundays with his mother, Lupe. I filled his life with positivity and laughter, friends, and teachers that he could experience God's love through the intercession of the people in his life that I steered him to, and their angels arranged encounters with their charges, all of us working together for the God's glory and fighting against the powerful influence of Charo and Riggs.

Pride and Lust had moved in, and I was limited as to what I could do to influence his spirit, his heart, and his mind we were not allowed to manipulate because, quite frankly, this is impossible for us since we exist in Love. When Riggs broke the laws of obedience, and directly challenged God's Supremacy all rules were gone for him, unless Elohim directly interjected. We must fight with one hand tied behind our backs and while sitting down, but we make some great strides, but the only, and best, weapon we yield is that of your free will, when you choose Love over anything else . . . wow! . . . does this give us power to move and act! There is always this celebration in the Heavens over one repentant sinner than over 99 righteous who need not repent. This remains truer today because in our encounter logs, we explain the difficult environment and the tactics undertaken by Riggs and his evil enterprise. We record our charges cries for help from God, although God pays attention to everything because He is everything, He knows better than anyone what is going on, and simultaneously assigns tasks and direction to us through the same Holy Spirit that you all can access with choice, your free will. This is the beauty of Creation, the access to God is constant and the Order of Orders in Heaven keeps an eternal record of every second of every minute of existence . . . in perpetuity until all is complete.

When Hope Dies

A tear rolls down,

and it screams as it runs.

Delicate and rare,

trying to catch up to hope.

A senseless race,

the tears dry up as the cold sets in.

Confusion and delusion

take me by the hand,

and walk me into a corner.

Wait here, they command,

as they kick me in the head.

Over and over again.

They tag out,

and in comes the abuse of legions.

Those demons of many restless souls.

Slamming my head

against my righteousness,

until I black out.

Awakened by my own screams,

fear and pride laugh and ridicule.

Like an old friend,

they know what buttons to press.

With a ton of weight,

they pirouette on each button they know.

driving me to visit the darkness

of my insanity.

How I long for this nightmare to end,

only as I realize that this has just begun.

We are playing the long game.

It's hard to remember

how I escaped the times before.

I almost remember.

A fog called uncertainty

stumbles into that corner with me.

A chill runs through my core.

Blinded, I struggle with reality.

Fight or flight?

Since I have no answer, I choose both . . .

I sit still in the corner,

and do neither.

Suddenly and violently,

hope is ripped away,

raped in front of me,

and the perpetrator grins at me.

It is gluttony,

who's appetite is never satisfied.

Disgust fills my spirit.

Wailing and gnashing my teeth,

I'm frozen in my nightmare,

and stuck on rewind.

I catch the scent of something

comfortable and familiar,

like bread baking in an oven.

The familiar smell of a loving memory.

It's faint, but distinct.

Question is, is it enough to hold onto?

Chapter 7

I'm staring at the shadows on the walls, as the moonlight and streetlights sliced through the windows and cast long shadows that sometimes moved but stayed the same. When I was sick, they always grew like ten times the size they regularly were, it was always disturbing. Nights in these parts were warm and moist, humid and the box fans in the windows did nothing to cool anything down, how could it? The fans just blew in the balmy air from outside to the inside. My dad, me, and Gus were always mending the screens on the windows because pop kept up with stuff and always had something going on, but later he spent a lot of time with God alone. The mosquitoes were bad if there was even a little tear in the window screen, and the crickets were loud like they were rubbing their legs together right in your ear. I loved it when the gardenias would bloom, the night air would be filled with its bold, floral, woodsy scent and would make the nights seem cooler somehow. I can't sleep right now, and while I stare at these shadows on the ceiling and the walls, sometimes closing in on me, I would lay there worrying of nothing, just about being lonely suffering, torturing myself with endless worry about this loneliness being forever, and I'm only twelve years old. I'm attending Crockett Middle School now, in my second year here and today was completely different and memorable although I didn't know it when I woke up this morning. My mom would drop my brother off at Fletcher and then drop me off at Crockett, I think, or vice versa, anyway I would walk home since we only lived two and a half blocks from my school. A regular morning excited a new year has started and getting used to the schedule now, especially orchestra class, I'm in heaven and it has only a little to do with music. More like surprise and confusion, like I needed anymore to worry about, already I was getting very little sleep for staying up half the night just worrying about loneliness and death, but not like fear of death but death being an escape from the emptiness I felt inside and having trouble with discovery, my humanness and God. I would talk to him as I lay in bed alone and worrying, I felt distant from God, like He was there but too far to be next to me. I knew that He was intimately aware of me, but I felt far away . . . distant, even to myself.

The bell rings, and I take my seat, something is amiss but with electricity in the air like something was about to really change my life. I knew about eighty percent of the kids in school because we all started at Fletcher together or we knew each other from the neighborhood, or church. It was still that small town, no need to lock doors, and you could run around all over town without supervision. I was still shy and introverted although you couldn't tell because I masked my loneliness so well, and my friends from school, I didn't hang out after school with those friends, I hung out with my neighborhood friends, and my church friends. Cristo Rey allowed us to know kids from all around the area because it was the only Parish that celebrated the Holy Mass in Spanish. Father Luis had established it under the auspice of the Mission of the Augustinian Order from Spain. I was always intrigued by the statue of Cristo Rey—Christ the King that was prominently standing above the front doors to the church, I always gazed or glanced, depending on the type of event and pace to which we were exiting the church, seeing Him so Kingly up there with the world held in one palm of his hand and a scepter in the other and a crown upon His head. I was in love, but I didn't know what love was yet, and I wouldn't for another twenty-five years, yes you heard that right . . . thirty . . . 25?

"Good morning class," greeted Mrs. Barns our homeroom teacher, of the G's, H's, I's, and I'm not sure about J's. We all greeted her back. "I want to introduce a new student, Santos will you please tell Rosa that you will be her class buddy and make sure that she understands what we are talking about and to assist her in speaking with me, especially if she has any questions." All I could concentrate on when she was telling me this, and all the boys . . . and the girls, were already staring because she was tall and beautiful. She had light brown to dark blonde hair with hazel eyes and light complected, it tripped me out because she looked white, and couldn't speak a lick of English. She rattled off Spanish though, and I had to ask her often to repeat herself and to slow down because I spoke and understood Spanish, that's all we spoke at home except among me and my siblings, we spoke English to each other. My older siblings, I'm sure, think in Spanish and translate in their minds to English, whereas I think in English and have to make that translation in my mind to Spanish so my Spanish has no regional dialect nor was it extensive, this would always give me problems especially when I became an educator for an International haircare company and I had to refer to the scalp, in Spanish! I had all those hairdressers rolling when I did my first in-salon class in Spanish, but they loved the effort, and it was the first time that company had a bilingual educator.

After we recited the pledge of allegiance, which I didn't translate because I just couldn't, I did explain what we had just done. It was so commonplace all the days of my school years, we always started the day with the pledge of allegiance, I can't remember if there was also a prayer. I believed in it, since I was born a Texan, so were my parents, my maternal grandmother was born in Texas, and Tía Juana tells me that she was Coahuiltecan Tejas Indian descent, my paternal grandmother was born in Mexico. My paternal grandfather was born in Texas, and my maternal grandfather was also born in Texas. The Hispanic community was small and tight nit. I remember many a house bar-b-que to celebrate birthdays or weddings, or baby showers, graduations, etc. Rosa turned out to be funny and very talkative, we got along fine from the beginning and as the years passed, her father Don Alejandro would become a close friend of my father. This was the first day I was tasked to be of service to someone outside of church and I know that Mel was around, I sensed him but I didn't know at the time that it was Mel, just that I had a Guardian Angel, because Scripture told us, and my faith accepted all Scripture as Truth revealed and I had no reason to question it. I felt a closeness to the Word of God, it was the only real tangible thing I had of Him, since I felt distance from Him in the Spirit.

After the bell rung, I asked Rosa if she would be ok for her next class, she said yes and thanked me for my help. She was glad that we met, and that the teacher put us together. She told me she had someone in her next class that was assigned to do the same as I did for her in this class. One of the boys from the neighborhood, one that I didn't hang out with much came up and said, "Santos, tell Rosa that she is really pretty and that I wanted to say hi, and tell her my name too.", "Yea, no. I'm not your interpreter, you should know Spanish you tell her yourself and if you don't know Spanish then learn it because I ain't doing it," and I walked away, and so did Rosa. Rudy just stood there stunned and embarrassed, that was not like me. I was changing and I knew it, I felt it. I didn't know what it was, couldn't put my finger on it but I was becoming uncomfortably aware of my surroundings in a way that I knew was way beyond my years. I was learning more of life in Sunday school than I was in public school, but I was making the most of it in school. Like I said my orchestra class was my favorite, not because I like to play music but because I enjoyed it more than sixth grade orchestra, same teachers but new students. This was probably the most relaxed class I had and looked forward to each day aside from art class. When I was in fifth grade, towards the end of the school year, and boy, was I glad to be getting out of elementary school! That incident in Mr. Busby's class when I got paddled in front of the entire classroom for the first time ever, still lived in my mind. Anyway, faculty from Crocket Middle School were registering and selling us on their elective classes, like band, orchestra, etc. I don't know what made me want to choose a music class, but I listened to both the band and orchestra instructors, I chose orchestra because they would loan all the students their instruments but band, I would have to supply my own instrument and I never wanted to be a burden on my parents when I was a kid. This is the year I asked my dad if he could help me find a job because he had to take care of so many kids, this way at least I could buy my own clothes and they would have one less kid to worry about, so he got me a job as a shoe shine boy at his Barber's, Mr. Oshea who lived a block away from us and his shop was down the street on 11th St. right over the railroad tracks across the street from Deb's Liquor Store, which is still there to this day, both the liquor store and the shop, although it's a hair salon not a barber shop now.

My worrying became worse as the months went by, and I was starting to notice that even at school there was a big change happening to everyone that I had grown up with during Fletcher days, and noticed it everywhere, in the neighborhood and Sunday School, there was electricity in the air and things were becoming clearer in some regards and more confusing on other fronts. I noticed that boys were starting to chase the girls more and the girls once huddled together in groups started being walked to class by their "boyfriends", which was totally foreign to me, this concept of "going together", going where I thought, but I knew it had to mean more than just walking a girl to class, and why didn't the girls walk the boys to class, never entered my mind back then in the early seventies, this is just the culturally normal thing to do. Boys and girls held hands, boys walked their girlfriends to class and carried their books. I didn't know what else they did together outside of school, but I really didn't care. I just started to notice, and I knew it had something to do with the girls because their chests were bigger than even last year, their grapes sprouted to plums and some to peaches but there was one girl, and her little sister, who were the talk of the school. They were relatively not known before, but this year they were in all the boys' minds and busy turning them down. Lydia was very pretty, aside from Rosa there was no competition, for distinct reasons of course, but I would have to say, among the Latinas, they were the belle of the ball. Lydia was pretty, nice, and had melons in the seventh grade while Rosa was breaking down boundaries and being chased by all the white jocks who usually stuck to dating their own race, not that this was noticeable to everyone, but I picked up on these things at a young age, probably starting in the sixth grade. Part of pushing me towards reality was the fact that we had an English teacher that one day had to be taken out of the classroom because she was too drunk and kept passing out at her desk. We all knew that she would keep a coffee thermos at her desk and kept pouring what we always thought was coffee, but we were woke now, adult teachers got drunk in school and their mother had to be called to come talk some sense into her to leave the classroom, and no, we never saw any police.

"God, I don't want this, please not this. I'm already miserable, let me know that I got this all wrong." From here I would spend the rest of the restless night tossing and turning, but mainly staring at those shadows. I pleaded with Him into the wee hours of the night, wrestling with whatever was pulling and pushing, stretching me, contorting my view and sentiment of loneliness, death, and now this! I couldn't bear it. It all started back a few months at the start of school, I noticed we had new kids in the 6th grade, and boys were rare in orchestra, aside from smart nerds, but smart nerds were popular or at least second to athletes in my middle school. I played out at third chair, second violin the first year, sixth grade, but now I had played out to first chair second violin, not a place I wanted to be, but happy I was able to get here, and yea a little bit of pride but not looking forward to the work and attention. Later that same year, I ended up in second chair, second violin, and just in case you didn't know second violin supports the first violin, who plays the melody, both harmonically and rhythmically. I always felt the melody was more fun, so I was bored right off the bat, not to mention . . . my first pick was not the violin, it was the cello. They said my hands were too small, who were they to limit my potential? I thought that then because I remember. My Tia Lucia asked me a very candid and straightforward question, but in curiosity and trying to understand this story, "How can you know what you were aware of at that early age? You are a different person, joonie (that's what my tias call me). I was honest, and replied, "Only with the Holy Spirit, I prayed, and God blesses me when I am obedient and I asked Him when I moved back to allow me to go back to see where it was that I welcomed sin into my spirit, and He did over several years." It has been a journey, but I digress . . .

I had to meet this new kid, something about him I'm drawn to, and we've smiled at each other a couple of times, and we always say hello to each other. I don't know anybody in the sixth grade, so I can't ask anyone I know about him, but I wouldn't anyway because I just wasn't that type of boy. I was shy and quiet, except for when we would sit around a circle in orchestra class playing a clapping game, where you sing and carry a tune and name all the cars by model into the beat. I know, I know it sounds crazy, but this is the time where we were hearing 'Ring My Bell', 'Le Freak Le Chic', and Anne Murray's 'Danny's Song' that sums up the love that was flowing through the hallways of Crockett Middle school, kids hitting their teens and classes like biology and orchestra! On the one hand I knew that as a young man from a respectful family, cute and smart needed a girlfriend because that's what was trending . . . LOL. Trending, before we knew what trending would become on social media. Dating was trending and trending big, it was like over the summer someone had flipped a switch and boys became bigger and girls showed new body parts that captured all the boys' attention. Much more activity and communication between the sexes unlike I had experienced at any other grade. The seventh grade was setting a new pace and for me, Jimmy was the first stranger that I was determined to befriend.

I can't remember how we met, but I think my friend Karen, also a cellist, really hit it off with him and she introduced us, from there it was usually the four of us; oh yea, my best friend Debbie. In sixth grade orchestra, we both were violinists (ha-ha, sounds better than we both played the violin, which would be a more accurate description). We had hit it off and it was always refreshing after spending time with her, she was someone I could hang out with all the time. I never let her know that, but I really liked Debbie but never thought that we could have been anything other than friends, but I did imagine her being my girlfriend and being happy. She lived close to the middle school and to my house on what was Railroad St. The trains that traverse this city have always been many and many a complicated, all-in-all it worked for several decades. The train tracks ran right through the middle of this street for about 3-4 miles. Driving right along or against the traveling train, you could reach out the window and touch the train, it seemed like, and was always a trip riding next to a train, much less, learning to drive. My father had a 1973 Dodge pickup truck, white, later he put a white camper on it. I remember going to Cheto for the summer and holidays and riding in the back with snacks, pillows, blankets the luggage and everything my mom would like to pack. Mom always managed to pack whatever vehicle to the brim, she thought of everything even to her favorite cooking utensils. Plus, if you have a really good mom, you always had tacos de frijoles refritos and some chips, like Fritos . . . and in those days they came with a little eraser in the image of Frito Bandito, it was a marketing scheme for Fritos . . . a revolution to instant migas. Migas are no more than corn tortilla pieces fried in oil until desired crispiness is reached and then you add the eggs. Yum, huevos con Fritos, but the traditional is with the frying of the corn tortillas. If you've never tried it, you are in for a good treat. Of course, we would also be traveling with a botella de chile, Trappey's Red Devil brand, of course. No other is as tangy and good. Ding Dongs, cold fried chicken, this one I remember one trip where we stopped in Houston to pick up my Tia Rosa and she bought a bucket of chicken, so of course it cooled, and the trip took eight hours so plenty of time to enjoy my favorite way to eat fried chicken and that's cold. Out of the fridge cold is delicious, same with pizza except that I do like pizza hot just as much as cold, not the same with me and chicken.

Oh, back to Jimmy, if he was absent, I absolutely would have had a bad day, and I couldn't figure out why he made me feel this way. I hadn't felt like this with anyone, getting lost in his big blue eyes as the light gave him a golden halo, wings . . . the boys and girls hairstyles were all the rage, and his soft very blonde hair was casually parted down the middle and was about earlobe length with a little wavy, soft curl towards the ends. He was my bright moment of the day when I reveled in his company. Soft white skin with salmon, pale pink undertones. He was an angel, or like the pictures of angels I would see in religious art during this time, never in my childhood, at least it started in this school year, did I ever think or realize that Jesus could have been any color. It was only later in life, that I realized that He didn't only have to be white, He could have very well been brown or very dark or whatever . . . we don't know. I mean look at Rosa, she was the first Mexican girl that I knew that was tall, beautiful, funny, talkative (interesting and intellectual conversations), and basically white in what you would think in that time. Light complected skin with no dark undertones, sandy sun kissed dark blonde hair, and light-colored eyes. Anyway, my Jimmy just captured my heart and I wanted him to keep it, I was grateful that we became very good friends and it never got weird between us, because I kept all this bottled inside and I was the only one, unless you were paying very close attention like in a stalker mode, because I was very talented in keeping things to myself, building walls, drawbridges, damns, levees', just to keep my sanity. Sometimes I felt that there was something tugging and pulling me in opposite directions, confused and conflicted as to my true love, but I was in a dark place during what should have been a beautiful experience in puberty. Except that I didn't know why my hands sweat in anticipation for orchestra class with Jimmy, it was the only period I had with him since he was an underclassman, but oh my how I had it bad for him, with butterflies in my stomach and if he missed a class, it was torture because I didn't even like the violin, I wanted to be a cellist but no, the teacher said my hands were too small . . . what a way to stifle talent. Overcome adversity, they should have let me try, I most certainly would still be playing a cello today, sometimes I think of taking it up, but I don't know what stops me . . . maybe the effort . . . how lame.

On the other hand, I was trying to live a life expected and readily accepted as normal. To get a good education, a decent job, a wife, and children, living out my life with family and children and love the experiences of bringing forth life, and leaving a little of me in another person. Biologically speaking of course, that little of something in someone else . . . some of my own DNA along with that of a wife, and continue the blood line of my father, and his father, and his father, and his father, and his father, and you get the point. I was suffering such loneliness because back then I wasn't deep into the experience of the Spirit, I was fumbling through it all, and there were obstacles, bypassing, and hidden paths in this journey. Aside from how I was feeling about Jimmy, which confused me, I was determined to figure out this whole girlfriend-boyfriend thing. It was time to start thinking about asking one of the girls to be my girlfriend, I just had to choose but this terrified me. Not because I didn't like girls, it's that I was a late bloomer in the whole puberty and finding your sexuality thing. It was as though I just stumbled into and with my sexuality, but that is a little inaccurate because I didn't know what I liked sexually, nothing was popping a boner in these days, probably worn out, but that was changing, and it all started changing during a game of chase playing cops and robbers. One of the neighborhood kids was riding on my bike with me that night. We were playing the police and the robbers were on foot trying to grab us and take us down. Now that I look back on that, we were training ourselves on protecting our streets in the Avenues. Little Mexico they call it now, and it has lived up to the name, where it is not uncommon to hear gunfire. It was during the summer because I remember it getting dark and we were still out and the only times our parents allowed this was on Fridays or summers. So, there we were, about six of us, with the two of us on the bike. We had just ridden through the others unscathed because of my speed and ability to dodge the kids on foot. I would make the block (not one of those huge city blocks, just a regular one with the church taking up half and what used to be six one-story houses taking up the other block). I would take the block to catch our breath from barreling through the street as fast as I could peddle, and it was after the third turn that it happened! The first time someone ever touched me sexually, the boy reached down and grabbed me with both hands and started squeezing, ever so gently. I was instantly excited, I wasn't repulsed by it, but I didn't acknowledge that it happened and he let go as I lifted my body off the bicycle seat to start peddling faster as I reached the last curve in the road before and I knew they were waiting for us, but all this was clouded by what just happened.

As I made it through the robbers trying to stop us on the bike and commandeer my bike, this would mean we lost and they would now be the cops, but all done in pairs . . . I have no clue why that was a thing. Maybe because cops back then patrolled in twos. We took it easy, laughing and breathing hard while celebrating our near escape. What we didn't do was talk about what just happened, but it was just that fast that I was not thinking about how wrong that was, not because we were both boys, although this was a big one for me at the time, I was thinking and wondering if he would touch me again. I tried to brush it off and act as if nothing happened, but I was nervous with anticipation as we made that third turn again around the block. I take it extra slow to give him ample time to do it again if he wanted to, but I also didn't want to be weird about it, just in case I imagined it all. It's laughable now to think I could have imagined a thing like that had happened. We finished our small talk earlier, and as we made our turn and passed the first house on the left and came up to the backside of the church, what was the church hall at that time. We were out of sight from everyone, he reached around and did the same thing, but this time I wheeled the bike to the side of the hall, we got off and I touched him back and we got a few squeezes in before I started to put my hands down his pants, and now he was timid?! He initiated this entire thing and now he is being shy about where my hand was going, where did he think it was going to go? Did he not think beyond the groping? He was two years younger than me, but he started the whole thing, and I hadn't even imagined touching someone else before this. There were some things going on like masturbating and finding my brother's great stash of porn mags hidden in the bottom of the bottom drawer in our bathroom. I don't remember how I found his stash, but oh my, it was an enormous collection. This kid gets nervous so I tell him that no one can see us, and then I told him that he could touch me the same way. He smiled big and that was all it took, we were groping our naked boyhood and it was exhilarating but we knew that we couldn't be long, the other kids were waiting for the cops, and we were already taking too long, those kids didn't miss anything!

Since it was a neighborhood thing, and he was two years younger than me, it didn't affect what was happening at school and I wasn't worried that he would say anything to anyone. We had made a promise to keep it between us. At school I was still maneuvering through what I think I should be doing, so far as girls, and I guess boys too because I was starting to understand that instead of having a crush on the girls, I was also crushing on one boy for sure . . . for Jimmy! I wasn't hating myself for it, he made me laugh, he was talented, witty, and very cute; handsome, like an angel. Even at that age I wanted it all, but didn't know that's what something evil in me was trying to convince me of, while I knew in my heart the right decisions I should be trying to make, I had grown up in the church across the street, I knew that I was a child of God and that God had certain standards and morals that He expected of those who love Him. I knew that He was present and alive, and gives forth life, I had a strong sense of faith in the Holy Trinity, our Mother Mary and God's entire family, but this also included the belief and awareness that the devil and demons existed. I knew they weren't on our side, these demons, and the devil, that they try to make us follow them, listen to them, make us their monkeys. Even back then, I was just unaware of the war, I underestimated the amount of hate and lies the devil was capable of and at what lengths he would go to corrupt someone like me. I always felt protected by God, I believed in prayer, and I loved God and spending time with him at church, this is why I participated and was involved in the church life. Already depressed, and everything else happening now to a twelve-year-old. Not to mention that both of my career goals were already smashed in my middle school years, the first was fighter pilot because my eye vision was right on the verge of blind, I came to know this by not being able to read the board from the closest row to the chalkboard. It was in Mr. Bryant's math class; he sat me in the front row, and I still had to ask him to approach the chalkboard to write down my homework assignments. The second was dually competing interests in art and music, and I was mediocre at both, but I loved it and kept signing up for art classes but left music alone after middle school, mainly because Mrs. Todd did not adequately prepare us, as one of our orchestra teachers, to prepare us for high school orchestra. It wouldn't have been so bad if me and Debbie noticed how her students she taught in the more affluent middle school were ten times the violinists we were, it was embarrassing, and Mrs. Todd made it worse by calling us out in front of the entire orchestra.

To make a long story short about my first girlfriend, because nothing happened between us, although she was the most well-endowed 7th grader. I was in the eighth at this point and so much was happening, including calls to acts of justice. I asked Lydia to be my girlfriend like a practice because she was turning down all the requests from the boys to be their girlfriend, and none received a yes. I had the advantage of being good friends with her best friend, we were both in Home Economics together and I started asking her if Lydia had a boyfriend and Maria was more than eager to say that she didn't and to inquire why my interest. In the interest of time, she became my girlfriend, I caught grief from my oldest sister about not being able to wipe my ass right without leaving stains in my drawers, but I had the nerve to have a girlfriend. Rough, but looking back on it, it was tough love. Plus, it had no effect because my other problems were bigger to deal with than the stains I left because as a boy, yeah, we weren't always immaculately clean and sanitary. Which further confused me about having crushes on boys because I didn't play with my sisters or girls or their toys, I was into marbles, chase, kickball, playing with bugs, hot wheels, army, cops & robbers, playing under the house, jumping off the house, and playing baseball and football with the neighborhood kids. Aside from being smart, liking art class, and orchestra, I was a normal boy who liked doing normal boy things. So, needless to say, I was a perfect gentleman with my girlfriend except breaking up with her twice, and the second time a couple of days before Valentine's day solely because I was expected to buy her a gift and I wasn't going to spend my allowance on her because I saw that as my parent's hard earned money, and the last thing I was going to do was make them pay for my girlfriend's gifts, so I broke up with her. This is how my twelve-year-old mind maneuvered that predicament.

At the very least this one less social problem was a relief, but then my interests were consumed by something else, the injustice of corporal punishment in school. Back in my middle school years at Crockett I made it all the way through until the eighth grade not being paddled, and it was rampant in our school. Teachers were getting creative with their paddle designs, some shaped like a tennis racket with holes drilled into the head to cut wind resistance, while others were narrow, skinny, and wrapped with tape designed to be aerodynamic and with a sting that made it hard to sit, if the teacher had an arm. This was the other thing the adults were doing in our school, they were taking their students to other teachers because they could instill more pain, and they made a reputation out of it. I started notic-ing how there were more and more children being lined up outside the halls of teachers' classrooms, but it wasn't until I was sitting in Mr. Lee's history class that I aimed to do something about this rampant abuse of power. Back then, at first, I didn't do anything but notice and thinking that kids were acting up more and more, but when Mrs. Lee told us to be quiet while she paddled Mrs. Main's students that she brought over, we were instructed to work on our history projects in silence. Kids being kids, especially those who liked to talk and had too much energy to stay still and quiet, started to get louder and louder. When Mrs. Lee came back into the classroom, she was angry, yelling at us that we had embarrassed her in front of Mrs. Main and that we were all bad and for all of us to come out and line up, where she proceeded to give each of us two licks (hits with the paddle). I was fuming, how unjust, I wasn't being loud, I had remained silent and worked on my history project, just as she had instructed, and I was still punished. As a child, I knew that the cards were stacked against me, but there had to be a way to make them realize that they were abusing their power over us, because if the innocent were being sacrificed for the sake of someone's pride, something had to be done. I say this so eloquently now, but then it was more like how dare you hit me when I did nothing wrong, and I can't do anything to you because you are an adult. This was not satisfying to me, I had to come up with another way. The days passed and the more I suffered with my depression, the social awkwardness of crushing on a boy, not feel-ing up Lydia (not even the feeling up but just the fact that I had no interest bothered me) and being lonely and not knowing why.

Every day after school, I would stay late since it was my last class of the day, and I would help clean up Ms. Reed's art classroom. She would let me work on my art homework if she had papers to grade or whatever and then we would clean the room and go. I would always walk home since it was only a few blocks from home, so I don't know where I came up with the plan to take as many paddles from the teachers' classrooms as possible. Just one problem, I didn't know how much time I would need, if the teachers left their paddles out, or who stayed late in the building. It was as if the plan was born within me and folding out as I let it take me. I started to take more bathroom breaks afterschool while I was helping Ms. Reed, I would sneak around, peering in the teacher's classrooms and noticed paddles laying out in the open, and took notice of who was staying late and the fastest route to take as I was putting together in my head, a map of sorts, upstairs and downstairs because I just had this feeling that I should not focus on only one floor but to take as many paddles as possible, especially from those teachers that were starting to develop a reputation or had a reputation of being able to inflict a lot of pain on some of the thickest skinned butts. Ms. Reed never caught on to anything, what teacher would? I was always a teacher's favorite; I was the smart nerdy well-known and well-liked kid from an honorable family with reputations of three older sisters and older brother that preceded me. The week that I was ready, I enlisted the help of my best friend, Debbie, to be the look out and keep Ms. Reed from coming to look for me (keeping her in her classroom was the goal but as long as she didn't come looking for me), since this was the only part of my spontaneous planning that I figured needed another set of eyes, and I remember only thinking I hope Debbie doesn't crush under pressure if we get found out and they start asking questions. I trusted Debbie, only to realize how honorable and tough she was after the pressure from the adults after they did find out what I did, was intense. The Friday came that I decided was 'go' day, I took one of those big brown paper grocery bags we used to have in the grocery stores, which I would like to point out today, were more environmentally safe than those plastic things they readily and eagerly bag everything with nowadays, they even try to bag a candy bar if you let them, but then complain about the price to buy bags. I hid the bag in my wall locker, and after school Debbie and I went to Ms. Reed, I introduced Debbie since Debbie didn't have Ms. Reed for art class and they hit it off. We had a great time and then I excused myself to use the bathroom, as I left the room I locked eyes with Debbie's, and we exchanged what to me felt like this charged energy that we were on the verge of committing a crime, ok maybe not a crime because I was fighting for justice, but criminal in the sense that we were about to piss off the entire ruling class of this middle school, all of leadership was going to be impacted, but not really, how could we know their reaction? We just knew we were doing something we were not supposed to be doing according to what we knew at the time, but something deep within me knew that something was wrong with the way the adults were acting in this power paradigm.

First thing I did was to go to my locker, which was close by on the second floor just in case I was caught in the middle of this heist at least the brown bag might mask the paddles except for those long ones, but I wasn't sure if the bag would cover all of them. I started just like my reconnaissance before and started violating the space of the power-hungry adults and stealing their source of power and symbol of authority over us, those treasures that allowed them to inflict influence with pain. I got comfortable with my ability and the speed in which I was performing so I got a little bold, but not too bold as to try to jeopardize my mission. Calculating and shrewd, I went room to room, that I liked or disliked the teachers didn't matter, they all were involved in a system of abuse and no adults were doing anything about it, this is why I had to act. I returned the grocery bag to my locker, but now it was full, if my memory serves me well it must have been like 8 paddles, may not sound like much in these days of oversized classrooms and such but back then that was six to eight teachers out of about 15-20, not including administrators. I walked home that day with a bag full of paddles, and only recently found out that I may have given Debbie one of them as a memento. When I reached the house, I realized I hadn't planned on what to do with all these paddles when I got them home, so I stashed them under the casita, the little house behind our house. When we returned to school on Monday, boy did I realize what an impact I had made on the everyday life of everyone, especially the teachers and administrators of the schools. Every teacher in every class reprimanded us, they said that the person that did this would be found, and the truth would set us free. They were angry, accusatory, and surprisingly obnoxious in their tone and speech. They told us that we weren't going to change anything, that we would get in trouble, fuss, fuss, fuss, arrogance, pride, warnings, and threats. Not the reaction I was looking for, this is not good, I thought. It only took me a couple of days to think of what I could do to alter or affect their reaction to this violation of their power and authority. Steal them again, all their back-ups they were so championing as they revealed them from their hiding places, like I didn't take notice where they were taking them out from, where they kept those back-ups safe from prying eyes or slick fingers. This time I would do it all alone, I did not even tell Debbie what I was going to do. I was impressed and honored that I had a friend like Debbie because she never broke under all of that pressure campaign brought on by the responsible adults. Again, I took the paddles from the same rooms plus some new ones, that I didn't hit the first time. All the while, being the little shy, innocent boy.

"Santos, do you need a ride?" Ms. Reed surprised me when she pulled her car over to me as I was walking with a big brown paper bag! I was toast, I thought, as I thought quick on my feet. "I have to stop and leave this at one of my mom's friend's house. She asked me to drop it off after school on my way home. "I can take you". "No thank you I'm almost there, and I like walking home from school". "Ok, have a good weekend, see you on Monday." I was a liar, I thought, that can't be good. I just lied to my favorite teacher, as I was in the middle of a robbery, and I did it all with a straight, and obviously convincing way. What was happening to me, I thought, on top of everything else that I must deal with and worry about, now this. What am I supposed to do with all these paddles now? I have the first stash and with this second stash, now I have double or more. So, being a small municipality where we could still burn trash in a barrel, that weekend I took all the paddles and set fire to them with our trash for the week. The only other person besides Debbie who knew and saw those paddles was my little brother Gus, with whom I've never spoken to about this to ask if he remembers. I was starting to think it was just some made up story in my head, not that I have those, but when no one said anything as I was posting to Facebook on our Class FB Group, I asked if anyone remembered and at first no one remembered, and then Debbie commented, and I drew a sigh of relief. She remembered, she said she may still have one of those paddles and that she told her children that story years ago! When I went back to school on Monday, wondering how much they were going to be threatening and fussing about those paddles, there was silence about any paddles being stolen or for that matter, nothing, zilch, zip, nada. Now, this is the reaction I wanted to begin with, but better late than never. The paddling halted, when they finally replaced their paddles, there were very few lines, fewer students being paddled over petty things, and there seemed to be a little fear in the air, emanating from the adult power class. Someone had violated them, invaded their personal space, and took away their source of what had become their power, while losing focus of their true power, their minds. I'm glad that I helped put things into perspective for them, but I didn't think of how I would get caught, or that I would get into trouble, I somehow knew that I was fighting the right fight, and that I had done the right thing. To me, their silence, was my success and their conformity to a higher moral authority would only be clear as the Spirit allowed me to journey in my own history to enlighten me on how God worked in my life and where I strayed. This was one of those times when God uses the less likely to be the force to cause change for justice and love.

Walking Alone

Loneliness descends upon me,
like a heavy fog on a hot summer night.
I'm alone and terrified of what I can't see
but I sense I'm not alone, and I tremble with fright.
Shadows behind shadows reaching out,
trying to drag me into the fog
where they do what they want on their walkabout.
I feel a sadness set upon my shoulders like a heavy log.
A never-ending nightmare, I suffer.
While the shadows laugh and taunt me in a loud silence,
I try to gather my senses, and I try to be tougher,
but I find myself drawn into a strange, lonely romance.
The shadows take me, and force me into a waltz,
while I laugh and scream in my lonely heart.
I try to run away, but I run back to embrace the false.
Hopeless, the shadows take turns in-kind, tearing me apart.
Trapped like sand in an hourglass,
everyone can see me running
but no one can see those shadows kicking my ass.
Their evil abuse is powerfully stunning.
I live in the death grip of loneliness,
breathing the night fog deeply into my spirit
as I waste away in my blindness.
The shadows tear out my heart and start to eat it.
The darkness settles in around me,

hope doesn't seem to stand a chance
as I tire of any effort to break free.
I dance with the shadows in a trance.
In my pride, I made my choices,
and one by one, they led me astray
even as I heard all their evil voices
telling me, one day, that I would pay.
The toll and stakes are high,
the shadows always paying attention
and listening for the fear in my sigh.
Like cats, they pounce at my spiritual malnutrition.
I try to break away
only to discover that I am lost,
a whisper reminds me to pray
and slowly, my prayers erase the cost.
The abandoned years of my youth,
mostly spent lost in that fog
with the shadows lying about truth . . .
convincing me that I was just a wild dog.
Not until I chose to listen
did I hear that whisper telling me to pray
which freed me from my prison
and never again to be led astray.

Chapter 8

M y eighth-grade summer was the best, I threw a fit that helped me take a trip to Asherton, to spend a couple of weeks before my parents and my siblings would take our yearly summer trip to Cheto, where my parents grew up. This is the summer I convinced my cousin Ari to help me put together a newspaper, it was all plagiarized, but I didn't know any better, this was the first newspaper and the second would be decades later and it was for Mom's Christmas village. I had a really enjoyable time, and it was the first time ever that I was without my immediate family, with my grandparents (maternal) and my aunts and uncle. I would go around to see my father's side of the family when he and my mom would take us with them to visit relatives and friends while we were there. Me and Ari had so much fun, we spent hours playing together, we especially loved playing in closets that were connected from my grandparent's bedroom to another bedroom. Ari didn't stay with us though, she slept over at her father's mom's house. If we weren't at our 'Beula's house, we would have been at Ari's grandma's house. This is when we negotiated the terms of our journalistic partnership, mind you I was only twelve but soon to be a teenager, this is why I threw the fit to be able to come here without my mom and dad, brothers and sisters, because as I argued, I was with my mom's mother and her sister, my tía Lucia. I was growing up and after my personal private justice crusade with the paddles was so successful, I was starting to get a little big for my britches.

"I don't think they trust you", I whisper into this boy's mind, just a little doubt brought to you by none other than by my cucchi cucchi coo, Charo strikes again! "You should get angry", I whispered, "They don't trust you, even with family"; I could see this was working. He was really making a scene and putting his parents in a bind, their little boy wanted something and didn't want to take no for an answer. This was a first for them, from this child anyway. It took me a while and a few years, but I knew I would eventually grind him down to this. Riggs told me I should have worked faster but

I decide what and how to do what I do, no one's the boss of me. I made up my own bad ass nick name, Charo! I love myself so much, the power I hold over people that are tuned out but think they are tuned in. Kids are easy, well most of them, and this was a hard little nut to crack. "The rest will be easy", I thought but this little kid was getting a lot of help, which wasn't making my job easy at all even though I was convincing him to ignore that good part of him that he liked so much. I've had a lot of practice, but the most famous and treacherous, besides the Garden, was Riggs' open invitation for Judas. I was jumping for joy, swirling about the sky when I saw him enter him, what a site. "Start prepping him for me", Riggs commanded of me, I was tickled because I had just screwed up big time with those who identified themselves as Legion when Jesus came upon them. I kept telling them to be careful and that they were getting too crowded in that worn-out human sack of nothing, too scared to believe anything. Those are my favorite! Those of you who think you know everything and are too scared to use that faith you don't deserve. I don't know why J (can't bear the pain to speak His name) would spit out all you lukewarm, you are the most delectably delicious appetizers, it's no secret we all think that He has made some pretty screwed up moves with His Majesty that just dishonors the very law that God set into motion. Not the brightest, but who am I to judge? Ha, ha, ha, I love that line! "Who am I to judge?!" I crack myself up, but you should see it when we all meet up to a corruptionade. A favorite concoction of corruption and persuasion to an evil thought, or action, which sets off a chain of events because it works so well with the free will defect within you all. Some call it original sin, I call it pretty stupid, but ok I will take the delicious freebies that don't know anything about anything but think they know everything about everything. This was a fun little project because it softens this little boy up for the big plans Riggs has in store for him. Right now, this little temper tantrum in disrespect to his parents for selfish reasons is enough to lay a good ground game after a successful initial onslaught in the physical dimension. Yep, on special occasions we can use the 'Free Will Clause Exemption" built into our contracts. We don't get very many, and they must be approved by Riggs G to use them, so they are effectively supporting our concerted efforts to destroy as many of you as possible. Fun! Fleshy viruses full of shit and air, never satisfied and always indulgent, and it's not just food which makes it so easy to corrupt and persuade. Thus, corruptionade, which is something I came up with described my feelings about you all and when I first knew of lemonade. Deliciously sweet and sour, with a hint of bitterness. He got his way, so this filled him up with pride and entitlement which is fertile soil for the lust I had set off in him recently, as he moved from rubbing one out to touching and tasting. I love this more than my fall, which was a wee bit painful and very frustrating. Wings clipped so we could go no farther than the Firmament. Such a beautifully 'sick' place, and I use sick in the good sense you humans use it. Your voices like nails scraped across the chalkboard, you guys have an annoying and feeble voice compared to other animals and us. I wonder why, those things that make you go 'huh'. We don't understand God's reasoning behind things, or whatever floats His boat, same as you but we actually did something about it . . . thanks to Riggs.

As much as I hate to admit it, Charo has been a tremendous help in my mission to destroy God's mud patties. Although he really pissed me off over the Legion incident, we lost all that work and effort in just one encounter . . . even as I told him to keep that under control. He ruined the plans I had for that community, they were so close to losing their souls to my darkness, but Charo took his attention away to play around with the Han Dynasty and his toy project Caligula. I'm not going to say that I direct Charo's efforts, because I do but he also knows that I had a plan and when he took his attention away from the Legion project, it ended the evil I had in store for that region. I had to start all over with another region and it's not like I have all the time in eternity. I'm glad he pulled this off with this boy, it is the first time he was openly disobedient and disrespectful to his parents to get his way. This seed of defiance will be nurtured by us to give him a firm foundation to obscure all of this trash talk in church. He spends way too much time at that church across the street from his home. This will give us a lot of time with him because with the amount of time that he is spending in church it doesn't give us as much time as I would like. This boy is very attentive and is like a sponge, but I'm determined to undermine this family, as I've tried and tried before so I know that this little boy's father is pretty tight with God. He has received all kind of attention from God's Holy Spirit . . . ugh, that has a bitter taste when I speak it. Like having skunk spray inside your mouth, don't ask. I laughed as I looked on, this was too important for me not to keep tabs on Charo, but he did a fantastic job, that little boy locked himself in his closet after making a great spectacle of his lack of honor. I would have him for a few weeks before his family joined him in Asherton. No church activities, at least he wouldn't be across the street from the church, and we could approach him any time we wanted in Asherton. At least that is what I thought, but you know we can't get everything perfect; you are all so damn unpredictable that some would say makes you all resilient, but to me it just makes my point that you are a weak and pathetic mud patty, created but made of dirt. It's a good thing most of you rely on your tormented souls to keep you company so this distraction lets me play on your dark desire to fill your pots with anything you think can make you feel full and not empty. It has begun with this kid, and I have great plans to destroy the peace within this family because God has been too good to this kid's father and mother. It was time to get their little beloved Jr to turn to me and be my puppet that destroys this family.

I knew their plan, and as much as I tried Jr was intent on going to his grandmother's and intent on leaving with them back to Asherton. I was taken by surprise at the ferocity and pointed attack of deception they unleashed on my little charge. As his protector and guide, free will is a tricky little nuance of human existence. I for one think it was God's greatest blessings upon man, because God gives humans the ability to choose to love and this makes the love extra special because you know that it is genuine, not ordered. Even ordered does not accurately reflect what it means to have free will. To be handcrafted by the hands of the Almighty, is quite an extravagant honor and then to receive His breath into you once He shaped and molded you, well . . . that's just God's perfection. Riggs' argument before the Tribunal was adamant that this creation was subpar and too fragile and frail to be worthy of God's living breath since they weren't formed and spoken into being. He convinced so many others and they would not be convinced or deterred in their disgust of humans, especially because he gave you all a kingdom, all that He created was subjugated to you. What an amazing love He displayed with your creation, and, sadly, those with Riggs did not see the perfection and beauty of man and woman. At the very beginning, even God was surprised by man, when He realized that up until man, nothing was unsatisfied. Only free will could surprise God, all knowing; this doesn't happen but free will was a first to Creation and exclusive to man. Another thing that drove Riggs-G insane with fury. It wasn't enough God favored man, you were given free will, and a kingdom to care and cultivate. Riggs lost it and launched a rebellion after God created woman for man because " . . . none proved to be a helper suited for the man." I don't know what Riggs had such a problem with, it is after all His Creation, He is God, our God. The thing that Riggs fails to realize is that while we were made to assist in God's Creation, it was made for man. There is nothing God must explain to us, we serve Him, but Riggs being the first and brightest of us all, the one that used to be God's morning star was privy to things that the rest of us were not. Not a free will but more of a free reign to manage the Heavens, which he warped into this notion that this position he held was fine enough, but that God would not listen to him about what this would do to his ability to manage the Heavens and his subjugation to the will of man that the moment had come that pride took an evil transformation and Riggs perfected this declension which became a virus in him, and he started to act defiantly. I was going to have my hands full because Riggs was up to something with my little charge, and I was determined to protect and guide him along. I knew that my little charge was going to have a rough time of it, because he was easily distracted by the confusion in his little heart. He was in a constant state of loneliness ever since the day he forgot his homework and was paddled for it. With all my efforts to keep him in church and family activities like instilling in his little brother a sincere ability to express love with his family. Gus' guardian could easily inspire acts of love towards his parents, and this helped Jr develop these expressions as well. They kissed their parents good night, which is what Gus' example was and Jr did it because I knew he had that love in his heart which would later prove invaluable to his not pulling the trigger of the gun when he had it in his mouth, but that's a story for later, for now I had to get him through the next couple of weeks because he was about to travel hundreds of miles away from his mother, father, and brothers and sisters, for the first time since he was just an infant.

I was twelve going on thirteen, over four hundred miles from home with relatives I barely knew but I knew that they loved me dearly. This was made known every time we saw them, and they always made me feel loved. I wasn't nervous, scared, fearful, I was simply happy in this newfound independence, this freedom, maybe this would help me not be so sad inside, so lonely, so scared. I loved the smell of the morning dew; it would fill you up with the history of the place where my parents grew up. Knowing you were on the roads that your parents traveled as children, youth into adulthood. No matter the distance, I found out this summer on this trip that you can't run away from your sins, you carry them around like heavy, familiar baggage.

"Puedo ir a la tiendita 'Buela?"

"Ten cuidado niño, y no te tardes." , my grandmother would say . . . be careful child, and don't be too long.

"Puedo ir más tarde a ver a Ari?" I asked before heading out to Raul's, mine and Gus' exciting first excursion each time we visited Cheto. I wanted to go visit my cousin Ari.

Sr. Raul would put up our school pictures inside a top corner of the big glass candy case atop a wooden counter with those old swivel stools. We loved saving our allowance, coupled with what my mom and dad would give us and going to Raul's (this is how we referred to it) and buying candies and answering Mr. Raul's questions:

"¿Y cómo les fue este año en la escuela, subieron grado?" Mr. Raul would always ask, I think he had a certain question he would ask all the kids, because we weren't the only kids' pictures in the glass case. I never knew why my mom would give us one of our school pictures to give to him to put in the case, but we just figured he was family somehow or a family friend.

"Si." My brother would say.

"Sí." I would also reply.

It was always a great visit; we would leave with candy that would last a few days. The coolest thing was the independence and freedom you felt not being supervised by an adult and walking to the store on your own. We did that back home, but we had bicycles and the store was not too far, but we were expected to go there and back only, until we got older.

"Hola, está Ari?" I asked Ari's grandmother when she answered the door.

"Pásale, pásale. Ari, tienes visita." She was very kind, and I felt very welcome.

"Tendrás hambre, estoy hacienda de comer." I said yes, I never turned down food.

"Hi Jr." Ari welcomed me with her signature huge joyful smile.

"Hi."

"Come play, you want to play Barbie?"

"Not really."

"Come on, I will be Barbie and you can play with the Ken."

"Naw, I really don't want to. Hey, I wanted to see if you want to help me put a newspaper together?" I didn't know where this was coming from, it was a surprise to me, but I didn't think it odd, nor did I spend a lot of time asking myself why I wanted to put a newspaper together.

"No, why do you want to write a newspaper and who are you going to sell them to?'

"I don't know, Tia Lucia, Tia Imelda, you know the family and maybe their friends."

"I tell you what, I will help you, but you have to play Barbie with me."

I thought about it, but just for a moment, I had her support, and this was going to be fun. I would get my stories from the local newspaper; at the time it was the Javelin out of Carrizo Springs. I would basically read their newspaper and then put it into my own words, with headlines, a header, columns, but unfortunately, I don't remember the name I gave it.

Ari and I would go with my Tia Lucia in the morning to her job and we would work on my newspaper and my Tia would run off copies on the copy machine. We would fold them, and I don't remember if I ended up selling them or giving them away. But it was a newspaper! And this little partnership only cost me one play date with Barbie and Ken. I would later kid around with Ari that she turned me gay because she made me play with dolls. Up to this point I never played with dolls, never interested in anything but boy things, marbles, Hot Wheel miniature metal cars, playing in the dirt, except recently as I hit puberty. I was starting to realize that I may not be like the boys I considered to be normal, you know straight. My faith also told me that I was supposed to get married and have children, this was the way of the world. It was hard being so far from readily accessible porn, like what my older brother kept at home. I was missing those, so I had to get by with other things like this paperback I found in Tio's room. He had a bookshelf with law books and such but this one was a love novel with some steamy sexual scenes in the plot of the story, just enough to let a boy's imagination go wild. Plus, I had my own few experiences already. Otherwise, it was getting pretty boring so I would pass my time with my Hot Wheels, playing in the dirt of my grandmother's garden. I spent hours out there, and since I wasn't much for reading nor conversation, I kept mostly to myself unless my Tia's would take me somewhere like the veterinarian's place my Tia Imelda worked. The most memorable was that she took me to a store and let me pick out a toy and I picked out a stuffed brown and beige dog with big floppy ears. I loved that dog; I still have him packed up somewhere to this day. The other thing was they had a big bulldog that kept farting and slobbering all over the place. I was thrilled when my parents arrived for the yearly summer vacation, because I had missed them and my family. My parents told me how Pepe, the eldest child of one of the only other Hernandez families in Beaumont wanted to talk to me about a job and that if I was interested to call him. I was excited about a more grown-up job, man, I thought, this summer is awesome. I was getting bored with my job at the barbershop because I had just about read all the comic books a couple of times over.

"Hey Jr. I was wondering if you wanted a job as a stockboy at Pic-n-tote. I have been working for Nick and Lena for a while and I got offered another job as an apprentice to a man that paints cars so they asked me if I knew anyone that he could recommend. I thought of you because I want to refer someone who I know will not let them down. What do you say?"

"Yes, I will take it. Thank you so much, I can't wait to start. I will call you when we get back home."

"No problem, I will tell Nick and Lena, they are great people so work hard and don't let me down."

"I won't, thank you again."

"Bye."

"Bye."

This was the beginning of adulthood, I thought, getting way ahead of myself, but I was high on this newfound independence and freedom. I would soon find out and learn the hard way that the kind of independence and freedom I was embracing, is costly.

I was so excited, and the work was a welcome distraction from the nights I spent awake staring at the shadows within shadows on the walls of my room. My mother or father would drive me to work at Pic-n-Tote almost every day, except on the weekends when I would ride my bike from our home to the north end of Beaumont. I was used to bike riding since this was my main pastime besides playing cars (that's what we called it), with the little Hot Wheel cars. We would spend hours on our front porch and around my mom's flowers and plants. We would pretend the brick walls that made up the flower bed were highways and within the plants we would create houses with driveways. We had our entire yard to play so it was like living in the alternate world of a make-believe metropolis. Often enough, the neighborhood kids would get together and play cars. Everyone would bring their favorite car; some would bring more. For those who didn't have one, we had plenty. Since it was mostly boys in our neighborhood we would also play 'war'. We would grab sticks that looked like guns, and we would take turns hiding and then when the countdown was complete the attacking team would navigate the front of the house, underneath which we didn't use that much, for the risk of getting shot without the room to try and dodge the bullet. Our imaginations were our playmates as well, and when we all came together to play there was so much fun and creativity. Good and bad. A loud "DisqualificATION!" would allude to breaking of rules or to prevent capitalizing on the impossible. Like shooting through things we knew bullets would have a tough time penetrating. Or using the roof of the houses, or a variety of different issues that would develop over hours playing outside with great friends.

The first week was Jose training me all that I would need to make sure Nick and Lena were set with what he said was a reliable and responsible replacement that he would feel good about leaving the store. They were great, honest, caring people. Old school Italians, homecooked Italian food. I was invited to their house on the West end for the holidays one year, where I tried stuffed artichokes for the very first time. They were ok, had them only once since then. There was so much food and desserts, it was a great dinner, and I was able to experience how people with money lived. Even though I was intrigued, I didn't pay all that much attention to all the wealth around me, because there was so much love, honesty, and frankness that I was enthralled with this experience of another type of family. Mr. Nick was funny, a tall man with just as large of a heart, and Lena was so pretty with her blonde hair and perfectly fitting outfits, but just so down to earth. She was just as sweet as she was firm when she had to be, which was all the time because Mr. Nick was the super nice, go lucky kind a guy. I enjoyed my years here, I spent nearly four years working for them, when I left, I was a cashier even though I was working the register since I started because we had two registers and sometimes, we would get a rush, so I had to learn how to use the cash register. I loved it when I was able to work the register because it was one of those tall old ones with cream and black, round buttons that you would push down to represent the dollar and cents and then the corresponding larger button to tally it up and then another to total it out. Every time you hit a button, inside the tall rectangle glass case running along the top of the register, these white tabs would come up corresponding to the buttons you were pushing, and then my favorite of favorites . . . you pull the handle on the righthand side to total it all up! Those were the days that you had to do arithmetic at a moment's notice to make change. Round up to the nearest ten with the pennies and nickels, the dimes to get you places faster and the quarters were the stars, especially later when Ronnie—Nick's son-in-law put arcade games in the store. Oh, how much fun and good we got playing these. Jose, Juan's brother, who I will tell you about in a minute, made a hole in a quarter, tied a thin thread to it and could drop it into the coin slot and pull it back up, but not before the machine registered a credit. We would load up but had to be careful so no one would discover it, but enough to have fun and eat up the time waiting around to stock, wait on clients, or clean the store. I loved it, and the smell of links bathing in simmering bar-b-que sauce (which we sold, and now that I think of it, we never tried to sell the bar-b-que sauce) and people loved these. We would put that link onto a hotdog bun, when they still baked fresh bread in Beaumont, and wrapped it up in this one page of foil we would pull out of a self-dispensing box. Simple, and delicious, but I had absolutely no interest in the most popular food item we sold from that cashier's counter, smack dab in the middle of the store with the double glass front doors right in front of it, no sir, I was not going to try those pickled pig's feet. They were sliced in half and drowning in a vinegar liquid, you could see the white cartilage in the little piggy's hoof. Oh, people bought these things up, we were always opening another big jar. Ooh, I lie, the most popular were the dill and sour pickles! Full size, lounging in delicious pickle juice. I have never cared for the taste of sour pickles, but I cannot deny that every so often I would eat about half of one before I got over the sourness. My favorite were the dill pickles, not just any brand, Del Dixie brand, the best, in my inflated opinion.

He starts school in a couple of months, and Riggs wants me to start the next phase with twinkle toes, this one is going to be a dancer from the looks of it. I do have to hand it to you all, you throw some good parties, those disgusting families you cherish so much, all of those meat on twigs living in one place, expelling the disgusting and toxic waste that comes out of all of you. I can't help but laugh so hard when I think about it, how you go from this small grubworm looking thing wearing something to catch their toxic waste to a grossly taller version of what you are at your core, your origin, dust . . . just a big ole dusty mini me wearing another diaper to catch that same toxic waste you've been shitting out all of your lives. Disgusting. I disturb his peace at night, when he thinks he is too tired to stay awake, I keep him from sleeping by whispering non-stop "Worry, fear, lonely. Worry, fear, lonely." I let him do the rest, I just keep repeating myself until he is in this endless loop of worrying about everything and nothing that matters because what can y'all change? What can you do? You are so limited in abilities, you're only something because of . . . cough, cough, spit, spit . . . God.

The plan, after the physical attack didn't work, is to torment his spirit. The special reserve instigators were making preparations, we would start with intensifying his lust for the material and the sexual, plus increase the dread and belief of being all alone, with doubt and envy thrown in. I found that the best way to start was to muster in his thoughts this spark of doubt that his parents were strong, intelligent people. I would whisper to his spirit how boring and long his father's talks were, and to drift away and not pay attention. For his mother, I would tell him how mean she was to him, compared to how she treated Gus, the baby of the family. I told him how unfair it was that his little brother would start fights, but then he would get spanked harder because he was older and should know better. He was all too eager to submit to my coercion and manipulation, the rest is easy for such a willing spirit. I took advantage like someone driving the ball down the court when his opponent trips and falls, while you dunk the ball to show off. I, Charo, do declare that things were running on time, and all starting to fall in place, Riggs and I are going to push this kid until he kills himself.

I didn't have anyone to talk to, I remember the friends in the neighborhood were all about the games, bike rides, and such but never about talking about your problems or feelings. I was a fourteen-year-old kid, from altar boy to CYO (Christian Youth Organization) president, Mexican folkloric dancing, retreats and conventions, performing for the nursing homes, I was a well-connected, well-rounded young man, handsome, and a good dancer although I did have a bit of a complex after one of my Aunts told me that I shake my booty like a girl. I was aghast, so close to what I'm uncomfortable about, not just uncomfortable, but downright horrified at the thought that the rest of my life, I would be attracted to other boys. I wanted the wife and children, oh, how I begged with God to 'fix' me. It was easy for me to think that I had to be 'fixed' because I was broken or felt that I was defective. I was all boy, except for this one problem . . . attraction to the same sex. I was already depressed, but this only made it worse. The church community would imply that I was an abomination while society exclaimed "Be free, live your life. Sex is naturally beautiful." This is the era when men started to become more effeminate. No more than the Elizabethan era with the powder, the wigs, and the ruffly clothing. Instead in my time, the 1970 through the 1990's you have what were once unappealing thin, scrawny, pretty boys wearing tights and engaging in overtly sexually free performances where the drugs allowed the environment a sexual freedom which included all that you can imagine and more. Boys that couldn't get laid before just had to put on some spandex pants, tease and perm your big hair, let your chest hang out, your crotch bulge, and join a rock band . . . this got them laid in a flash. Girls were digging it, even the boys in the neighborhood of pick-n-tote were wearing tight, short shorts with half tees, cropped midriff. Although I was confused and refused to accept who I was, it was a real turn on for me, especially my type . . . those blue eyed, blonde haired, Caucasian boys. I hated that I was also predictable, opposites attract.

It was working at pic-n-tote that I became best friends with Juan. I met him through my little brother, Juan was a twin, Jose was his twin and my brother's best friend. I knew they were my brother's friend because he would bring them around the house, but they were loud and would get on my nerves so I would yell at Gus to go play somewhere else with his little friends. I pulled this card because I'm two years older than them. Sometimes I would have to chase them, but they were acting like it was a game and I was being serious. So that same summer I started working at the store, Juan's family moved into the house right behind the store. Ooh, these little turds would wait until I was bagging ice in the back of the store. Mr. Nick had an ice making machine enclosed with a chain linked fence about 8ft. high with a tin roof. I would go out at night to bag, because in Texas you wait, if you can, until dusk or nightfall when the temperature is cooler. I say cooler like there was any coolness to the scorching summer air in Texas. One evening, as it just turned from dusk to night, I was bagging ice, sitting on an empty pickle bucket (Mr. Nick would buy those 25-gallon buckets filled to the top with whole pickles). I was about halfway through and never had I been anxious but this evening there was something disturbing in the air, this energy I couldn't explain. I was fearful and didn't know why, the small hairs on my arms and my neck stood at attention. I didn't know why I felt this way, so I started eating some of the ice. I loved eating ice, crunch crunch crunch. It was a terrific way to cool off!

"ARGHHHH!!" I heard as I saw these two shadowy figures clinging to and rattling the cage. I ran full speed out the cage door, and without looking back, I ran around the side to the front of the store and ran inside. Barbara, Gloria's daughter the senior cashier, would usually work nights with me and she was startled. I told her what happened, but she wouldn't let me get Mr. Nick's gun, so I grabbed a knife and a broom and went back outside. I was raised to be chivalrous, so I had to protect Barbara. When I went back outside there was nothing, just the crickets. It was eerily quiet, I looked around and nothing. I sat back down and started bagging ice again, and once again I felt the hairs stand on end. Suddenly, I heard the rustling of the grass as these two shadows ran towards the fence, which I caught in my peripheral. My senses were heightened so I was able to pick this up, which I couldn't before because of all the crunching. When I whipped around, the two figures jumped into the light, which was cast from this one bulb above the ice machine, and jumped onto the wire cage and rattled it, yelling "ARGHHHH". It was the twins, Juan and Jose, I acted like I was irritated, was dismissive, and acted unimpressed as they made fun of the way I ran out of there before. They kept taunting me until I ran after them and chased them to their house which was only about 20ft away if that. My ego was hurt, my pride offended. Since I worked every weeknight and pretty much all day all weekend, and since they were so rambunctious, this happened a lot when I bagged ice until no matter how hard they tried, I could ignore them and stopped getting startled. Jose eventually lost interest in coming around the store, but Juan and I became closer. I didn't understand why he wanted to spend so much time around me at work because to me this was my job, I had to be here, but he didn't work here but he enjoyed hanging out with me in the store. This was the first time I felt like I was fun to be around because he wanted to be there. Often his mother would have to call the store to tell him it was time to come home, which sometimes was close to quitting time. I don't remember what we talked about, or what we did together except we enjoyed each other's company, but he was becoming the person I was closest to besides my family which was new to me. I never felt this close to someone who was not family so I knew this was special, I just couldn't figure out in what way. I was really struggling during these years in high school to figure out who I was and what I liked. But even with this blossoming and special friendship, it was not enough to distract me from my misery, my loneliness.

I could feel him pulling away, and becoming more confused, my poor little young man. To see him growing, learning to drive, working and being responsible and building a lifelong friendship, well he didn't know this at the time, but I did, one of the perks of being a guardian. He shared with kids at school that knew, he always had a dollar to share. I am so proud of him right now; this little gem would always lend that dollar in the snack line because a couple of kids wanted something from the snack line but didn't have any money or not enough. I don't think he ever said no, but don't ask him to share the brown bag lunch that his mom prepared, you weren't getting any of that! Such a fine young man, I just wish that Charo wasn't so convincing, and Jr not so anxious to grow up so fast. He would notice God's gifts within himself. When Riggs intercepted communications between me and Juan's guardian, he became aware of the significant role that Juan would play in the life of my charge and how important Jr would play in the life of Juan. He ordered Charo to create chaos in Juan's family's lives, so Charo tried to burn it all down, fortunately I warned Juan's guardian of Charo's plot and that's why they went to the beach that day. So, because we can use a saving grace like a reverse card in the game UNO, I was able to use a saving grace to put things in an order that will benefit your charge. We don't get many of these, but Juan and Jr needed to be allowed to become important in each other's lives. I know this was going to be confusing for Jr at first, after time he will understand the role Juan would play in his life, later when he moves back after leaving home to "Find himself."

"Will you take a look at that!" Riggs huffs.

"That boring soul, used a saving grace for these two."

"I wonder what this could mean", thought Riggs.

"That was an interesting move".

I know these two are supposed to be in each other's life, but I couldn't figure out how until the saving grace was used. Now, at least I have an idea and I am going to have to try to destroy what was set in motion. Charo and I will be having to drop in more often. Things are going to become much worse for this little boy, that humble mess Ahava Mal'akh, whom I refer to as AKH (like a gag that makes you throw up a little in your mouth) is up to something with this kid and I will not let it deter my plans to use him to cause this family some grief in hopes they fall apart.

I will use this little kids longing for God's love to entice him to things in this world to distract him from the very God he wants to love, turning him away out of distaste for God's evasive yet available love. Since you will always long for His-majesty-full-of-it, I use this longing for want, so that this want and desire builds up inside you like the pressure in a pressure cooker, until you explode into fear, anger, rage, and prideful arrogance. My goal is simple, to entice you to join my ranks, and then work with me to destroy the peace, and eternal rewards that God has bestowed upon you, through His goody two sandals chip off the Old Block.

Longing for Love

Two stars kissing in the night sky,
so romantic and bright as I look on,
and take in this glorious sight.
I wonder where my kiss is tonight,
all alone and without love,
not least of these, my God,
I scream, where art thou?
Where is my heavenly kiss,
do you not promise me this?
My lover rules the night and day,
my lover taught the stars to shine,
but what about mine?
That intimate time we spent,
where is my kiss . . . my embrace?
Are you not my spouse . . .
my parent . . . my friend?
I would never be alone,
is the promise You made . . .
Where is my kiss, my embrace?
I see it all around me,
romantic hugs and kisses . . .
lover's holding hands,
speaking of intimate things.
Where is my kiss, my embrace?
Why don't you let me see your face?

Why no whispers in my ear,

expressing how much You love me?

I can't endure this pain,

longing for Your love . . .

expressed in intimate embraces,

loving kisses all over my face.

Where is my kiss, my embrace?

How I long for the day,

that I can run into Your arms,

into the warmth of Your embrace.

Where I will no longer feel a longing,

nor cheated of your touch,

Your love will fill my spirit, my soul;

I will finally arrive at my real home,

but what can I do, what shall I do,

to feel close to You now,

as lovers should?

I know the answer,

but it is never enough.

Where is my kiss, my embrace?

so, I wander, and stumble,

and fumble through this torture,

looking for love

in all the wrong places.

Satan notices, and exploits,

my desires to feel loved

so, he mocks our love for each other.

"Where is your kiss, your embrace?"

He taunts me with my own question,

and offers me a choice . . .

keep longing for God, or better yet,

I will satisfy your need,

just heed my advice,

and I will satisfy your vice.

I've made the wrong choices,

in heeding Satan's advice

to look for love in all the wrong things.

When I reached a low, lower than low,

this is when God came to my rescue,

He kissed my heart,

and embraced my soul . . .

the only way a sovereign God can do,

He touched my spirit.

and made me whole.

Chapter 9

My God in heaven, why does it have to be so hot here, I asked God? I often have conversations with God since I live a life without a spouse, without children, it's different and foreign to many people but some of you relate. Even if you are in a relationship with a houseful of kids, sometimes life is very lonely inside your head, or heart, or both. I've lived with several forms of loneliness, there's that one you feel in your mind, the one felt in your heart, the one felt when you walk into a strange place and know no one. There's the loneliness of being in the same lonely room, after being there for five minutes, or more, and you don't make a connection with anyone, or worse still you choose not to engage with anyone. There is a loneliness, deny it or not, they exist. There is this very dark loneliness that some of you may know intimately, others just for a brief period or periods of their life. This type of loneliness cannot be positively affected by anything, it can't be filled just by waking up and knowing your alive, nor can it be replaced with joy because this dark loneliness smothers and fills every orifice that it becomes a dark cocoon which envelopes you into yourself denying you of anything outside of it. I recall this loneliness today as I drove back from picking up lunch. I try not to turn on the oven during the summer, yea it's that hot. I love to eat my own cooking, but I don't like to cook, how is that for a twisted-up existence. Everything is so high right now. This lunch I just picked up, delicious fried chicken, white rice with brown gravy, and sauteed spinach with a white roll, oh what a southern delight. I'm thinking of this book's deadline and I'm freaking out because I still have several chapters to write. It shouldn't be that hard, but I found that it has been because it is forcing me to recall everything I can dig out of my memory box. Today I'm thinking of what brought me back to Beaumont. Why I haven't moved to a cooler place, especially because it is so close to the Gulf of Mexico that our hurricane seasons are intense. Especially this past decade. So much has happened, hurricanes, major illnesses-surgeries, historical flooding, except everything is historical nowadays. Even our politics is historically cyclical, and not all in a good way. But for now, lunch! I didn't eat breakfast and it's about one in the afternoon, so the sun is out proud and angrily pushing its heat onto us, unforgivingly. As I'm driving, my mind and spirit start asking God's forgiveness of my, what did I call it? Gluttony, selfishness, whatever explains how I have food in the fridge, people in the world are starving or cannot acquire food, who are going hungry but here I am, leaving my air conditioned icebox, getting into an air conditioned car, driving to Market Basket (a local grocery store with a deli) off of Eastex Freeway and TX HWY 105, which is right at seven miles away. All because I want a particular lunch, they have a decent deli and a great price, but still high for someone working at a non-profit agency, in an entry level position, which is the position most readily available in the non-profit world around here. People in leadership, in a small city (but yet produced many a national heroes, that we know of, I can image those silent saints that achieve just as much or more, but are never heard of by the masses like my Mom and Dad, and so many others I have known . . . those that keep the world going just by living life), they tend to move around and keep each other in power without engaging the whole of community, much less are they able to unite all of us to obtain a greater standard of living.

Today I am drawn to drive into and through neighborhoods that bring back plenty of memories of growing up here in my teenage years when I bought my first car. It was a 1973 Dodge Charger, metallic emerald green, with American Racing AR61 Outlaw I Silver Wheels Good Year Eagle GT II P 285 /50 R20s on the rear and as small of a tire that I could get away with on the front. Some referred to it as the avocado, but everyone wanted to ride in it with me, but in those days, it was pretty much just Juan, my best friend, and me. I would pick him up and we would drive around Southeast Texas, just listening to music, talking, going to Parkdale Mall, Sonic, and then take in the view of the drag in mid-county where everyone wanted to race me. I only raced a couple of times, and one was a cop pulling up fast on Hwy 69N heading back to Beaumont on my left-hand side he was gaining, and I thought they wanted to race, and my car was fast once it was moving but almost anyone could take me on a sprint. My sister Cruz was the speed junkie; I remember she would come pick me up from Pick-n-Tote on the corner of Delaware and Renaud, which I was passing by on my drive right now. She would pick me up after closing at 10:00PM and before she would take me home, she would take Concord heading North where there was a sharp S-curve that she would try to take as fast as she could in her canary yellow 1967 Camaro SS. Juan said "Junior, Junior it's a cop car, it's a cop car," so I took my foot of the gas and they raced past me, either glad they won, or they were on their way to a call. Either way, I was relieved, and we had a good ole laugh about it.

I was making my way towards Magnolia Cemetery, where my Mom and Dad are buried, a place I had to visit daily for almost two years before I was able to deal with the fact that both were no longer physically present in my daily life. I was remembering my mom's last words as I passed where there used to be a Church's Chicken, where my parents would buy a family meal on a Friday that my mom craved fast food. She loved her junk food, I tell you, and I'm no different! I remember we would stop there, and my mom would tell me to take out a couple of pieces as they dropped me off at the store to work. I miss them both so much, and I think of how they made their life in this part of Texas after leaving their hometown. The courage, the fear, the stress, and anxiety of moving their family across Texas, which is so different from driving in the Northeast where I could get into like three to four different states in one day's drive, but they moved anyway to give us a better life than they had. This, according to them, would be the better life. My Dad, when I returned home wouldn't even teach me how to weld because he said, "No mijo, no quiero que trabajes tan duro como yo en este calor." In other words, no, because he didn't want me to work hard in this heat. No wonder that he suggested that I take typing if it was offered in high school because if I learned to type, I would never have to work outside. He was right, even in the military, during my last two and one-half years I worked out of the harsh elements. I wish I had had more talks about God with him. Same with Mom, I wish I would have had more talks with her about our blessed Mother Mary and God. I knew her mother, my grandmother whom I spent those few weeks in the summer with, she was an avid Rosary praying Catholic, and devoted to praying protection over her family, and others, I'm sure. As I made my way to the cemetery, I contemplated why I was still in Beaumont, asking God to show me the way, to enlighten my path . . . my journey now. It was much different having conversations with God today than it was back then when I was in junior high and high school. I was so messed up as a kid, depressed, shy, lonely . . . that loneliness of the mind and heart. It was not the loneliness of being rejected or isolated from others, because I had a loving family, friends, I had a job that forced me to interact with the community. It was a loneliness of mind and heart because I chose it, and relished it, but I didn't know that at the time, in those days it was just something I was battling and knowing that I was battling it alone. Battling loneliness with aloneness before you are spiritually ready can drive one mad and crazy. I often reflect on the Gospels of Luke and Mark that tells of the man (in Matthew it's two men) with legion as the demons were many.

As I look back on those days, because now I know I had many, but I didn't know then that I would be enslaved by many more before God would intervene. Not that he hadn't tried before, I knew that I had a guardian Angel, although I never felt, or recognized who it was. My faith was strong as a child, I even got the calling to follow Christ in a particular way, as part of the Clergy of the Catholic Church, a priest. Unfortunately, I had no one encourage or approach me about these choices, even as it was obvious to everyone that I was in love with God. Maybe it is because it was hard to notice, I mean I was very shy and introverted, not as much as my cousin Magda (Ari's sister) but shy and quiet, nonetheless. So, I never really talked about my feelings with anyone until Juan came along. He was so easy to talk to, he was the first person outside of the family that loved me and it's that type of love you can feel before your mind accepts it, and recognizes it. I remember he was the first person I shared that I thought I might be gay, because of my crush on Jimmy in junior high, it only became stronger in me, especially after that incident where I first felt another person's privates. I mean before that, I was already feeling a crush on Jimmy and definitely not having those feelings for girls. In high school it was no better and was only getting worse. I remember that I was so ashamed to dress out in PE in high school because I had it with Brett, only the most beautiful boy at BCP, in my opinion at the time anyway. We weren't even friends and didn't travel in the same circles but that didn't matter, the type of person he was didn't matter, there was no crush it's just that he was what they called "fine." I remember making him laugh one time, the whole class did but the only one that mattered was him, he laughed, and I still remember that! Even in high school I was shy but when you are around the same kids during school you start building a certain confidence of fitting in, or not, I guess for some. We were in biology class and that day were we dissecting frogs, we were teamed up and I can't even remember who my partner was, but the teacher had to excuse herself for something and you know what happens when the teacher leaves a bunch of ninth and tenth graders alone. Well, there were two (partners) at a table and I picked up our frog and took the forceps separating the top and bottom of the frog's mouth in a way that it appeared it was talking. I did this as I sung, "La, la la la la la, la, la" just as the singing frog from the cartoons we watched as kids, everyone around me was cracking up. This is what caught the class attention, and they begged me to repeat what I had done, and I only did it again because Brett also encouraged me, and like I said we weren't friends and we never spoke to each other but this day, he was encouraging me to do something and I oddly felt obliged to make him laugh, and I did and he did laugh, and that was a great day! But having him in my gym class, this was too much. I dressed out only a few times before I decided that it was too much to keep my eyes to myself, not out of fear really, but more out of respect. I knew that most boys weren't like me, attracted to other boys, and because I didn't want to be either, I knew how disrespectful it would be for me to look at them at their most vulnerable. They never said or did anything because I didn't goggle over them, I couldn't help myself when I would take a glancing look but I always felt bad because of this feeling that it was disrespectful to them, especially if they didn't know that I was checking them out, I felt like a thief that got away with the jewels (pun intended). I stopped dressing out and failed PE for two years, ninth and tenth grade. To graduate the counselor pulled me into his office and was asking me what was wrong and explaining to me that if I didn't get my PE credits in the next two years that I would not graduate high school. I didn't dare tell him why, so I just said OK and forced myself to be like the horse with blinders on, I wouldn't even shower unless I absolutely had to because of how much I sweated and what class followed. A lot of how I felt, like my eyes were stealing forbidden glances, stemmed from my relationship with God and Church. I followed in the steps of my older brother, I became an altar boy as soon as I could, I was confirmed by the first Mexican-American Bishop in the U.S., Patricio Flores, I became the first president of the CYO (Catholic Youth Organization) revived by Alma because she saw too many kids hanging out in the streets, the CYO had not been active at Cristo Rey for a long time. When I turned eighteen, I started a young adult group and taught Sunday School. My heart ached for God and everything holy. I took everything I learned from my teachers, the two I remember had a great spiritual impact on me were Mary Nell Lopez and Sue Ramirez. They gave of themselves for the sake of others, they taught their faith to the next generation and guided us spiritually, while some of the kids only went because they were forced to go, I couldn't wait to go, and learn about the things of God. His loving family, which included me. It was the only place besides Mass that I would forget my loneliness and would find some relief from the constant pain of depression. I didn't know how this, coupled with the love of my parents and their prayers would call on God's protection later in my life when I would tell God to take a hike.

After leaving my parent's grave site, I drove towards downtown by way of Grand Ave., passed empty lots with pecan trees, and empty houses. As I make my way pass downtown and the American Legion, I remember how Cruz would take me and Gus to this place, I think it was close to the corner of Park and Langham, where we could jump on the trampoline, play table tennis, basketball, and all kinds of other things to do. I remember when I had my Charger I drove around Irving St., just to remind myself of my blessings. This was a depressed part of Beaumont, and dangerous for those who did not belong to that community, or at least this was what I thought at the time. I remember that I started crying because of the pain and misery of living this way. I don't know why, because many others could say the same thing of where I grew up, but the biggest difference to me is that my area of town was safe, we knew each other, our friends and family lived amongst each other, and we lived across the street from a Church. Seeing this neighborhood today, it reflected the failures of both religion and politics to heal the suffering of people, to help them achieve this American dream everyone talks about, but only a fraction obtains any form of it. I remember what I read about Beaumont after being old enough to care. The KKK parades down Main St. in the 1920s, the Beaumont race riot in the summer of 1943, only 60-40 years ago (from the 1980s). The disparity continues today for most, because generational injustices last for decades after justice is won, and even then, both Scripture and history attest to their long-term harm to communities and nations. I felt this all back then in a spiritual sense, but I didn't know it from a personal or historical sense, because we didn't hear of these major things in the public schools I attended around here, but I could see it all around me. I remember this time when my Dad picked me up from school and we went straight to the county courthouse to renew his truck registration and when it was his turn this lady was so rude and condescending that I interrupted, which was totally unlike me because I was reared better, but I saw an injustice and I 'felt' this to be really wrong. "Get me your supervisor, I will not let you talk to my father this way," I ordered her, an adult, and I was only fourteen years old, but my voice did not quiver, nor did it falter. "What?" she replied, shocked because she probably knew what she was doing and was caught in the act. "I said, you are rude and condescending to my dad for no reason, and I'm not going to stand by and let you do it, go get your supervisor." In perfect English with no accent, which probably surprised her as well, and she tried to explain, but I stopped her before she could even get the first words out. "You had your chance and you decided to treat my dad rudely, I will not allow you to wait on him, so go get your supervisor." By this time everyone around us, including her co-workers had heard our exchange and were staring. She went and called her supervisor, "Yes, how can I help you?" "This woman, who works for you, and for no reason whatsoever began speaking to my dad rudely and condescendingly and I will not tolerate it." "I'm so sorry," he said looking past me to my Father, he turned to his employee, who was looking down, "You need to apologize to them," but I quickly interjected, "No, she had her chances and it took you to make her realize that her behavior is wrong, I do not want a person like that, waiting on my dad." He stared at me, and I stared back for what felt like an awfully long time, but I wasn't backing off. "I'm very sorry sir," he addressed my father, "Let me get that for you, and trust me, I will discipline her for her behavior today." I instantly took my place behind my father and became that shy and quiet child that was not supposed to interrupt adults conducting business or having a conversation . . . no matter how long the conversation lasted. A lost art and form of rearing today. My Dad and I never spoke about this incident ever, we didn't even acknowledged that it happened the day that it happened as we left the courthouse, but knowing my Dad, he was probably beaming inside with pride that he had reared this child that spoke with confidence and defended his honor in a community that had a sordid past when it came to the way people looked at us, not knowing anything about us or where we came from or where we were born. Not much has changed, only about three years ago, as I was attending the announcement of a local political candidate as I was paying my water bill at city hall, I ran into someone I knew, a sheriff's deputy, because he served security somewhere I was working and we were having a conversation when someone in a nice suit, cowboy hat and expensive boots walked by, and the deputy called his name and introduced us. "This is Santos, he is a fine man . . . a good man, he's a keeper, he has a green card so we can keep him." "I'm a third generation native Texan, for your clarification, just so you know." The man in the cowboy hat nervously smiled, and couldn't get away fast enough but the deputy, oblivious to what he had just done, just kept talking, luckily for him (before I started to educate him on what had just occurred), a new artist friend I had made only a few months before, invited me to walk down to the Beaumont Art Museum just about a block and a half away because she wanted me to see a certain artist's collection. Since I was not raised to assume a person's character, but to know the type of person they are, I have never judged anyone based on things like appearances, status, education, or anything else that does not fully represent what a person holds in their heart. This would go a long way to protect me from people who wanted to use me for their own interests without having any regard for me. This helped me a lot, but things were about to get darker for me after graduating high school.

The twinkle of my eye, my little charge is in high school now, and although he is miserable and depressed because of Charo and Rigg's manipulation and my little charge's weak faith, they have been able to coerce and entice him to do evil. I gently apply the gifts intended for him, which he reacts well to, just can't keep his focus, but fortunately they stick in his heart. This child has a great propensity for good, because his mother and father instilled strong values, he seeks God in everything. This, of course, is a double-edged sword, on the one hand he understands and fully accepts Scripture as a reality, he also is easily swayed to take pleasure in those things that are forbidden, but only because he can't quite fully master that which God spoke to Cain, that you master over your sin. I gently whisper into his heart, verses of Scripture, that universal Truth which comes from God, but it's a constant battle, and on-going war between good and evil, because although Riggs and his supporters were cast out of heaven, they linger in the earth to devise an individual, but overall, plan to move people to partake in their view of Creation, and promote it in your minds so everything me, and other guardians, whisper into your hearts will not be heard. As many times as we try, as hard as we work, mankind and especially my little charge is fascinated with what Riggs represents. Maybe not so much as others, I'm recalling someone who turned out to be a general for Riggs back in 1925 in Germany, where even after being imprisoned, believed his cause was just because Riggs and Charo cheered him and those around him on. Their tactics do not change and have not changed since the Garden days. He is a timeless charmer and extremely effective perpetrator of evil, but he makes it appear fun, innocent, and exciting. Nothing could be farther from the truth, but how is my little charge to know this? So, I whisper, and he does listen and then puts it into action, like when this righteous seeking young woman begins a long dormant organization at Cristo Rey, what a beautiful name for a church, where it is a family affair. Her mother, who they call Micky, is like the CYO mother for them and they are a praying family, very involved in the church in my little charge's tender, turbulent teen years. He is voted in as the group's first president, and they are doing a lot of good, they are living the Scriptures, they are brining awareness of their church to others, even traveling out of town to attend youth conferences. They learn their traditional Mexican dances, and even this thing called break dancing that is catching a craze, and while my charge cannot break dance, his brother Gus and others are exceptionally good at it, so they take their dancing on the road to perform at community events and in the nursing homes in the local area. At the behest of my charge, they spent, not only an hour, the entire night inside Cristo Rey because of one question that I whispered into his heart over and over and over again, " . . . you could not stay awake for one hour with me?", so Junior (what they call him in the physical world), suggested it to Alma and the group, but not before I had the chance to call a group session between all of their charges so they could whisper into their charges hearts. It was a remarkable success, the kids are thirsty for Jesus, and they loved it, and they stayed awake with Jesus during that Holy week before Easter Sunday. He was really growing spiritually, and seeds of faith were being planted in his heart and he was nourishing and tending them well, which was bearing fruit, the only problem, of course, is Riggs and Charo, and all the others. Swirling around them like flies and mosquitos waiting and attacking constantly. They didn't like the free will God gave mankind, but they were using it to their advantage.

"Bring me the amulet I made to commemorate the red dragon of Germany," ordered Riggs. "Hurry up!", such incompetence. "Charo when are you ever going to get it through your feeble head, that timing is everything, didn't you learn from the bind with the red dragon?" "What do you mean?", Charo replied, "What amulet?" "The one I told you to use to make the red dragon believe he was being directed by The Bully, this is what I call the G-pops. It scours my throat like swallowing brimstone if I try to use His names. So, I made up my own. "Oh, yea, that's a great amulet but its affects are unpredictable." "Shut up, did I ask you for any of your feeble-minded opinions, you didn't use it the way I told you to, and our mission was cut short and before we could wipe out more people back then, so just shut up and do as I say, can you do that?" "Yes", Charo replied, he knew when it was time for one worded answers to Riggs, and he was perturbed that the goody two shoes was keeping this kid from going completely dark. "This amulet is just the beginning, I created it with the fires of the lake of fire and used the skins of many of the tortured souls who are staying with me, go place it under his pillow without disturbing him and don't get caught by twinkle toes." "Yes, sir," Charo exclaims as he salutes Riggs, always the Riggs pleaser, and cheerleader, he loves this special attention from Riggs, it fills him with pride. "Leave it there until morning and keep stroking the boys head, but do it in secret, so use this flaming cape to disguise your approach and once there, turn the coat inside out and it should shield you from those who are trying to prevent this from happening. Riggs was excited to use this robe, he is immensely proud of it. It belonged to Joseph, the son of Jacob and Rachel, and being defiled by jealousy and hate, I turned it into something we could use to hide our approach to one of these bags of mud, this way their guardians could not sense our approach but we only had a certain amount of time before they became aware of us once we took this coat off. "This will set his mind to such an unease that I think we can make him take his own life!" I am so pleased with myself that I was able to groom this kid to such a point that he would take his own life. I know I've tried it before, but I didn't know how long I had to stroke his head, but I know now that it will take all night, and I was intent on seeing this through. I thought that when his father had the heart surgery that I could convince him to take his life, but instead it backfired, but it was not all bust. Like I told Riggs, something is better than nothing, I was only able to get him to ignore and be aloof to his parents struggles during this time. He did nothing to help his parents during this time, not even concerned with the struggles they were suffering through, all he was concerned with was riding around in that green goblet, getting high on Mary Jane, and riding around town like there was no care in the world. It was about this time also that I convinced him that he was so miserable, and that G-pop was ignoring him, that he stole his best friend's codeine pills and swallowed them all, sending him to the hospital, but still alive, argh. This time would be different, because I have a clever idea how to convince him to blow his head right off.

Sitting on the beautiful hardwood floor of our living room, Father Luis, from our Parish across the street from our house, once commented "You could hold a dance in this Livingroom", I sat cross-legged, alone, desperate, and had lost all hope. I had just turned twenty, home from college, but our home was empty this Christmas which only worsened my loneliness. I sat there with my father's gun loaded, and the barrel of the gun inside my mouth with my finger on the trigger. His revolver was heavy, I am not sure if it was the same one that he would shoot rabbits with in Asherton, but we only fired it on New Years. After some silent cries for help, because these are the only cries that I was capable of, instead of expressing my emotions or even talking about them I resorted to a couple of silent actions that I now realize were silent cries for help. On this day, only a few days before Christmas, I was determined to realize my fantasy of ending the pain and loneliness I had been suffering from since the sixth grade. I sat this way for hours, putting the gun down every so often because it became heavy in my hand, but with each time that I put it into my mouth, I wanted so badly to pull that trigger and end my suffering. A life of endless loneliness, alienating myself to the love and happiness going on around me, I was living like an outsider to all the good happening around me. Each time I lowered the gun, I felt like a failure and all I could think of was that soon, this would all be over . . . I would be free of me and my pain. I was angry with God and with myself, I longed to just be a normal kid, doing kid stuff, but the world was getting darker and scary for me, but not because of society, community, or family, it was because the loneliness I felt deep inside was consuming me from the inside out. I didn't even know where it came from, like a thief, it had snuck into me and made a home for itself. Slowly devouring me until every waking moment was lived in a state of nothingness because nothing mattered to me except this loneliness. It was so confusing to me, this loneliness because I had five siblings, loving parents, and many friends but none of that mattered to me because I existed in a lonely world trapped inside of myself and my self-loathing, while having high expectations of myself to achieve great things in life but lacking the desire and motivation to chase my dreams with a loving heart. I would learn later in life, that what I suffered from was a lie that the devil had sold me . . . I was nothing, you are all alone and no one can help you. It all culminated to this point in time, me sitting there with a gun in my mouth desiring with all my might the ability to pull that trigger and end this, because a life like the one I was living was not fulfilling and I was missing everything, even today I retain no memory of many of my childhood years with friends and family because I was lost and living inside my head, like a dungeon with no sunlight, and all alone.

It didn't go as planned, I would not be here telling you this story, this account of things in my life and my thoughts. When you encounter Jesus, you cannot contain the love, joy, excitement, and wonder that living in Him and He in you, that just makes everything ok. Back then, I was getting truly angry with God. Knowing He knows what's in my heart, I did all I knew to do to be closer to Him for nine years. I had planned to cease to exist, knowing this was a Judas move, to deny God's redemption, His mercy, and His forgiveness. No hope, no faith, no love. I didn't pull the trigger after what seemed like forever and I also realized right there, I did not want to speak to God anymore. I had already stopped going to church every Sunday beginning shortly after graduation, high school graduation in 1984. Socially and economically from like 1975 to 1995 seemed that a big shift was occurring in all aspects of life and spirituality, corresponding to the years of my waltz with satan, giving to the whims of demons setting up a home within my disorientation and aloneness, setting traps and delectable delights.

I felt a failure after I wimped out on blowing my brains out in the middle of our family living room, while mom and dad were in Asherton, my older cousin Jr. and his wife Odette (Ramon Jr., my dad's older half-brother) had picked them up on their way. My younger brother Gus was living with his girlfriend at the time, so he wasn't around, my older sister Cruz was in the military in Oceanside, CA. Everyone else had their families, and when the parents are away, we tend to retreat to our own, like every family, unless those that are wealthy enough that everyone depends on each other to support the family enterprise, like I've seen on T.V. and movies, but never in real life, not me anyway. I was all alone and with no God because my exact words were, "I know you made me this way, and I have been begging you to change me so that I could have a wife and children, this is what I so desired to live this life and you haven't done anything, you don't even talk to me. So, since you ignore me, I will ignore you and will not go to church, I will not pray, and I don't ever want to talk to you again."

It took me a while to get over the excruciating pain of still being alive. I believed the lie the devil sold me, and I bought it all up and asked for triple scoop of lust, with pride sprinkles on a confusion cone, one soul in payment. The lie he convinced me to believe that I was a coward, I couldn't do the simplest thing of taking my own life, it's me, I'm in control, I say when . . . and then nothing! Oh, he worked me good, day and especially at night, sometimes all night. Although this was the lowest time for me, God was working on me, unbeknownst to me, in silence while the noise got louder and the darkness, darker. It would later be revealed to me when I was thinking clearer that the reason, I didn't pull that trigger that night, sitting there all alone with regret stroking my lasciviousness. I could not do that to mom and dad, I knew that it would hurt them, and traumatize them because I knew how much they loved me, my mom had just recently told me as much after I was dropped off at the ER because I took a whole bunch of codeine pills, which I stole from my best friend Juan (playing football in the front yard we both went for the ball and his collar bone hit my shoulder and knocked his collarbone out of whack). When we got home from the hospital my mom locked my bedroom door after she and I walked into my room and after mom did not let pop come in. Mom asked me to promise to tell her the truth and that's when she asked me if I had tried to kill myself, I was shocked and taken by surprise because at the hospital she did not say one word, not even on the ride home, not even when we arrived at the house, went inside and she followed me into my room, shooed my dad away, and then locked the door to ask me this. I couldn't tell her the truth, so I told her that I wasn't trying to kill myself. They didn't have to pump my stomach so it wasn't that bad, but boy did I have a splitting, pounding, headache, like my head was going to explode, an experience that let me know pills were not the way, how could I get enough anyway if there was going to be a next time. Even as my mom was telling me how much she loved me, I knew it already, I knew it because both mom and dad were so loving to me, yes they both had their ways to discipline but there was no question of how much they loved me, and I knew that but at that time, my loneliness and misery overshadowed everything in my life at this time. Love had won that day, the love I have for my parents, this is what kept me from pulling that trigger, but at the time I did not know this . . . at this time, I just thought how much of a failure I was turning out to be in this life so far.

I became so angry with God for creating me this way, that I didn't come with instructions nor directions, I just came into this world and had to figure it all out inside, and I had no idea what I was doing. I didn't want this life, I blamed God for robbing me of the life I wanted, that most boys have. Why me Lord? You can do anything with just a word, a thought, you can bring people back to life, I was only asking to be straight. "I know you have heard me, you hear my heart's pain, my soul crying out for Your mercy and grace." Silence. Things have only gotten worse, and still nothing. "FU, I don't want to have anything to do with you. What have I ever done to You, but be in love with you, learn everything you have shared with us, I served You in the church across the street, dedicating my free time to serve the church. "You answered all kinds of prayers for my father, so I know you can, and you do!" I was beyond angry, so I decided no more prayers, no more church, no more anything that had to do with God. You ignored me, and I was going to do the same. I decided to shoot the middle finger up towards the sky and screamed, "FU, you haven't done anything for me! You can answer prayers, but not mine. I will never speak to You again, and with that, my life was about to get very interesting, and extremely dangerous, really fast.

I decided to move from Beaumont and far from my parents so that I could live the life I was given, at least that's what my young twenty-year-old self was thinking. I would finish the Spring 1987 semester and join the military. Juan had put that in my head just by joining, not because he was trying to recruit me, even though we later told his recruiter that we meant to join on the buddy system, this was where they encouraged friends to join together. This won him his mosquito wings (Private E-1), just one rank higher than everyone else in your platoon, plus a little extra money. I would do almost anything for Juan, especially after we made up. He got pretty angry with me when I ended up in the hospital because he had stopped me before, and he was mad that I didn't come to him and try to let him help me. So, I joined the Army, and I was able to finish out the semester, flunking grades, and an eagerness to get far away from Texas, like across the ocean far, so that I could go explore what society considered was love and happiness. This was my first really huge mistake.

"@!#%," I yelled, and shook hell to its core. "So close," and these hurt because I can tell something is going on, that he sat there for so long. That's the thing we don't know what's going on in the heart, that's restricted space, a bit #@!$*&# unfair but there are safeguards that we don't go meddling. We can push it, contain it, envelope it but when G-pops says 'No Entry' yea it's a big deal. Loser. Anyway, it didn't work, too much of that L stuff, argh. It is not over, I will have to devise something else, I thought for sure this would work, but not only does this kid have a powerful guardian he absorbs things like a sponge and his heart does it like led to weight, doesn't look like it's that heavy but the led surprises you when you pick it up. I would just like to squeeze every one of your hearts until it bursts in my hand. I would love it on those days when the Aztecs would sacrifice, tearing their hearts out of their chests on a platform right under G-pop's nose, in the light of His days he created on day one. What defiance, what pride, ooh I loved it. Heads rolling down while someone at the bottom made a game out of catching their severed heads. Ah, such barbarians at heart, so easy to convince them until later, but we will not talk about our setbacks. I hate it though when things don't work out my way because you all are too stupid to know you are fighting a losing battle. Most of you are oblivious to it. I told a few people as they held me in bondage for a spell with their spiritual weapons, they unfairly can employ these creatures' called exorcists. Freaking horse flies if you ask me. But you people don't even believe that I exist, much less pay attention to what's going on around you. I couldn't stand it when the J dude was walking around revealing all this truth, He even told you all that you were skilled and learned enough that you could forecast the weather, but you had no clue about spiritual matters. I thought there would be a revolution, but yea, at the time I was feeling pretty damn good about myself. I would only learn later what was kept hidden in plain sight. This idiot thinks that thinking about himself all of the time is worth killing what G-pops created because he's sad, he's lonely, he doesn't know what to do, he's scared about nothing, he scared about everything, worrying and worrying about the future, like he can do anything to change anything or else I would have already done it. But you empty pots have your mind's and all you can do with them is be obsessed over the what ifs, the how abouts, the whereabouts, the nothing that will get you nothing. Ha, ha I laugh myself silly when I sit here and think about it on my break. Yea, I must take breaks, you are wretched, vile, good for nothings. Like picking up shit, the runny kind that spreads out over the grass and then there is no cleaning it up, you stink, oh I would love to go on but for now, I have to get on the plan to destroy this kid and his family.

"Come on, get out," they yelled at the top of their lungs, sounding like they had bullhorns attached to their mouths. "This ain't a vacation, your mamma ain't here to get your bags, there's no valet, get the hell out of those trucks! Hurry, hurry, faster, faster!" It was crazy, I thought to myself weighed down with all this gear, not just a ruck suck on my back but two huge duffle bags. Green, long, about three- and one-half foot tall and a circumference of about 24 inches full of Army gear. I chose infantry, even after my recruiter tried to tell me I could choose better, to keep looking at the tape. I had my reasons for choosing infantry and once I saw that particular job as I sat at the recruiter's office deciding what I wanted to be in the Army, I knew it was infantry. The video showed men in full camo, even the face, holding an M-16 above their heads as they were treading through water chest high. They were engaging the enemy in hand-to-hand combat, checking for mines, attacking the enemy . . . this is what I wanted to do. Ever since I graduated high school and flunked out of college, I never played any sports and by this time I knew I liked boys and that I had no interest in girls besides being great friends, I mean great friends. Girls are exactly how God created them, they are so different but the same, they are the only ones that really get us and us them, even though most think there's a better gender and some are even wrestling with gender itself but yea, great friends but nothing else for me anyway.

I knew one day I would come out to everyone about being gay, and when that time came, I vowed to prove myself in the Army Infantry so that no one could ever doubt or say that I wasn't a man. Only one to one half percent of the U.S. population serves in the military ever since they went to a volunteer military and of that one-to-one half percent only fifteen percent of those go into the infantry. So, yea, no one could tell me anything. "Who are you?" "A lean, mean, fighting machine!" we would yell in basic training. I was going through my basic and advanced individual training (AIT) at the home of the Infantry, Fort Benning Georgia. They recently changed the name to Fort Moore, yep again it's about racism. I had my own incident regarding racism when I was stationed at Fort Drum, but it happened when we were deployed to Somalia, Africa. We had been deployed to protect the supply routes so that the U.N. could get food distributed to the Somalians because the warlords were intercepting the food and supplies the world was donating and they were deciding who received it. So, they wake me up in the middle of the night, I'm a corporal at this point and out of the Infantry and retrained when I reenlisted after two years to a central switchboard repairer. I was the one they called if they couldn't' get their satellite phone operator system on-line. Yea, I went from the front of the fight to the back, because I learned that my contract included fine print that they could call me back up in something they called a ready reserve (what they would later use like a backdoor draft for political reasons during the Iraq war). Anyway, I was all warm and comfy in my bed, in the barracks on base when the CQ (Charge of Quarters), those who stood watch if we had to rapid respond to a threat against the country (every unit had to have one), someone to take the call after the unit had been dismissed for the day, while in garrison. I had to report to the battalion and sign in and come back to pack what wasn't already packed to go. I had one hour to report to the company armory to check out my weapon. Once we had everyone, we loaded up the buses and drove us to the airfield. I was sick the entire flight from Griffiss Air Force Base in Rome, NY to England, to Egypt, to Mombasa, Kenya, Africa. I was sick because of the malaria pills they gave us. In Egypt we couldn't deplane for security reasons and every seat was full, in full gear, and I was sick from the pills. We had to wait while they refueled the plane before taking off for Kenya. As soon as I walked out the side door at the front of the airplane, I was hit with this intense heat, and what felt like a wet, smothering felt blanket that instantly wrapped itself around me. I mean, I knew Africa would be hot, but not more than hot but humid as hell in the middle of the night! I was back in Southeast Texas but worse. I started freaking out inside, I was having a serious discussion with myself about what I could do, what I should do. "I should just get back in the plane and tell them I'm done, but yea, no. Not a possibility you better get used to it, calm yourself down and remember the briefings about snipers. This is real Junior, Mr. Infantryman". I didn't care about the bullets; the heat and humidity were the immediate threat!

I finally acclimated, we were ready to move in the morning as our vehicles were retrieved and as Captain Kieffer's driver I got my shit together fast. We set up about 45 miles north of Somalia in an old World War II Russian Air Bunker. Several rooms were converted to offices and since I was part of the headquarters company of headquarters Battalion, we had the medics hospital with us, as well as a unit of marines for security. The Battalion HQ was about a mile away from us. I was also tasked for the physical fitness (PT) training of our company. Just before deployment I had convinced our first sergeant and Captain Kieffer to let me incorporate aerobics into training to improve everyone's PT scores and they had agreed. I showed that improved their scores so by the time we were in Somalia, they were used to it, and everyone enjoyed it. I chose music as I designed my aerobics class, all this I had learned while stationed in S. Korea for fifteen months during the first Gulf war. My friend Juan went, but then his howitzer was separated from the unit, so he missed the battle and they reunited with their unit afterward. We still laugh about that today. I'm glad I joined because he and I can relate when we speak of the time we were in the military, and that we knew each other growing up before that, and are still best friends. God has truly blessed me with a great family and a friend like Juan. So, this one day I'm putting on the music, we are warming up and I changed up my tape a bit and used different genres of music to appease everyone. Now that they were getting built up and most could keep up with me, they started having opinions about the music. I liked it before when not one of them could keep up with me. This day, there was a Caucasian and a Black soldier in the front row and standing next to each other, and both were the same pay grade as me, but I had the chevrons on my sleeve, the Corporal, so I was in charge. We stretched to country music, and the Black soldier would berate the music, we warmed up to some rap music, and the Caucasian soldier would berate the music. I had enough when it became heated, and they started to throw racial insults around.

"Attention!", I commanded, and everyone shut up and locked up at attention. I proceeded to educate them of the reason's we were here in Africa, thousands of miles away from home, where there was no running water, where Somalians were rifling through our trash and walking around with orange water, and it wasn't Kool-Aid, it was orange dirt mixed with water because of the civil war. I explained how when the French were here they

got with the local Somali women and had children, and now there were Somali and French Somali, they discriminated against each other and started
warring against each other, destroying all things modern, which they had,
now they had nothing and food wasn't getting through, food that the world
was sending to them but hate still prevailed and here we were, thousands
of miles from home because of the same shit they were doing right in front
of me. "I'm not having it," I yelled from my diaphragm. I smacked my hand
against the Presidential Fitness award that I had sewn on my t-shirt which
reflects the highest achievement of physical fitness, and you must maintain
it, and they all knew of it, this is why I was able to convince them that I knew
what I was doing. "We don't have to do aerobics, I can take you on a five-
mile run, or you know what? We can do a practice twelve-mile road march,
so it doesn't even count on your qualification for the year. Since they all
knew that I had an EIB (Expert Infantry Badge) they knew I wasn't joking.
So I stared both of them down, looked past the both of them an addressed
the company, "These guys are about to make you run five miles in total
silence (it's harder that way, than when you sing cadence), or we are going to
change and do a practice twelve mile road march, and I will be the one making the decision, all because they can't realize that they are as ignorant as the
people that have destroyed their own country from within, and too stupid
to realize the ramifications of hate." I look back at them, "So, it's on you two.
Are you going to apologize to each other, and shake hands, and never ever
let this happen again, or am I about to smoke all of you with the run or the
road march?" I didn't have to wait long, they immediately took each other's
hands and shook as they apologized to each other and we continued with
the music and aerobics and had no further incident again, in Africa or when
we returned to the U.S. It was when we returned that I started doing a little
crystal meth and drinking a lot more.

Come August, as a birthday present to myself, I decided to tell Captain Kieffer that I was gay, so that I could get thrown out, but ever the clever one, I formally requested and received an honorable discharge because,
yea up until this point I had not disrespected the uniform or violated the
military code of justice so there was no legal basis for them to do anything
but give me an honorable discharge. The fact that I had done a few days
at the psychiatric ward of the VA hospital in Syracuse helped solidify my
case, that I was going crazy, and it is because I met someone that made me
question my sexuality. After all, I told them I thought I had fallen in love,
but I couldn't figure anything out while I was in uniform and that this was
starting to take its toll on my ability to continue being a good and effective
soldier. He was amazing about it, I remember that I couldn't look him in
the eye, and he ordered me to look him in the eye and I did, "Corporal

Hernandez you have done nothing wrong, I mean who is to say what is normal and who is normal? I mean who can say that when this is all said and done you were not what is normal? I am going to handle this, and this letter you wrote and the copies of the law, this is why I'm going to miss having you around here, because you're so damn thorough". I will never forget him, my friend Austan, who you will meet later, he asked me if he could read it and was so impressed that he asked me if he could have it. It had served its purpose for me, so I agreed, I let him keep the letter along with a chess board I bought on RR (rest and relaxation) in Mombasa, Kenya. I challenged him to a game twenty years from when I dated the back of the chess board itself. To this day, we are still friends but haven't played the game and it's been twenty-three years and I have visited since then, and we have even played chess . . . on one of the many other chess boards he has collected by winning them from others.

When I get out of the military and ready to live without boundaries, and completely free. Free to do what I want, far from my family and where no one knows who I am. Such a completely dissimilar experience for me because up until this very moment I felt that I had been living my life for others, which is strange since I was pretty self-centered. I was excited, gleefully afraid of the unknown, and knowing that I was going to be going to beauty school. I must laugh, excuse me, because I never thought of myself as a beautician, I guess that is the easiest way to explain it. Maybe a barber, since I really liked the atmosphere of the barbershop I worked in as a shoeshine boy. I loved the men coming in to get their haircuts, talk about what was in the news while I asked if they wanted a shoeshine for a dollar. If I had no customers, I would just read all the comic books Mr. Oshea had laying around his barbershop. My mom would make me a sack lunch or dinner depending on when I was working and I just thought it was all great, the smell of the hair tonic he would put on the men's freshly shaven face and neck. I would sweep up for him as well and he would give me a small pay each week for the things he had me do around the barbershop, but we both knew that my main job, and what my dad had asked Mr. Oshea, was shining shoes. My dad let me use his shoeshine box, the square wooden type where you put your foot on so that someone like me could shine your shoes on the spot. Pop taught me how to use it all, the shine, the brush, the liquid shine that you applied to the side souls and heels to cover the scuff marks while filling them in so that the shoes looked good as new. This would help me out so much when I was in the Army.

I was happy to be out of the Army. I had everything lined up, I had a place to stay temporarily while I looked for an apartment. My friend Bug had moved to Syracuse because she had got a job working for Matrix as an educator. Bug was the whole reason I looked at people as canvases and that cosmetology was another new medium, for me anyway, of art. The color in color theory, the design and geometry of cutting hair, it all interested me and piqued my interest now that I didn't know what I was going to do in life out of the Army. I knew one thing for sure, I was staying for a while because I was in love with the friends I was making and the geography of the Northeast. I love the crisp chilly air of winter, the lake effect snow that covered everything in white and before anything disturbed its peace, it all looked new. But it was still too cold to melt the snow, even the night was day because the white snow would reflect all light and just light up the night. Don't try this at home, because it's just not a good thing to do, but in blizzards, it was almost easier to see if I turned off my headlights, but this is illegal folks don't do it. Would you jump off a cliff if I did? Ok, then.

A new chapter in my life, and an old one gone but not really if you know what I mean. On the one hand, I could have made a hell of a green beret, and I would have been among the Army elite skydiving and ready to fight, but I was an anchor in the water, I didn't float easy. I'm not a water person, I tense up and start drowning. You see how I went straight to drowning? Yep, that's me and water. So, once I knew that this wasn't going to happen, it was yet another disappointment in my inability to achieve a desired goal, just like my life has been up to this point. Maybe this time will be different, this abrupt change of lifestyle from military to civilian was as surprising and abrupt for my family and friends as it was for me. Yes, I was just stumbling through a mirrored maze with glass windows, but God was steering me through it, even though I had stopped talking to Him long ago, but I wouldn't know this until later, way later, ok a few years later. After a lot of partying, drinking, drugs, sex, and all of what the world has to offer. I had never lived like this, but I was determined to give it a whirl. My friend Bug was the inspiration behind it. I remember Craig and I went to hang out with Bug when she called us in a managed panic, because I never knew Bug to do panicking so we were surprised and went right away to be with her at the Marriot in Syracuse, NY because Bug was having a model call for a hair show that she was responsible for in her new job with Matrix. She was like, "Guys, I've bought pizza and the artists are late. Can you get over here and help me entertain the models and keep them here until they show up?" Sure, Bug was Bug, so we got over there quick. It was an interesting event that stuck with me because Bug was a hairstylist in Watertown, NY when Craig introduced her to me. Craig would come to hang out with Bug because he grew up in Watertown, but I met him when I was in Syracuse one evening. It was like driving from Beaumont, TX to Houston, TX which is about 79 miles but a much more scenic and beautiful drive that I had done

many times. I walked it once, when I was in the Army only about a year
before I moved to Syracuse. I wanted to rough it, sleep in the woods, and
then keep going the next day, smoking some weed as I walked. This got old
quickly so a car full of young kids offered me a ride and I happily accepted
because now I could go to the club tonight. The gay club, which I loved since
I was living the life now, I was free, I was free to do what I wanted . . . finally.
I met Craig in an adult bookstore, in a video arcade, where if you wanted
you could push a button and a black screen would lower between the glass
and you could peep into the other booth, if that person also pushed their
button. Usually this would lead to a rendezvous to engage in sex, but this
time it was different. Craig left his booth, and I was determined to meet this
guy, which was unusual for me because I didn't want to date anybody I met
in these places, because I was looking for sex. I caught up with him outside,
he had just got into his car, and I said hello. He was surprised, but I could
tell he was interested so I asked him for his number, but he said he had
broken up with his boyfriend, but he said I could give him my number and
he would call me next time he came to Watertown since that is where he
was from. I thought he had very kind eyes and he was very cute, but I think
what made me fall in love with him was that he did not make excuses for
being who he was, he didn't wish he was something else, he was just living
his life. I wasn't prepared to meet Craig and where this would lead but on
the journey of tormented and forbidden love.

After Craig and I showed up we learned that the artists for Bug's model
call were held up at the Canadian border and would be late, but they still
had to choose the models they wanted to use for tomorrow's hair show. Poor
Bug had to use all her people skills talking most of the models into staying
until they arrived, which they did over two hours later. It was tense after an
hour of waiting, much more than tense, Bug was getting nervous, and the
models were getting very antsy. When the artists showed up, you could feel
the immediate elimination of all things negative. You laugh, but that was the
instantaneous response to the 'Artists' of hair. The models were giggling as
the artists grabbed them with a gentleness but firmness that only a hairstylist or barber can do, running their fingers through manes of hair. The girls
were eating it all up! I loved the impact they made on the models and how
their presence filled up the space with excitement and hope. Not the type
of hope that is of the spiritual kind, it was hope that this artist can make
me more beautiful than I've ever been. Feeding into that pride. Not that I
knew this then, that the beauty industry was not a good place for me to be
with the demons that had set up shop in me. I know it's Charo and Riggs
G, at least now I do but back then it was just good and bad, evil and holy. I
didn't care too much about holy or good, I was done with those. I can only

imagine what this did to Mel, but again, I didn't care during this time in my life. It was a new chapter, one that I would write, one of desire, lust, greed, disillusionment, and despair but in the moment, I was excited to be living life . . . whatever that meant. I knew one thing at this moment of seeing what one or two people can do to affect such a behavior change, I wanted some of that, I needed some of that because up until this point in my life, I was shy and reserved. I had served in the military just for this moment, when I would decide to live my life as I wanted and without any boundaries and no one was about to tell me what to do or how to live because I have proven to be a man. I served six years in the Army, three years in the Infantry because I didn't even want men that had served in the military to be able to tell me that I was not a man. I proved myself in the Army Infantry, overachieving and being the ideal infantry soldier. A lean, green fighting machine. I was ready for someone to step to me; I had such a big chip on my shoulder that I couldn't see what was coming. I turned to Craig, and I told him that after leaving the military, I wanted to be a hairdresser, an artist, like those that showed up and changed the entire mood of Bug's event.

That was years before I became a hairdresser because I was still serving in the military when that model call happened. The show was a big hit, by the way, and Bug made a great impression for her first show. Years passed and I was moving to Syracuse now, with eyes wide open and shut at the same time. I've always had this push, back and forth no matter the issue, the problem, the exercise, the drive, and what not, but I have always sensed this rivalry and comradery within in me. Always searching, questioning, and thinking of the right and wrong of each side of the coin only to find that I'm at both sides of the coin, arguing with myself. "A walking contradiction," as my best friend has proclaimed, like only best friends can do because they know you so well. I'm proud of this, because it makes me more aware of the stakes at hand in any situation be it material or spiritual. I'm not the only one but maybe one of the few that share it out loud. What I didn't expect, was that Bug would be out of town a lot and Craig had moved to Florida while I was deployed to Somalia, Africa. I would have to make new friends for the first time in my life, which were made not forced upon . . . let me clarify, when we are in school, you're forced upon each other, when I was in the military, we are forced upon each other, when we work for a company, we are forced upon each other. You don't have to be friends, but you make them because this is just the way of life, otherwise you're a hermit living in your own seclusion. That's strange, unless of course it is a holy or spiritual experience. Otherwise, not making friends when you are together with people for so much time out of the day, it is a bit weird, don't you think? Anyway, this was the first time in my life that I chose what city to live in, my apartment, and the school I was going to attend: Phillips Hairstyling Institute.

Before I returned from Somalia in March of 1993 I wrote Craig a letter because before my deployment to Somalia, I had already been admitted to the psychiatric ward of the VA hospital in Syracuse, NY because I could not guarantee to my military psychiatrist that I would not harm myself so he contacted my unit and my first sergeant and a soldier from my unit escorted me to the hospital in Syracuse where I stayed about four days. I'm telling you this because it was my sexuality that I was having trouble with because I wanted to tell everyone about Craig, but I couldn't because they would kick me out. Craig and I would see each other when he would visit Bug, and his family although his family, aside from possibly one family member that I knew of, did not accept his lifestyle so they shunned him, what a shame for them to not experience the loving and caring person that he was, full of life and love for life. I was in love with Craig, and we became so close, he introduced me to Bug, his best friend. Hanging out with them while I was stationed at Fort Drum was just spectacular, we would hit local dive bars as we followed Bug's first love around as he performed his music with his band. They introduced me to great music I had never heard before, new foods, they welcomed me into their world and Bug introduced me to her friend Andrea who was just a fun and funny mature friend. I had a life outside of the military, a civilian life, and I wanted more, but I wanted it with Craig. Unfortunately, I was the other man. Craig had an on again off again with an abusive boyfriend who he lived with in Syracuse, so I would only hang out with him when he was not with his boyfriend, which was usually when Craig would run away from him and into my loving arms, but we both knew that it was impossible to have a serious relationship while I was still in the military. This was driving me crazy, so before we were deployed to Somalia, I basically had a break down, my depression (which at this point was suppressed because of my military career) was rearing its head again and coming back like a thunderbolt. I got into crystal meth right before I went to the psych ward. It was a great feeling, all my body tingled, and I was horny when I did drugs, especially any type of crystal meth, cocaine, or pot. Alcohol and mushrooms, not at all horny, which I found out with one boyfriend who wanted to have sex while we were shrooming one night so I called my friend Leslie to explain to him why I couldn't have sex on mushrooms. I found myself one night, horny as hell because I'm high on crystal meth and so I tell Dean that I have some crystal and if he wanted some so, he did some and then we end up walking the roads of Fort Drum . . . mind you, this is an Army base, at about 2AM. Luckily no MP's (Military Police) ever passed us by, nor did we ever get caught but this is what I was doing right before we were deployed to Somalia because I was overwhelmed with feelings for Craig but having a relationship with him was painfully impossible, and it was driving me crazy. I wouldn't call on God, because I had turned my back on him years ago and I wasn't even giving Him a second thought. I could feel some pulls and tugs, like when my dad would talk to me on the phone and before hanging up with me, he would tell me to find a church and be careful to make good friends. I would ignore this part, but it would have a profound impact on me later but for now . . . yea, I wasn't about to step foot into a church, and the friends I was making were good friends which God has blessed me with all my life.

In the letter to Craig, I explained how much I loved him, because I had never told him that before because I knew I could not give him the relationship he deserved . . . fully committed. I also wrote that I was going to get out of the Army, I was not going to reenlist but only if he felt the same way and wanted to start dating and living together. Something I had never thought of doing with anyone else up to this point, so it was a big step for me. Not being with Craig had driven me to the psych ward and I was determined to be with Craig, to love Craig, and to make him happy and support him so that he could do remarkable things with his life, and I could be at his side conquering the world together. I mailed it and several weeks passed with no response to my letter, even when I was receiving letters from others I had written. I started to get sad when Bug, Andrea and even Andrea's mom, my family and friends were writing me letters, but I never received a letter from Craig. I thought I had scared him away and so I started to feel heartbroken and that I had pushed him away and he would no longer even want to be friends, knowing how I really felt about him. I didn't know, I had never had a boyfriend, and I never had a girlfriend, hell I hadn't even had intercourse until I was 25 years old with a man and 26 with a woman, so this was very new to me at 27. Ok, I did have two girlfriends, one in junior high that lasted a few weeks and another in high school that lasted only a few days, but I was married to her. Oh, I forgot to tell you about that, so maybe I can work that in later or somewhere else in this horrid affair where Riggs G was pulling the strings and Mel was unable to do much except protect me because I was completely entangled about sin. My choice, my most unfortunate choice. Just hang on to this for now, I married my childhood friend Karen for financial reasons having to do with the Military, not because of love or sex, or anything . . . just a contract of mutual benefit and rewards. I really believe she got the short end of the stick, but at least we both have a story to tell when we run out of other stories. That marriage was never consummated. With Craig, I wanted to spend the rest of my life with . . . happily ever after . . . .but I never heard from him, so one night and after getting high on the hashish I had scored on R&R in Mombasa (Kenya) I pick up the reenlistment NCO (Non-Commissioned Officer) in my Humvee (I was the Commander's driver) where I reenlisted atop an old War World II Russian air hanger. It was old and no longer had the roof on the hanger part, but it served well as a headquarters base about 262 miles north of Mogadishu.

So many things were going on in my head and heart, I became colder so as not to get hurt again, I decided love was not for me because I didn't like the feeling of helplessness when someone doesn't love you back in the same way as you love them. I wouldn't have it again, I was just going to have fun, so needless to say my new theme song was Girls Just Want To Have Fun by Cindi Lauper and I was also listening to a lot of Depeche Mode, Morrisey, the Cure, and Bob Marley but I was in a transition because this is the music I bathed in when I was stationed in S. Korea right before being reassigned to Fort Drum. I returned to the U.S. in April of 1993, and with a fresh new contract to serve another four years of active military service, and I was already coming up on my sixth year in August 1993. But it was something familiar, and sure, unlike relationships which were turning out to be an emotional disaster for me. I wasn't back a week before I received a letter . . . from Craig! I looked at the post mark and he had mailed it while I was still in Africa but because the mail takes a long time to reach you, and this time because we had redeployed back to the U.S. it delayed it even more and it never reached me in Africa but now, I was holding it in my hand. I was both nervous and excited, my heart started beating faster and I think I even started sweating, I mean it was the response to my first I love you and want to be with you forever letter and admission! I hesitated; do I really want to know? Would you? I opened it both dreading and elated to finally know what Craig was thinking and fearful that he might also be letting me down and not wanting to be friends. I read his letter and I was full of joy and sorrow; in his letter he proclaims his love for me and that he felt the same and wanted to date and live together and he couldn't wait until I returned home and discharged from the Army so that we could start a life together! My first love loved me back and wanted the same thing I wanted! At the same time, I had reenlisted, and I didn't know how I was going to break it to Craig because it's not like I could say, I take it back I don't want to reenlist. I can't describe how reading that letter felt, all I can say is that it is the hardest letter I've ever had to read. We did connect later but who can get over something like that, a missed romance, after the pain you feel of a betrayal not betrayal. All about timing and Army logistics. He went to Florida, and I was making my way new, exciting, striving for an exhilarant experience at this thing called life . . . whatever, it is what I choose it to be, and boy how I did that while something was pulling me into the darker corners of the cave I was in. All alone but excited that this was going to change, because I was now responsible for me and didn't have to answer to anyone and do whatever interested me. What I know now, that I didn't know then, was that I would meet and be accepted into a family, we would inspire and encourage one another as we devoured life one day at a time, with as much love and drama that would be both amazingly tantalizing living of legends in our own minds, the populars, the stars, the life and owners of the party, while strong forces nipped at our heals and whispered into our hearts to push it to the limits and see if anything, or anyone broke.

Evil History on Repeat

In a time long ago, but only yesterday,
hate ruled many minds and hearts.
Most unknown, was hate itself,
it passed itself as mockery
and everyone laughed.

Hilarious was attributed to its forays,
its laughter recruiting evil stalwarts.
Love lost all of its wealth,
with uncivilized debauchery
served on draft.

Pettiness ruled in all the parties,
lying so cleverly, it became art.
Con artists employed stealth,
while puppets peddling chicanery
improved their craft.

History repeats its malformaties,
while not ashamed of its part.
Opinion crafters gain their wealth
on fear, pride, greed, and misery,
creating an army of the daft.

Chapter 10

G od and I weren't on speaking terms, my choice of course, even though He had never actually spoken to me in the many ways that I know now that He communicates with us. I especially had not given Him a second thought up until now, and yet, I'm still a little angry, ok not angry anymore, but definitely my last resort after all the things I had gotten myself into after getting discharged from the Army in 1993. About a month after my 27th birthday I was free to live the life I had chosen, carefree, with a check in one hand and a dream in my head, none of which would come true during these dark years even when it did seem to be glamorous if you only consider the sinfulness of my indulgences. I invited my friend Renee Givens, I called her Givens because we both had served together in the Army, in the same unit at Fort Drum, NY. She was still in the military, but I had just been discharged . . . honorably . . . in case you were wondering. Anyway, we went to NYC in my little black Nissan Pulsar which so fit me and served me for a long while. When I believed in luck, I would say I'm lucky with good cars, but now I know better and I'm a little wiser to know there is no luck in this world, at least not mine. You believe in luck if you want to, but I like to give credit where credit is due, you can't give credit to a word . . . luck, lucky, luckbox, maybe luck is related to some type of energy for some people? I don't know, and don't mean to offend. So, here we go on a long weekend trip, and I am done with six years of military service. Thank you very much USA, it was my distinct honor and privilege to serve to protect you, my dearest. My misfit countrymen, no, no, I'm kidding, just checking to see if you were still with me. I get kind of windy and chatty after I put on a little sweater. Big wooly sweater in NYC and our first stop is Bumble and Bumble at 146 E 56th St, New York, NY for braid extension. Nope, not Givens, they are for me. I had been letting my flattop grow out, I kept my hair in a flattop in the Army, and it was about three inches maybe, so I decided that I wanted a physical transformation as I entered this new chapter in my life. No longer a soldier, no longer in my hometown so I'm not going to embarrass anyone, and I am a grown, fit, young man with a check in one hand, and a dream in my head. Next stop, getting my ears and my nipple pierced, the nipple was the worst and on top of the pain I bled pretty bad and stained my white tee. Renee and I were having a blast, driving around we ended up exiting after I noticed I was going the wrong way but when I turned, and because I was really high, I hit the curb and blew out my tire. I stopped at a corner store and fearlessly got out, knowing the reputation that Harlem had from the movies, I knew I could hold my own against almost anyone, everyone if I could surprise them. I knew how to change a tire; I mean what young man from Texas doesn't know how to change a tire? I had the tire and jack out and started to undue the lug nuts when a white beat-up cargo van pulled up, I told Renee to get in the car and lock the door but before she could even hear me, the guy was next to me. I was surprised that he moved so fast, but I was on my guard, and he insisted on helping me, but leery of his intentions, I was hesitant and told him that I didn't need any help, I could change my own tire. He was unfazed, and I started to feel at ease because he didn't give off any bad energy. You see, God has always protected me from shady people, with the gift of picking up negative vibes in people. He did not give off a vibe so I figured I would be more at ease, and I wasn't wrong, he changed the tire in record time, and I tried to give him some money, but he wouldn't have it "Naw man, glad I could help. Be careful." And he gone. Just like that, it didn't take any more than ten minutes, Rene and I were back on the road whooping and hollering ready to take on NYC, or otherwise known as Manhattan . . . to the belly of the beast. It was my liberation tour, my wind through my hair (albeit fake) moment.

My dearest charge is growing up fast, at least the military occupied his time, but I was unable to sway him back into good graces with Elohim, such a strong willed and stubborn spirit. Aside from this, he has so much love bottled up inside of him, but he fails to realize that as strength. He still feels like a failure living through his suicide attempts, failing at them actually. He failed them because the love for his parents is really strong, such respect that he has always had, from an early age he admired their strength of raising a big family, going to welding school and then moving the family across Texas to start a new life. He admired and respected that they could read and write both in English and Spanish, my mother better than my father but they were able to absorb knowledge and wisdom. Their family loves and respects each other when Riggs isn't playing around with them and trying to cause them to divide them from each other, it is a lot harder nowadays that both of their parents are no longer in this realm. Jr, what his family and close friends call my charge, doesn't know it right now but if he survives Riggs and Charo, he will be helping so many people, immigrants to be exact. Something he knows nothing about, since the only time his life was ever affected was when he came home from school one day and saw his mother crying for the first time he could remember. It was a very disturbing experience, being ushered into the living room. As he passed his and his little brother's room, he noticed that his grandmother, Natividad, was comforting his mother while she was crying. He thought someone had passed away, someone close but no one said anything. It was only later, in his adulthood, that he found out that his oldest sister had run away and eloped with Jose. Since my little charge was so young, the adults felt no need to explain things, not that he would have understood. It would all turn out fine in the end because Elohim would not allow this family to be destroyed but Riggs sure was testing his limits. Alicia, his sister, had to grow up fast, being the one his parents relied on to read and write anything and everything in English for his parents which would continue all her life, this is the way most immigrant families must raise their first born, out of survival in a place with a foreign language. The unique experience with Jr's family is that they are native to Texas but Asherton was a primarily Spanish speaking community, so English was still a foreign language, but Riggs' hate and division tactics instilled into humans a great capacity to be afraid and resentful of foreigners, even while the Lamb King walked as a foreigner, a fact blinded and choreographed as a very effective lie.

I did make a special trip to Heaven during this time to strategize because he was free from the confines and strict disciplined life that kept him from idolizing death. I was genuinely concerned with his newfound freedom, with no family to keep him focused on life and God. He was making new friends, some were placed in his path to keep him safe and grounded because they had these characteristics, like his friend Dawn and Andrea, but Riggs would soon attempt to destroy these by convincing him that they were selfish and privileged, but these were all lies, and I couldn't intervene with free will, his free will to choose what he believes and at this moment in his life the only thing that he believes in, is living a life of discovery and with no filters whatsoever. He was going to experiment and experience a life of drugs, alcohol, sexual freedom, a network of lies, and a life of glamour and to become a person that got what he wanted, when he wanted. After having served in the military, and a distinguished military stint, he swore that no one would have the right to deny him his manhood when he let the world know he was gay. Riggs and Charo had convinced him that he could conquer anything and say anything no matter who was hurt in the process, this was his life, and no one could interfere. He would live his life boldly, loudly, and dared anyone to make him even feel disrespected, much less actually disrespect him. He was intimidating, obnoxious, rude, and physically threatening. There were so many times that I had to whisper into his heart the hurt he was causing, and he would be physically sick and exhausted from acting out his wild side. I was losing my ground to Riggs and failing to comprehend the resolve behind Riggs' fascination with him. I had to figure that out, and this is why I had to take a trip to Heaven to strategize, I was getting very worried about the direction and decisions my charge was making, including the experiences he was seeking now on a regular basis.

Oh, boo hoo, it's nobody's fault except for this little shit. You all have your own will, and you can decide what you want to do, don't blame your shit on me because you can't handle it. I was the one that called it from the beginning, you can't handle free will! The first of your kind couldn't handle it and they used to be visited by G-pop as dusk descended upon that shit show paradise, he made just for them. What makes any of you think you can deny me, ignore me, or defy me? I was the one they called G-pops Light! You can't begin to fathom the power I have, so you ignore me and blame the Old Man for everything, which is fine by me because I can carry on with no resistance. You may not know any of this, that I rule the earth, I can cause as much chaos and destruction as I want and can get away with anything to test your humbleness, your love, your free will, your desire to follow what's in that fairytale you gave a special name, I call it trash, full of lies that don't even match up to reality. Even better for me, truly little attention is paid to any of it, and even if you open its pages or hear its contents, you may have a reaction to it (most don't) but you definitely don't live by it, hoorah for me!

My strategy has to change with this one, he was safe these past six years but he was about to jump into my world, my domain, and he was ill prepared for it because he is all alone in a big scary world, brought to you by no other than the Riggs-G, living up to my new name and proud to destroy as many of you as possible and this little shit was a good challenge, there was something about him that really disgusts me, and this can only mean the L word, the same thing that saved him from me before, this kid sure did love his parents. They are the only reason this little shit is still alive, because if he didn't, he would have splattered his brains, or driven his car off a bridge or into a pole because I pulled out all the stops with him. He was also assigned a protector that has been a formidable opponent throughout the ages, sparring with Mel is as much entertaining as it is frustrating, but I was determined to have this kid destroy himself and I was attacking physically and spiritually, this kid has no chance. It's just going to take some more effort; this is why I'm meeting with Charo and his team to come up with a new plan to destroy him. It would entail working from the inside, and moving those around him in a way that would make him question his friendships, make him distrust them, and wish they had never met him. I would have him all to myself to do as I pleased without any interference from any of his new friends and his new makeshift family.

For now, I had to settle to achieving a dream of living, whatever that meant. I say I had a dream, but the only dream I had was to live something I thought I was supposed to be, not thinking of any broken things or people I left along the way. I looked forward for this moment, and it is my friend Dawn whom I credit for inspiring me to pursue another art medium of art . . . hair and people. I decided to enroll in Cosmetology School. Phillip's Hairstyling Institute in Syracuse, NY to be exact, which was memorable, and I surely relate to Frenchy in the movie Grease because I was also a beauty school dropout. I went back and finished, but that doesn't excuse the almost eight months, and almost didn't go back until my very good friend Warren, a boyfriend at the time, encouraged and convinced me to go back and finish. The only reason I dropped out was because I was disgusted, ok ok just drama, but this was my life back then, so bear with me I promise it will tickle your tickle bone. There were these two guys that were all the rave when I was in my junior year and stole some of my attention away from me and during this time that I was on the outs with God (by choice, I'll explain later) I was very hung up on pride because I felt that I was owed a good time since I had been living in a deep depression for seventeen years at this point, and I was still not ready to make amends and start talking to God. I was too busy settling into my new home, wow, this sounds crazy as I'm telling this story because I had never lived alone before, but I had my own apartment. I found an apartment on the second floor of this old home that sat on the corner of S. Geddes and Stolp Avenue, and it was pretty drafty but the view out of the dining room was just awesome. It overlooked part of the city because it was higher up. I was living in the Strathmore neighborhood and across the street from the Woodland Reservoir, .8 miles of easy level walking/running and such a beautiful place to exercise because of the stairs and just so beautiful all year around it was a suitable place to live for my first time alone, but this was soon to change.

Charo do this, Charo do that! WTF, I didn't give up the upstairs to come down to this awesome place, just to be a slave to the boss. Yea he can be the boss, but he's not my master! Don't get our relationship all wrapped up in something your little minds can handle, there is much more going on that you can feel than what's going on in those peas for brains. It really isn't your brains, they are more than capable, it's all that pansy stuff, that sissy stuff, that everything is lovey dovey shit. Wimps! Cry about this, cry about that, hand me a tissue, oh my I don't want to die! I'm scared, I'm just a punk . . . admitting it would give you a little dignity with me. Getting drunk on evil one night, I stumbled onto this little jerk Jr., they call him, shouting at the top of his lungs to me in his apartment on W. Onondaga Ave, where he lived in the restored attic apartment. It was when I wanted to let him know it was me. He really irked me that night, and I hold grudges, this pathetic little man was going to pay, but that night, I had to stick to the plan, and it didn't include me revealing myself. I had done it to his ex-boyfriend and to one of his roommates, I was trying to scare them away so I could economically ruin him, get him to become a begging junky and o.d. on crack. That's what was really doing it back then, the crack! You dumbasses try anything to escape, you already know there is no escape, there's only two real choices, although Riggs has you all convinced that you have all these choices. Yea, the rest of us know, there are only two. I'm not going to say anything else; you know what I'm talking about, you all do but some of you juggle around in your little brains that you know something about something, or you know enough to come up with, what do you call them . . . oh yea, theories. A fancy word for 'I got this idea, and this is how I'm proving it so.' Whatever, you don't know shit. Your stuck in a make-believe world of denial, and plain dilly dallying yourselves through the motions of trading your talent and intelligence for material and coin that represents a broken promise . . . money. You are all too dumb to realize that it has no real value, none, zilch, nada. Broken promises are what you all live on, and I would dare say, after so many a millennium dealing with your type, are just playing out a part sucking up air and taking up space.

During the time I started going to school, and buying what I could to start furnishing my apartment, Craig started calling me and convincing me to let him move in. He assured me that he wasn't with Rick anymore, but I could sense that Craig was not being himself. I agreed anyway, it wasn't the same between Craig and I after that missed opportunity, I think those are maybe once-in-a-lifetime things. I still couldn't stand Rick, and especially seeing them together, so I told Craig that he wasn't welcomed. I don't know what happened, but after we fooled around a couple of nights, he disappeared and when he came back, he showed up with Rick and continued to explain that Rick was moving in and sleeping with Craig. I was appalled, out of nowhere, but I knew this was Rick's doing, and I was so angry with Craig for being so weak. I didn't understand abusive relationships because I had never been exposed to anything of the such. We all argued that night, I called the police and since the lease was in my name, a detail I always tried to take care of, the police told them they had to leave, and then I told my landlord, and he changed the locks. Problem solved, and the first time I called the police on someone I called a friend, and I wondered why everyone was so surprised and made it my fault. How dare I call the police on a friend, they asked. Who does that, they asked. I did, I thought. Screw them, they hurt me, they lied to me, and I wasn't going to be pushed around and told what I was going to allow and not allow. Sorry that I must instill some type of morals into your life, but I pledged that if someone lied, cheated, or stole, they were gross and meant very little too nothing in my book.

I had one friend that I made at beauty school, her name was Jenny, short for Jennifer. We got along great! She had this country twang to her voice but not like you hear in Texas, this was upstate New York. She was married with two children, and she always wanted to be a hairdresser, so she started at Phillip's the same time I did. I was starving for friends, because Dawn was hardly in town anymore, traveling all over with Matrix, Andrea had moved to Albany, and I didn't have any other friends yet. I still went out, but my depression was kicking up into high gear, and I didn't go out as much anymore, plus I didn't ever really meet anyone that later became a close friend in a bar or club except for Warren, who would become my first boyfriend and the only person to ever ask me to marry him. It was through Warren that I would gain a family . . . a grams, a mom, a sister, and yes, we started out as boyfriends but ended up as brothers. I almost didn't meet him at all, again because I hardly went out to the clubs anymore and I definitely avoided gay bars, because the environment was more cramped, some would say cozy. This one Friday night, this guy I knew through one of Craig's friends, Larry. I can't recall his name, but he called me up and begged me to go out with him, I got tired of his begging and thought it would do me good to get out of the apartment because I was feeling especially lonely. I told him I was only going for one drink, so I met him at Ryan's, just this local bar, except it was for gay men, I mean everyone is welcome, but it was a gay bar. Nothing different than the Copa in downtown Beaumont. Drinking and dancing, and whatever tickles your fancy between two consenting men. We went to the bar, grabbed a couple of beers, and then sat down. We didn't talk much, because we hardly knew each other and it's not like I was into him, don't know what he thought, it never occurred to me to ask, and I have a really bad gaydar. You must understand that although I knew I was gay since the seventh grade, I didn't live it. I didn't have friends that were gay, I knew of guys in school who were gay, but I never had the opportunity to befriend any of them, not like there were many in my class or school for that matter. This was all new to me, being able to just swing down to a gay bar to have a few beers and maybe meet someone without lying or misleading anyone about where I was going or anyone asking about my social life. Everyone so far, after leaving the military, knew I was gay because I didn't care who knew or not. I walked with this chip on my shoulder, daring people to disrespect me just because I was gay, yea it wouldn't bode well for them.

I kept checking out this guy, as soon as I spotted him, I thought he was beautiful, I knew he was beautiful. He was the most beautiful man in that bar, that night and I had to meet him. I caught him looking back at me and returning my smile. I asked the guy I was with if he knew him, knowing he had lived here a long time, he at once said "Yea, I know him. I can't stand him!" "What's his name? I asked. "Why, you interested?" What's his name, I asked again in a more forceful tone that made him sit back and slouch like a child who was just yelled at. I didn't care, I hardly knew this guy and I wasn't about to take any advice nor any gossip about the most beautiful man in the place. "Warren, his name is Warren. You need to be . . . ." I got up before he could finish his sentence, I got everything I wanted from him and was done with him for the rest of the night. I came with him as I had said, I drank one beer with him, and my interests lay elsewhere. He had become a person sitting at a table that could hold my seat while I got to know this Warren fella.

I walked up to him as he was speaking to someone who appeared to be a friend, and I put my hand out to shake hands and introduced myself, "Hi Warren, my name is Santos, it's very nice to meet you." "Hi" He took my hand and leaned in closer, "How do you know my name?" "I have my ways." Thinking I was flirting, I was so bad at it since I just started living openly and was never the flirting type, I was so shy growing up. Thanks to the military, I wasn't very shy anymore. I thought I must have sounded so stupid, since I already knew that the guy I came with and Warren knew each other, so I didn't walk right back to my table and instead went over to dance on the stage, which was darker than the main dance floor, less people and it was higher than the main dance floor. I often did this, and then wondered why I would go home alone, and not meet anyone because I loved to dance and would drink and dance, often oblivious to any flirting or any moves. I was very insecure about my looks, all my life never really thinking I was handsome or cute or whatever. I thought myself to be simple and plain. I was short, but since I was recently out of the military, I was in really good shape, and the men did like that.

I sat down with that guy at our table again, and we made some small talk, and Warren and I kept exchanging looks and smiles. I must have taken a long time, because I still wasn't sure if he was into me, and it wouldn't do my ego any good to be rejected, although he was genuinely nice to me when I went over and introduced myself. Beautiful and kind, what a great combination, and he could dance really good. I loved men who could dance, because I loved dancing and I had to stop myself from staring at him, I didn't want him to think I was stalking him, just flirting with him until I could work up the nerve to ask him to dance. I eventually asked him to dance, and we hung out the rest of the night, one beer turned to two and

I don't know how many, but I was too drunk on Warren to be drunk on the beer I was drinking. We closed the bar down, and walked out together, I don't remember anyone else from that night, and I don't think he was there with anyone, because we both got into our cars, after exchanging numbers and saying goodbye. I don't remember a kiss; I think we were both just wanting to get to know each other. We may have hugged each other good night. He was tall, about 5'11", dark short curly hair, light complected, with a hint of rosacea (red cheeks I had just learned that in school, but my crush Jimmy had a little as well) which I drool over. My type completely, and such a nice butt, tall and beautiful. I was gaga stricken (not the singer of today), more like coco for coco puffs (if you're old enough, it is a cereal). I think he called me the next night and we were on the phone for hours, and then the next night and the next, until he invited me to his apartment. I eventually moved in with him, since he was more established and had a better apartment, plus his roommate agreed that I could move in. We were inseparable after this, and I had my first boyfriend, and I was loving my life. I was excited to have a boyfriend for the first time in my life and I was 27 years old. I never dreamed that I would be a boyfriend to someone so beautiful that was my perfect type, except for colored eyes like hazel, green, or blue. I had hit the boyfriend lotto!

We were smitten with each other, and it was a beautiful love story. Warren was the first guy to buy me flowers, telling me that he loved me without any prompting from me, and he is the only marriage proposal that I received. Yea, Karen didn't count and plus she was a girl who had her own wedding ring, but Warren got down on one knee in my apartment on Stolp and took out a ring and proposed. It broke my heart to say no, it was because I was so messed up and terrified to allow someone entrance into my dark heart, especially someone so kind and loving. I loved him dearly, but I was an emotional mess, and he didn't know the half of it. I believe that although he said he was ok with my decision to wait a while so that I could give him my whole heart, it was the beginning of the end for us. It would be a slow and painful transition to friendship. How could I possibly blame him? It takes so much courage to propose, and to say no, or wait, well that just has a long-lasting effect on someone. We made the most of the year that we were boyfriends, and whoever claims that maryJ is not a gateway drug doesn't know what they are talking about, because it wasn't long before I jumped into the deep end of mind altering substances so that I could numb the nothingness in my heart, this constant feeling of loneliness even while surrounded by fun and exciting people and opportunities.

One of my friends I met through Dawn rented the attic apartment that this guy had remodeled in this three-story building he owned so that he could live in it. It was an amazing apartment, albeit a lot of stairs when you came through the door you encountered fully carpeted stairs (the entire apartment except the bathrooms were carpeted) that circled up into an open design, at the top of the entrance stairs you could go right into a very large dressing room, at least this is what Warren and I made it. I say Warren and I, but it was him with the skill and eye for design and style. If you went straight you went into a full bathroom with black and white tile, or you could go left, stepping up about three steps into what could have fit a dining room table, but we were just starting out and didn't have much at all, both of us being in school at the time. To the left of this area was a small kitchen, but since we were far from throwing dinner parties, it suited us fine. Warren did some amazing things with spaghetti and spaghetti sauce since this was the least expensive meal we could cook that would fill us up. We also hit a lot of local places, especially up around Syracuse University, there were two places that were cheap and delicious, one was Munjeds serving middle eastern food and Varsity Pizza on South Crouse Ave for some great slices of pizza, you could watch them making the pizza, and the smell just made your stomach jump for joy. I haven't had food this good and inexpensive since I lived in Syracuse. We had our other places to hit, a diner on Sunday's after partying all night and waking up late and hungover. We had uppity places where we would go when we had the money and as we lived, worked, and played we started earning more and were able to live a great life on a shoestring budget, although no one was budgeting! We were living one day at a time, and I was one of the oldest, and had just been discharged from the Army so I had quite a bit of experience.

Past the kitchen was the bedroom where some shadow silhouette of a man stood at the foot of the mattress and called out Warren's name. He said that, while I was visiting Texas, he saw that shadow figure walking through that space on the other side of the kitchen, and it kept moving towards what was the open living room with cathedral ceilings, huge picture windows, white stucco, all carpeted and step up to open nooks in front of the picture windows, the ceiling was about 8 ft at the tallest of the peak. Warren said it was so real that he wondered why I was ignoring him, and something had happened in Texas, so he looked in the room off this living space into what was a huge room with a pair of seven-foot windows and a whirlpool that could fit five adults comfortably, a couples sink counter, and a sauna. Neither the sauna nor the whirlpool worked. You could fill up the whirlpool like we did, and Leslie did even after the landlord told us not to use it because it leaked downstairs, but being who we were we did it anyway, but after we got in trouble with our landlord, we turned it into a place to hang out. Warren, our interior designer, had a great idea and we put an oval futon in there and pillows, converting it into something we could use. Warren didn't see me anywhere so as he was coming out of that room, to the left was a black iron staircase that took you into what we converted to a workout room. It also had a window that gave us access to a flat rooftop on top of a three story, four with our attic apartment, which had to be like 1,200 sq ft. easy. We were high up, but so were the two buildings on either side, with two informers in the building to the left of ours who told Peter (our landlord) every time we went out there, well not every time, it's not like they were that bad. Although we did think that the lady next door stole our Pansy (our calico cat), who surprisingly came home after we called Peter and even tried to get her to answer her door, but never did . . . I think it was that evening that Pansy shows up meowing at our back window off the dressing room. Warren didn't find me up there either, so he forgot all about it, and chalked it up to whatever he did, but even when he told me about it, I didn't think anything of it.

The only other bedroom had cathedral ceiling with like a four- or five-foot skylight and I put my mattress right under the skylight and it was so relaxing to lay there and stare out into the night sky or the blue sky in the daylight. When Warren moved out, after our knock down drag out fight, which I started with my smart-ass mouth at Trexxx, the gay dance club in downtown Syracuse. After we beat the shit out of each other, which turned into some hot sex after we got out all our anger, we realized that this was very disturbing. This is when we realized that I was not able to handle my green monster and for the sake of our love for each other, we had to live apart. He moved into the front apartment which was almost as cool as the attic. I ended up renting the room to Josh, who had just graduated high school and wanted to move out of his house in Skaneateles. I don't remember how we met, but we spent a lot of time on the phone until he eventually moved into my apartment. I was grateful to have someone paying half the rent, but I missed Warren so much. One night I was sleeping in my new bedroom, the one that was our guest bedroom when we were together, plus the other room had too many memories. I was sound asleep one night with my bedroom door open, which I liked because of the Army, I needed to be aware of the entire apartment in case someone broke in, not closed up in my bedroom. Suddenly, I'm waking up to Josh running into my room, shutting my door, and getting under the covers next to me. "What the hell is going on Josh?" "I don't want to talk about it", " Josh, you are going to talk about it, you just jumped into my bed and slammed my door, what the hell is going on?" "I just woke up to this black silhouette of a man calling my name." I'm not going to lie, it made the hairs on the back of my neck stand up, but this was my house, and I don't care who or what it was, you are not supposed to be here, you weren't invited, and I was about to kick them out. "Don't go Santos, don't go, just stay here." "No, this is my apartment, stay here and do not open the door." I closed the door behind me and charged towards the room, knowing damn well it was some sort of spirit. I didn't know how I knew, but it did the same thing to Warren and now to Josh. Warren and Josh did not know each other well enough to have shared that story, I was the only one that knew what had happened to Warren and because it didn't really bother him, we didn't make a big deal out of it and forgot the whole matter without a second thought anyway. I crossed that space where tonight, I was glad nothing was in my way because I couldn't get to the other bedroom fast enough. The nerve of this spirit, scaring people I care about but this time he was messing with my money, the person that was paying half the rent, after seeing how he reacted, was not going to live here for much longer and then how could I afford this apartment? I would have to move, and I absolutely hate moving. I crossed through the kitchen and started turning on all the recessed lighting, there were about four switches and I turned them all on, and started using my Army voice, "Ok, you are scaring everybody showing up and calling their names, say my name! Come on, you can't be scared, say my name! Ok, ok, you need the lights to be out?" I closed the doors first and then started turning off the lights. I'm standing there in the middle of the room, doors closed, lights off, totally dark and I start again in my Army voice, stern, authoritative, intentional and from the diaphragm . . . "It's dark now, let me see you. Show yourself to me, say my name! Come on, say my name . . . scaaare mee! The worst thing that will happen is that you bring me into the spirit world, and you will still have to deal with me! Scaring everyone, come on! Scare me! Show yourself!" After I stood there for what seemed several minutes just waiting, and nothing. No silhouette, no calling my name. "One last chance, say my name, Santos, say it! Yea, that's what I thought, you chicken shit, stop showing up around here or we are going to have problems!" I went back to my room, left the door open and climbed in next to Josh saying, "Don't worry, I took care of it." "What do you mean?" "I mean I took care of it now go to sleep; you can stay here with me tonight if you don't want to sleep in your room." Needless to say, whatever that thing wanted to accomplish it was successful, Josh didn't stay much longer in that apartment, but I knew that something had appeared to both Warren and Josh, and I was totally surprised and very happy with the way I reacted to it, I mean, you never know how you will react in a situation like that, and I performed marvelously and courageously . . . What a story this will make, I thought. I was proud of myself, as if I needed anything more to do with any more pride right now.

Warren and I started having problems when he went away on a trip to Provincetown, I later realized that the problem had really started after I answered when he proposed. It just took us this long to finally realize that it was coming to an end. I guess with the pain of me turning him down and coupled with the fact that I never addressed his proposal again, we had been living together for about a year and things were getting stale and too comfortable. I am more of a homebody, and he was younger and loved music and dancing. I loved it too, but I had done so much of it that I was becoming bored with it and becoming extremely comfortable staying at home. He came back from Provincetown, and he confessed that he had cheated on me, I was devastated as much as I could be because I really didn't know how to love, but I wasn't aware of this when he came clean, it would only be much later that I would realize the empty love I doled out to friends and family. I was as hurt as a duplicitous person can be, but I knew this fairytale with Warren was over, but I forgave him because I had also fooled around with some young blonde headed kid in the parking lot of the same bookstore, I met Craig. He was so cute and we didn't even go in the bookstore, we spotted each other in the parking lot while I was driving up, I motioned for him to come over to my car and he got into Warren's Taurus where we fooled around, I don't think straight when I'm blinded by lust, we didn't do anything but give each other a hand job, but I still felt dirty and cheap. I had cheated on my perfect boyfriend but when Warren came clean, I kept this a secret because I was that shallow and I was not going to be the cause of us breaking up nor giving Warren the satisfaction of blaming me for our problems, at the time, I blamed him for the downward spiral of our relationship because going out with him would make me furious because he was usually the most handsome guy in the whatever place we went to, not only beautiful but he has a presence. Wait until you meet his sister Leslie, she was the upgraded female version of her brother Warren. Blonde, blue eyed, perfect proportions and we were so comfortable together. She was the one that really consoled me when we finally broke up and ended our relationship.

She knew her brother well, and she comforted me through the entire year it took me to get over him. Gram, their grandmother, was another kind soul that I connected well with, and I sought her out when I would get so lonely, I thought I would kill myself and she would listen and feed me, being around her was like the perfect sunny day with a light breeze that makes you feel that everything is just fine. Gram and her husband, pretty hard old timer, whom I never really connected with, but we had a mutual respect, must have been that I had served in the military. Warren had also introduced me to his mother, Tracy, who passed away too young. She had her problems as a young mother, but as I would soon learn, everyone has their demons. This was the end of something beautiful and romantic, and the start of the wild and out of control drug, sex, and alcohol frenzy that would ensue. I was also beginning to feel and see a change taking place inside of me, something dark and foreboding, a feeling that I may get my wish after all . . . to kill whatever it was that was keeping me alive. I couldn't stand peering into mirrors because I could see the evil emanating from within me, and no longer recognized who that was looking back at me, and there were many things staring back at me, prodding me and beckoning me to become colder, angrier, and more prideful with a good dose of self-righteousness. Everyone was getting scared of what and who I was becoming, and I couldn't give two shits about it.

After dropping out of Phillips Hairstyling Institute, due to the need to be gainfully employed in order to survive I decided to work full time and soon forgot all about cosmetology. It was Warren, even after having broken up, that convinced me to go back and finish school. It took a lot of work and effort on both our parts to continue as friends, faithful friends not just a fake and cordial relationship between exes. We genuinely loved each other, whatever love meant, and wanted to remain in each other's lives, so we put in the effort, and this meant that anyone we dated had to also deal with the fact that we were close friends with an ex-boyfriend which is like having three people in a relationship. The feeling was mutual, there was no way that we were going to give up the friendship because someone could not understand that we were going to remain friends, no matter what, but most couldn't handle it, and I was one of those people for the first year, and I made it very difficult because in a way I felt that terminating our relationship completely would protect me from the pain and sorrow of failing at my first relationship, and from someone who I thought at the time was the love of my life, but I had failed at keeping his interest, and making him feel safe and loved. I tried hard, but Warren's heart was bigger and stronger than my efforts to push him away and out of my life. His family felt the same way, they were not going to push me away, their love was genuine and it was only much later that I recognized the true importance of family, love, commitment, forgiveness, patience, and everything else you must hang onto in order to deal with someone like me, intent on smashing to pieces anything that resembled something that could hurt me. I was working at Key Bank as a data input clerk for their loan department when Warren's aunt Val helped me get a job at Federal Express, which allowed me to leave Key Bank and go back to finish cosmetology at Phillip's. I worked the night shift, and it was part-time, but I made more than I did at Key Bank, so I was able to return full-time to school. I was incredibly talented and by then I was in my senior year shortly after returning, which meant that I could apply my skills to real people during our clinic hours. I was also excited about being taught directly by Mr. Phillip's but to my surprise and disappointment, he was not going to teach! I asked for a meeting, where I told him that I felt shortchanged and neglected because it was his name on the school, but he was stepping away from teaching, and I was not ok with this. I'm not saying that my conversation with him changed his mind, but he announced that he would be doing some of the teaching for the seniors. I was happy about that because he had a way of teaching in three separate ways, for his students, like me, to really get it. Many people think that what cosmetologists do is easy until they run into one that is extraordinarily talented and artful, you have them in every profession. You have some that barely know what they are doing, you have those that are really good but are distracted so never reach their full potential, and then you have those that are totally committed and it is more than just a job, it is more than just showing up, it is about service . . . about caring, about achieving and growing, and sharing. It was upon graduation that Mr. Phillip's would recommend one student to Best & Co. which was the premier salon in Syracuse. They had these packages that one could buy, where there would be a day filled with pampering, lunch, and you would get to and from the salon in their limousine. It was the salon to be if you wanted to live large as a cosmetologist, your future would be secure and financially rewarding. I was that person the year I graduated, and the recommendation only guaranteed your interview with the owners, but you could bank on being hired into their assistant training program on his recommendation. Of course, at my age, and with my experience anyone would be impressed with my resume, and then gaining this recommendation, they hired me on the spot. I worked there for about two months before I had a falling out with the owners, I felt that I was not being taken seriously and that the whole salon was a façade of fake and cheap, both talent and product, wrapped in a golden blanket made to appear something glamorous. I just wanted to leave, but the owner insisted for commentary on their assistant program, "To improve it". I'm sure they were stunned at what I told them about their training, their assistant program, and their products from someone with so little experience and right out of school. What they did not realize was that I was much older than most students, with more experience, and plus, I was very astute, and I did everything I believed in as best as I could, throwing all my abilities and talents into what I wanted to achieve. I left that day, without giving them any time to get another assistant and left them stunned and reeling at what I had just told them about their fake, cheap, glitzy salon. I was done being nice to people, especially those wasting my time.

I got my resume together and one day, as I was heading to my job at FedEx, which by the way, I was still in great shape and looked really cute in my uniform I remembered seeing this cute salon on a corner down in the Armory Square district of Syracuse. This area was up and coming, it was right across the street from what would become the Imax theater but was a real Armory before, thus the name they used to promote that area of businesses in Syracuse. I was driving my little black Nissan Pulsar, and I pulled up to an empty spot right in front of the salon, where two beautiful women were sitting and smoking outside sitting on a bench. Not easily intimidated, well let me clarify this because at this point in my life nothing intimidated me, nothing! I had been through too much and I was trying to get somewhere, achieve something that I wanted to accomplish and right now it was getting experience as a hairstylist so that I could get on stage with my talents, just like those guys that I had experienced with Dawn's event. How their very presence completely changed the mood of an entire room, just by showing up. I walked right up to them, I couldn't get over how beautiful they were, both were smiling, and I asked for the owner of the salon, after explaining that I was a hairdresser looking for a job. Their smiles became larger and Carrie, the little blonde bombshell, said, "That's Michalle, she is with a client . . . ", "Oh, that's ok I don't want to interrupt can you just give her my resume; I was on my way to work anyway." "Hold on a minute, she probably would like to say hello" and she disappeared into the salon. It was a small but very eclectic salon, beautifully befitting an art community, with lofty ceilings, must have been 15 ft, taking up a corner space in a bigger red brick building renovated to house businesses on the first floor and apartment lofts on the other floors. Michalle came out with her scissors and a comb in her hand, and I introduced myself. I explained to her that I had just graduated and was looking for a job. I couldn't get over how beautiful she was as well, three female goddesses, fashion forward but with a sophisticated taste in clothes, makeup, hairstyles, and their presence seemed to radiate this down to it excellence. I really wanted to work with them, and I didn't go to any other salon after having met the three of them. Michalle took my resume, and I thanked her for her time and said goodbye to all three. I got in my car elated at the experience and I haven't even seen the inside of the salon! I couldn't' stop thinking about Sasha, which was the name of the salon, named after Michalle's grandmother. I don't remember how long it took for Michalle to call me, it wasn't long, and invited me to come do a haircut for her, "Bring a model and we'll see" was what Michalle offered, and the day we had settled on I was there on time and with Warren in tow, he was so excited for me, and just as nervous, he has always been so considerate and committed to people he loves, even to strangers, he was always the kind and considerate one in our group of friends, although some would beg to differ, but this was a misconception because they were usually jealous or Warren was just not interested. It was usually only the boys that Warren was not interested in, that would talk badly about him.

We show up and to display my skill, because I wanted to impress Michalle, I felt that I had this one shot to show her my skills and the best way to do this was to cut Warren's hair with scissor over comb, no clippers. Clippers are great, but I wanted to impress, and clippers don't impress anyone but the kitchen beauticians (nothing against y'all, just distinguishing professionally licensed from natural talent without a license), and with his curly hair, makes it way more complex and skillful. I was nervous but confident in my abilities, plus Warren had a way of making me feel that I was not alone in this, because he was so supportive and loving towards me even after all that I had put him through. I wouldn't even have had this opportunity if he had not convinced me to go back and finish what I had started at Phillip's. After I finished his haircut, Michalle came over and as she is checking out the haircut, I am looking around at the salon and there was no other place I wanted to be to do this. It was so cute, but not at all pretentious, which was totally opposite from Best & Co., it only had four stylist stations and there was only one open. Michalle had the most prominent one closest to the front door, opposite her on the other side, basically hidden was for this part-time male stylist who was married to a wealthy woman who only worked part-time because of the trade not because he had to, and they knew each other for a long time. Carrie was right beside her; she was my favorite, and we had this great relationship, we were both very independent, strong personalities, and beautiful, but she was more responsible, being a single mother and working fulltime while taking a few classes to further her education, majoring in English literature, I think. The other Michelle was the receptionist who sat at the front door, she was the sweetest of all, and beautiful blue eyes, reddish brown hair, and a calming personality. Snapping me back into reality after checking out the haircut, she said the haircut was good, and asked me why I chose to use scissors over comb, "Why didn't you use a clipper?"

"Because I wanted to impress you, and with his curly hair I thought this was the best way to show off what I can do". She smiled and said, "Thank you for coming in, I will call you." I was both disappointed and elated, she didn't say it was a bad haircut and she did say she would call me, but oh, how I wanted to know more! As Warren and I were leaving, there was a light snow starting to fall, that big fluffy snowflake type of snow, where it looks like the snowflakes floating and dancing down from the sky. I was so excited and happy, I remember that I thought that was a great sign of things to come, because it was my favorite type of snow and it just started as we were leaving. I don't remember how long it was before she called me, but she did and offered me a job and we talked about when I could start. I started right away,

I believe that she called me on a Friday and that night, to celebrate Warren and I went to Trexxx, and who did we see on the dance floor but Michalle, with a group of people! I said hello to her, but I didn't want to seem that I knew her so well that I could encroach on her fun, especially without being invited so after the brief hello, I pretty much kept to my group of friends and proceeded to party like we usually did, but it was a good sign that I was going to be working at a very cool salon with very cool people because you have to admit, a group of hairstylists, especially very talented ones, are set apart when seen in public . . . you cannot mistake their style and beauty. This would also prove to be the best and worst time in Syracuse, because I was achieving my goals, making friends, and experimenting with everything and anything that tickled my fancy. It was the start of me losing control, and forces I would have no power to control because it was only experiences I was after and started to look at people as objects of desire. Things were about to get dangerously complicated, but for now, dancing getting drunk and visiting the bathroom for the occasional bump of cocaine, while considering that I just ran into my new boss at the coolest place (only the cool straight people came to Trexxx to dance) in Syracuse to dance and run wild, all confirmed that I was living my life free, and without caution or considerate to anyone else's expectations of what I should do with my life.

temptation

i wink at the moon
as it moons the heavens
i bend into its glow and swoon
its mystery speaks of impressions
and of a romantic honeymoon
while imprisoned like prideful felons
a far cry from opportune
and as the vengeful moonlight beckons
we make love in a cocoon
with a tidal wave of concessions
i stare and wink again at the moon
and speak of greedy possessions
while we gyrate in tune
through recollections
from a pornographic cartoon
and a slew of broken intentions
it is too late while too soon
for apologetic transgressions
the sun screams "Get a room!"
while i buy more sessions
and seal my doom

Chapter 11

"LOL and LMAO, you are becoming all mine!" I yell into his mind, but Jr is so caught up with finally fitting in somewhere, but I know what he is really preoccupied with, defeat and failure. I know this because I have been working towards this by putting in that extra time, keeping Mel from really having any influence over him. This kid used to be an altar boy and lived at church as a kid, but now he was living only a few blocks on the same street as The Cathedral of the Immaculate Conception which he never sets foot in. I'm wining this soul! I have him believing he failed at family life, he failed at suicide, he failed at college, he failed the Army, he failed with his first love, he failed with his true love after investing a year, and he failed at keeping his mouth shut and having a promising and financially rewarding career at the best salon in town. He was trying to save face, he was trying to convince himself that everything was fine, he was trying to convince himself of many things, but he was becoming all mine! This is what happens when you convince yourselves that G-pop doesn't test you or allows you to be tested, I mean you all know the stories of your beloved book. You think that G-pop would allow His Son to be tested but then protect you from my tests! How foolish and arrogant you all are, to think you are better than me, or his Son for that matter, not that I care for Him, but I say this because you all do, you think that just because He left his safe place with G-pop that you are the same, that you can ignore me and be fine. This is exactly why I can wreak the havoc I do in the world, because you believe what you want to and make up the rest, you spend all your time trying to understand and confirm what your book of mighty stories says, when you dumb empty clay pots have what you need to make me take a hike, but just like Jr., your too busy hating yourselves than to pay attention to the damage I'm doing to your minds. You believe my lies, and I am not going to convince or con someone trying to explain away my lies or call it truth, because I know what I do, and I am proud of it, this is why I'm the father of lies, because I was the first, and the best. You weak, pathetic mud patties are so full of self-hate, self-doubt, and fear that I hate you even more than when G-pop told us what he was going to create. You wouldn't be shit, if it wasn't for His love and mercy for you, but what I love is that you blame Him for everything, and you give me a pass on everything. I love your weak minds, and your desire for vainglory, this is what attracts me to you, what gets my attention, and then you place yourselves into my crosshairs! I dispatch Charo for each of you to determine the extent of your disobedience and your lukewarmness, so I can devise a personalized plan of demise. Each soul comes with a cost, and I can't be wasting my time with those who are secure and living their faith, I do get some opportunities but why go after the strong when there's plenty of the weak that I can destroy with hardly any effort whatsoever. Sometimes it only takes one infraction of your happiness or comfort to make you curse the very existence of your G-daddy, treating him like a piñata, you beat Him and beat Him for blessings and when He showers blessings you all fight over them like hungry wolves or you say you are the master of what you accomplish, because you're so very smart. I call bullshit! LOL, you are your own enemy, not realizing that I'm only as strong as you are distant and divided from G-pop. You go it alone, you are like that slow one in the herd when lions are hunting, I pick you off one at a time. I devour souls all day, every day, 24/7 I'm working and robbing G-pop of His precious creation, proving to Him that you are not the breath He breathed into you, nor are you worth His attention, you destroy everything you touch, and you appreciate less.

I'm working on something pretty big, trying to coordinate everything so the timing is perfect to completely engage, simultaneously achieving mayhem on several fronts. See, you little brainiacs don't tap into the great potential that we can only dream of, well the third of us that know you were a mistake, G-pop doesn't see the benefit of complete control and dominance since it belongs to Him anyway . . . I could deal with that, but to have you running around like you were only half naked on a nudist beach, or show up to class with paper but nothing to write with. You're lazy, you're confused, you're smarter than everyone else, you wake up with nothing to do, you wake up and go to a thing you call jobs, that only feeds the machine I created to keep you idiots under a web of lies on top of lies, buried and soaring in lies. Like a maze with no opening and so you assume there is no exit, so you don't even look enough until you find it only to not accept it because it's labeled entry, securing your slavery to what I offer, death from it all. Why be an actor in a shit show, with a promise, when I can only trust in myself? So, when there is a five-dimensional game of chess going on, and you are barely playing in one, imagine the evil I can whip us in this fertile soil. Charo is spending a great deal of time on that project, as my project manager he oversees all my endeavors to devour souls, it's no wonder why

G-pop threw us down to the very place he created you all from, it was His intention for us to be at each other's throats. A fair fight, in my opinion, because you are unfairly greater and more powerful, shit we were created just to agree that we were to serve you in the end we all have our place and as His most favored creation, in His image made, His breathe and spirit living in you, but with a free will, how freaking stupid! And put all that encased in a clay pot, I sometimes stare up and into Heaven just to laugh and taunt the old man. He is right there, but not. The great mystery of daddy invisible to those who most need Him to be present as you so rightly demand. In that aspect I can agree with you low life.

Hey boss! Things are going great." "I'll be the judge of that, how many times do I have to remind you that I only want to hear the challenges because I expect everything to go well, it's my plan! The only time things have gone wrong, is because of you." "Yea, but some of the things you want done, only you can do, but you have your spoons in too many dishes. Then, you tell us to do it, knowing we ain't you. So, get over yourself because we are all in this together." "Report any challenges or get out of my site, or you can go back into the pit, you're a dime a dozen." Ok, I think I pushed it too far, and I know he has been busy lately, and why he is so hands on with this kid, well he ain't no kid anymore except maybe romantically—it's fun to watch, and it's easy to get this guy to sway way over to the dark side. He is blaming himself for everything, doesn't even have a clue. Riggs thinks he's dumb and naïve, but I've been around this kid for a while, he was on Riggs' radar since he was born, maybe he got clued in when Mel came with him. I have battled Mel before, and he ain't no joke . . . he can battle you without you ever thinking you in a battle, like winning a gun fight but you ain't got no gun. First time I went rounds with him was that time we owned the place, doing what we wanted and taking what we wanted, creating our own creations, we living like gods and then the Ark. Whatever, we have other great times since then and the old man, in his infinite wisdom, further shackled himself because of this stupid promise that he wouldn't do it again. Like that's gonna keep you from doing something, don't do that because I will not punish you if you do it again . . . Riggs is right, what kind of sick logic is that? Somebody is trying to drive a car without a steering wheel, and his solution is to put handcuffs on himself! LOL, oh ok, yea I will take that handicap every time, thank you very mucho!

"Any, any challenges whatsoever?" I asked Charo, he doesn't like the way I do things, but he also knows that he is dumber than a box of rocks, and if wasn't around to tell him what to do, he would just be swirling around in pain from the fire and molten rock of the lake. So, he can hate me all he wants, he doesn't know that it only feeds me, and I gain more strength.

"I'm worried that those idiots keep taking flights to California to feel comfortable, but they might get found out."

"What about Andras? How is he coming along in Mesopotamian?"

"He says things are going as planned, and that he is ready to go when you are."

"Fine, anything else?"

"What about this kid, Jr, you told me to let you know when I was finished with him."

"What do you mean, I got a lot of shit going on right now. You got less things, so be more specific when you talk to me about these people."

"The Mel kid, Jr, you wanted me to get him to the point of suicide again, and he's ready for you."

"Oh, right. Ok, what's got him to the edge?"

"Failure."

"Oooh, that's a good one. Excellent job! It suits him well."

"Yea, I thought you would like that."

"Ok, how much time we got? Did Andras mention a timeline?"

"Yea, he's ready when you are, at a moment's notice if need be."

"This is great, this is really great."

"Anything else you need, boss?"

He didn't answer, but that's Riggs, when he is done, he just leaves, stops answering you and that's when you know he's done. It makes sense and saves a lot of time. See, we don't have emotions, we have states of existence, we either exist in love or in hate, but you guys have all these different things called emotions that are like drugs, I've noticed. Some are preferred over others, some satisfy urges, some are senseless no matter how you look at it and all of them working together and against each other at the same time, causes like a short circuit and then you are just sitting there, staring off into nothing. This is after a very violent experience, there's always a violent experience. Thank you, but no thank you to emotions is my opinion! I'm glad he was good with the planning, and where I was with Jr., I was pretty pleased myself with it, it's not very easy to get him to believe in failure, because this kid has always been something. He can achieve anything he sets his mind to, very rare trait, he just lacked in the drive compartment, which I exploited. I had him burning the candle on both ends while holding a fire to the middle as well! I exploited the hell out of his lack of drive, I drove it so fast, at speeds so fast he felt he was drunk! Which was his favorite pastime right now, drunkenness with lust running nose to nose, and drugs were a close third. He was working two parttime jobs, FedEx, and Sasha, he was going to college, and he was going out drinking every night but Mondays, and I could only get him to include drugs on the weekends, but weekends started on Thursdays through

Sunday night. Sometimes during the week depending on how many of them we could bring together.

Riggs didn't even compliment, he never does, how I separated those two awkward lovebirds, I thought it was cool, they beat the hell out of each other. Mel ruined it when he encouraged Jr to ask Warren why he wanted such a bad friend, sick, he continued, "A friend is not someone who has to keep saying I'm sorry, because that means I've done something to hurt you, and I don't want to hurt you, I love you." Warren had already been looking down at him, sitting atop his chest and holding his hands over Jr's head and held to the carpet. Things melted and I lost control of the situation, damn your free will! I adjusted, but that one slapped me in the face, they both got passed that because of the love Mel was making them aware of, and that shit is like repellent to us, Love, yuck! No thank you, I'm good. I would get to them another way, but it was going to take time and planning.

After he blamed himself for everything so far, I had him getting into all kinds of debauchery, like those sex bookstores with booths, bathhouses, parks, everywhere but the bedroom, where your required to be intimate, which requires some conversation, and he would have to let people into all his mess behind that curtain no. 1. What's under curtain no. 3, 4, 5, 6 . . . how many curtains depends on a man's duplicity! Man, it was fun putting all that together and then watching you all just go at it, such a FU to the man upstairs, we get off on that shit! We cheer you on, "Drink more, take another shot, don't worry about the freaking money, it's about the now." One time I had this boy wrap a wooden Rosary around his neck like a choker with crucified Christ dangling on his hot chiseled chest for all to see. He was on the dance floor of this basement club in Syracuse, where he liked to hang out when visiting Syracuse. This was when he was stationed at Fort Drum, NY. He was really in shape, had on an embroidered vest from Guatemala, and jeans. He felt the eyes on him, he felt the thoughts of men having their way with him, doing to his body only he and few others had done. Tasting him, the sweat and everything else. His pride wouldn't let him grovel at men's feet so he would put himself on display, knowing how to move and knowing that he drew the attention of many. I thought it was funny when he was putting that on, I helped, of course. He did look really cute, but I knew something was going to happen, especially if what Riggs thinks of the kid is true. I knew that he wouldn't be wearing it for long, so when he started touching it, pulling on it, and then ran off the dancefloor and into the bathroom to rip that Rosary off his neck, I know he got scared, I got my fix by that fear. It didn't last long though, because I only tasted a little fear, didn't get a full dose. He put it in his pocket, got a stiffer drink, and went back on the dance floor, so he could be gazed upon. Trying to attract something that would satisfy his thirst and hunger for debauchery.

There was another time that I got him to jump out of a moving car just because they wouldn't pull over when he wanted them to, and yet another time that I convinced him it would be a good thing to color his hair dark red while leaving two black horns on his head, put on fangs and hazel contact eye lenses, go out to Easter Sunday dinner with friends dressed all in black, to a high end restaurant in Skaneateles, NY and ask if the lamb was fresh. Oh, there was so much fun with this guy, and he was game for anything! Orgies, yes! Does the number matter? No. Cocaine or pot? Can't we do both? Drugs, alcohol, and orgies? Don't mind if I do. Tonight? What about the next night too? What about your job? I got it, and if they don't like it . . . FU . . . I'll get another! Men or women, I'll do both right now, but men are better. I'm telling you this guy was really hating himself, didn't know himself, and at this point didn't care about himself. Riggs and I made it all look so glamourous to everyone who gazed upon his life right now. On the outside, he was working hard, he was going to college, he was popular, he was living freely and fun, he had a place to call home, he was having the time of his life. Traveling, hanging out with other celebrities in their own right. Walking and partying in the streets of places like Los Angeles, Toronto, Montreal, NYC, Miami, Boston while working with beautiful people as he was living in vanity, heightened by his very trade . . . beauty. Oh, it was fun times with him, but he was slowing down on the inside, I could tell there was an irritation developing over the very things that made his life exciting. This is what made Riggs ask where I was with him, because I had alerted him to this, and Riggs said it was time for him to act before Mel could dissuade what was happening to him, what we were doing to him. I'm surprised that Mel has let us cause so much havoc in this guy's life, both spiritually and physically, we were hardly getting any push back except lately. But overall, I must say I ran him and for someone who is built to be lazy, the rat race is the last thing he is interested in. So, run the rat, until it fell out with exhaustion. This was my strategy with him, to destroy any ambition, drive, or dreams. Failure . . . one of my favorites!

I had to just walk away, Charo sometimes thinks that we have time for chitchat, and I get off on division, hello . . . by this time he should know that I only interact because I have a job to do, not because I want to, because it's the only way to get as many of you to feed my lake. Your hate, misery, cowardice, lust, envy, pride, sloth, it all feeds the fire. Jr is one that will burn bright, and I'm not sure what it is about this one, but I am extremely interested, he is very interesting in the complexity of division and unity, love and anger, trust and flagrancy. This kid is comfortable existing in contradiction. I'm on my way to meet with Andras, a fine Marquis always looking so elegant atop his strong black wolf. He was facing east, as the sun was setting to the west. We were atop the north Tower gazing towards the East, laughing at what was to come. Death was coming and Andras was working on the reaction both from Meso (Mesopotamia) and here, we play the long game. As I walked up, he turned his head all the way around to make sure it was me, I always thought how cool that was. "Hey" he said, "How long you been waiting?" "Not long, just reveling in my work." "Everything ready? Charo tells me you are ready to go on a moment's notice, but I'm concerned with how many practice runs are going on." "You're only worried because he messes up everything, glad you kept him busy with other things so I could get this done in the time frame you were asking. Yea, we're ready to go." "That's great, I will let you know, stay ready." "Yea, see you." I could always count on Andras, I secretly like Andy, but he hates it and with thirty legions of demons you really want to keep him happy, although we don't do happy, just so you know what I mean. Our job is just to destroy you, and we are really going to have fun.

Knowing everything is set to go, I have time to go put the nail in this kid's coffin, failure is always such a sweet way to go. It comes with an especially sweet taste in my pride as it feeds the fire. You get a blast of sweet bitterness, with notes of earthy fear, but I savor that pungent note of envy. Yum, ecstasy! I'm going to use his friends to drive him over the edge, it may not be him pulling the trigger, but he's dead anyway and he'll be thrown in the fire. That "Is the lamb fresh" on Easter Sunday, in public was enough without considering all the other stuff but you never know in these matters until the soul has been harvested before it is ripe, once it sours is the time, and now was his time. I had compiled a team, led by Charo, that I believed could get me the results after I underestimated the kids capacity to love, which became a huge problem because this could have fed the lake a long time ago and the sins would have burned greater, his being so young, but I have to hand it to Mel, he was really outdoing himself which makes me wonder what this kid is meant to do if he was ever to get on the G-pop train. The team was Asmodeus, Orius, Seir, Leraje, Naberius, Gapp, Andramalius, and Raum, with their combined legions, they could put their best people on every person that had to be manipulated and convinced to do what we were encouraging.

I have to give Charo a lot of credit because it ain't easy managing a group like this without being eating alive, but I knew Charo could handle it, even if he does get distracted easily by the things he thinks are cool about this world, especially all the lying and hating that leads to the type of violence that only you humans are capable of. He can't get enough of it. I don't blame him, but I must keep my attention on the long game on five different dimensions plus the physical world itself and what that brings or takes away from the battle. We can't always depend on nature doing its part, because of this tricky thing about the human compact after G-destroyer gets all mad at the Watchers (well, the ones that, yea had fun with the humans and some fell in love and created an unsanctioned creature) and killed everyone. Except there's always someone that must ruin the party, the goody two shoes, those that choose to believe and trust the way G likes it . . . their choice, but once you are all in, it's worse if you are in and out. I was so surprised and at the moment I really believed that I may have loved Him for saying it, He told them that He would spit you outta his mouth if you were lukewarm. Oh, I loved it, because that's most of you . . . lukewarm! I think I could have hugged him, but that would be breaking all kinds of rules, laws, pacts, contracts, all that formal shit that G likes. I love chaos, because that's what He created so I'm giving it, living it, ordering it, and it is working far better than I could have ever imagined it after I realized He had reconnected you trash to G. I was furious, but then you all restored my faith in your ultimate demise, because y'all learned nothing, and as sure as the sun will rise (for now, at least), you trashy humans will repeat the mistakes your ancestor make, again because we have you convinced that whatever you believe, is truth. You can't wrap your mind around the fact that there is only one truth, and it's not the one with the biggest gun or the biggest bank account. No sir, it exists because G exists, and the only way to make my truth, the truth, is to get rid of G, but that is an impossible dream, so I focus on you, and every time I take one of you to join our army or feed the fire, it hurts Him more than if we could kill Him. Shit, you saw what I put His Son through using only a few of you, what do you think I could do to each of you, so when I conquer your soul, you can't even see us coming, you don't believe in us so while you blame G, we are carrying out our mission to kill your soul. Sometimes we make things happen in the physical world directly, but we need permits for these actions, but we can manipulate, entice, tempt, and anything like this to make you act on our behalf. You are like remote control cars, and we, the controller plus the added skill to speak to your hearts and minds, often times we also use feelings and emotions by encircling you and taunting you with our energy until our energy turns your energy sour, and we don't need any permitting for this type of temptations and manipulations.

I've been pretty busy traveling between Heaven and Earth, getting this just right because what Riggs and Charo have been up to, not just with Jr but with the coming wrath about to be suffered by his native country and the city he often travels to, Charo has been really busy and Riggs meeting with Andras confirmed what I knew was going to be a huge interference in moving forward with Elohim's plans for earth, particularly as it also had to do with my charge, my complicated boy. Just like a parent, and because we don't age, to me he will always be my little boy, because this is how I see his soul, still young, bright, and full of life . . . he just hasn't tapped into it yet. He's been asking all the wrong questions, looking for the wrong answers, but blaming it all on Elohim, as much as I've been trying to steer him, free will and Riggs' meddling has not helped things at all, made it so much more complicated especially that strong capacity and desire to be good vs. to be evil, both he finds interesting but he cannot comprehend the consequences of his choices, but he will soon enough. Just like the Persian Prince, kept Michael from fulfilling David's prayer, so with Jr, he has believed all this time and, even more of late, he doesn't believe that Elohim is paying attention to his prayers. Elohim answered it, but down here we have had some powerful fallen ones keeping us busy. It all started with a three-pronged strategy, one, to answer his prayers of curing him of his depression, two, to make him realize that God is present, forgiven, and that His mercy is immeasurable, and three, to send him an earthly spirit to plant a very powerful seed that will let my little charge finally learn real love, that love is unconditional but to understand what this means. It all started when to all our surprise, especially Riggs, without any prompting from any of us, me-Riggs-Charo, just his own free will, dropped to his knees and begged Elohim to cure him from depression, he wanted to live. Oh, how this was such a joyful day in Heaven, you may not realize it but there are celebrations, pep rallies, cheerleading, you name it, and it has to do when you all make some pretty amazing choices based on your free will alone. They are made in pure love, and that is Heaven on earth, cutting through all that society tells you is just and true of this world, but it is all Riggs' lies, because he was given dominion, unsettled the balance of the war, and had brought the war to you all. This was all part of the punishment, all part of Elohim's strategy to make the way to finally take on human form, as everyone else comes into the world, but this time it would be Elohim sending a part of Him to become what you are, in order to break that bond of punishment He was forced to instill because of your disobedience and the lies introduced into paradise. I was given the secret weapon, because Riggs was not going to be able to block it, but first was to cure him of this depression that was again putting thoughts in his head and the fantasies of ways to die, but different this time.

I noticed that Charo took a different route this time, by way of all the things that may bring temporary relief, but causing more damage every time to use it to lessen the pain of those things that he would also make profound when in fact, they were only small speed bumps in the whole of life. As Jr was on his knees and as I was guiding his prayers to the Congregation of Saints tasked with categorizing the spiritual pain on the souls of our charges so they could present them to Elohim in much the way burning incents fill the room with an intense fragrant. Jr's must have satisfied Elohim because all are mixed with others' and each a distinct aromatic flavor which must satisfy the will of Elohim and he must also recognize the amount of love within each note to identify sincerity of personal will and proper use of free will. Well my boy had done it, finally, he begged that if Elohim had a plan for his life, which was spiritually intelligent—how is Elohim not going to have a plan for each and every one of you, because He does, and then He starts to explain how he knew that Elohim knows everything (another required point) and that as a child Elohim never answered or listened to him. He had a frank and honest appeal, that now as he is on his knees after all of these years, was he going to be ignored, were his prayers going to go un-answered knowing that he was on the verge of taking his life in a different type of death, but death none-the-less, dangerously courting the dark forces roaming the world. Up until now, he knew how evil he could be to those who live life as bullies, and those self-centered souls that thought they could treat people like trash and live without consequences. Lately, he was getting more self-righteous with his friends while living hypocritically by acting in the very manner and considering some of the same tactics with his friends. He was able to make a case for his prayer to be answered, and he even threw in that he knew that Elohim knew what was in his heart, and knowing the evil it was capable of, this was his last hope to be cured, that only Elohim could do it at this point. He didn't know it, but he had presented a sound case to Elohim. Elohim granted it, and my work began but I was informed that it was not going to be easy because of the way Jr was wired and the influence that evil forces had on him. It took five long years with me and Charo doing a spiritual waltz you would call a battle (I'm going to let you in on a little secret, things will be totally different than they are now, where love will rule and no more tears, no more sin, no more pain, a place of everlasting joy and peace).

I don't know if he is going to answer me, but as I drove through my route through Skaneateles as a FedEx courier, I thought about what had happened last night. I actually spoke to God, and I still remembered the Lord's prayer. "First time He speaks to me is to tell me to talk about it?" What was I supposed to gain from that? If it was that simple, don't you think I would have tried that already, it didn't work. I even spent that time in the psychiatric ward of Syracuse VA Hospital because I couldn't promise the Army psychiatrist that I would not harm myself at our last session together. Our last session because I was done with trying to talk about it. None of anybody's business what I'm dealing with, if they wanted to know what was wrong with me, they would tell me so that I would know as well. Why does everyone always ask, what's wrong? Argh, if I knew I wouldn't feel the way I do! Ok, calm down, that was years ago, and you are just hearing this story for the first time. Excuse me, let's continue . . . What did this mean? Talk about it. Ok, I thought and after a lot of talking, a lot of blank stares, of no one cares, none of it bothered me, I was putting God to the test, I was this full of pride, and I was not liking the way this circus show was developing and continuing. I talked, and talked, and talked about it until one day, nothing. No talking about it, no emptiness, no loneliness, no black spaces, or holes. It was gone. It was gone. Dare I ask again? Is it gone? No answer. No answer. No answer. I lived my life the way I had created, no real difference in my behavior only to get a sound career building future in what I thought I loved and was good at, plus I was partying with the populars, the make things happen(ers). I was loving hating life, my life. The line I would not cross was feeling this way about my friends. So, I asked the question, "If you were all alone on a deserted island with nothing and no one, would you take your own life?" I waited for me to answer, or better yet, the Holy Spirit answer for me but it was that He didn't answer for me that I was able to see it for myself, where I was blind, I now can see, and this can only be God's working and blessing. "No, because I'm not alone. I have God, the Son, the Holy Spirit, and my entire spiritual family." "Thank you, God!"

No faster than Jr realized that he had been cured from depression, after battling with himself for five years, Riggs' diabolical customized steering strategy that had to be filed before any action of this gravity and in so short span of time between one grave attack with another, legally bound to the nature of Love, that I get served with a notice and given a certain time to prepare for the occasion. This sounds cruel, but the cruel part is having no notice . . . and ever since the great Resurrection and Installation Ceremony there are no surprise attacks, they are now opportunities of strengthening of the soul. This makes the soul shine brighter and Riggs gets an insight that this soul will be called to live in service and love, and if the spirit triumphs, each triumph gets a special glow of the light. Wonderful thing, but gives the enemy like a bullseye, theory being it can only strengthen against these attacks each time. By this second grave attack, now that he is cured of his depression Riggs now starts to convince him that humanity is a virus, and we were a curse on Elohim's creation. Diabolic in that he convinces Jr to self-deprecating behavior, emotionally and psychologically. This is when he was jumping out of moving cars, banging on someone's window to fight him in honor of a friend he had hurt instead of comforting the friend, and getting into sexual promiscuity, drunkenness, and gluttony with both lust and greed as it pertains to the drug choices and frequency of those occurrences. It was after he had sideswiped a guardrail, drunk as all get out and blaming his friends for his current situation, drunk, alone, on the side of the highway on the way to a bath house in Rochester, NY which was a frequent place for him to visit and have as much sex as he wanted. Yes, I tried, don't judge me but it is not all that simple, again you're blessed with free will, it can only be influenced, enticed, exposed, and capitalized on, but we cannot make the choices for you. Elohim knows what He is doing, in this we have faith. But now that he wants to be a hermit, go bury himself alive somewhere, I'm elated and thankful for his second drop to his knees, "God, it's me again and I'm hurting again, and only you can fix this. Thank you for curing me from depression, I am a new person, but now I feel you made a mistake when you created me, and worse, when you created all of humankind. It is a blite on your Creation, and I'm part of this virus, eating away your perfection. How can you possibly love us? Please send me an Angel to restore my faith in humanity, I can't kill myself because I no longer desire death, nor see it as something to solve my pain, but I see too many demons, I feel them inside and all around. If you have a plan for my life, please hurry, you know how bad I am, how much I get in Your way." Oh, my little man, had grown up! He followed that with, "God, your Son, whom You sent, and You love, gave to us a prayer. He said that this is how we should pray, so now that you know how much I love and believe in You, I pray this prayer to you . . . "

> "Our Father,
> Who art in Heaven,
> Hollowed be Thy Name,
> Thy Kingdom come,
> Thy Will be done,
> on Earth as it is in Heaven,
> give us this day,
> our daily bread,
> and forgive us our trespasses
> as we forgive those
> who trespass against us.
> Lead us not into temptation,
> but deliver us from evil. Amen."

I had authority to act as soon as Jr finished his prayer. I began by having his sister Cruz call him only about an hour after he prayed that prayer, he was still reflecting on all that was going on and just sitting there trying to have a conversation with Elohim, as best he could, good thing the Holy Spirit can help you pray. He spoke of how he wanted to be a hermit, but Cruz discouraged him, saying I tried living that life, and it's not all it's chalked up to be. I wouldn't recommend it. But he waited and hoped in God, he knew that God cured his depression, so He fully expected God to not abandon him now. He was correct, and so it was.

I'm staring into my reflection at Styline's in Armory Square, looking out into the night covered patio, large patio, full of snow, closed off for the winter, and I could feel the cold down to my bones. Same group of friends, same senseless and meaningless conversation, same drunkenness and same backstabbing people recognizing faces of people who I had run ins with, because of my friend's honor or something. I'm asking God why it's taking so long, like I can demand our sovereign God commit to a time-line. I swivel the bar stool in the direction to my group of friends leaning up against the bar, deep in their conversations, but some feeling is lit up in my heart and it is being drawn past my friends, past the bartenders and I felt this emotional connection to this guy paying his cover charge and the entry to the club. The connection was intimate, and I could see and feel the light he radiated, see it but not with my eyes but with the love in my heart. He glowed, it had nothing to do with physical beauty, although I thought, this guy is hot and just my type. He couldn't be older than twenty-one, Caucasian, blue eyes, sandy blonde hair, slim and beautiful. The bar was about 15 feet long, and I watched him making his way towards the part of the bar me and my friends were gathered. About halfway, we make eye contact, there is an energy, a connection. We exchange glances as he moves towards the pool table that is right in front of me if I swiveled my barstool away from the bar. I had a clear view, he set his quarters saving his place in line and then made his way to the bar to get a beer. He found a place to sit opposite me on the other side of the pool table, and it didn't take long for a couple of girls to introduce themselves and they no doubt found them an interested young man. We continued to exchange glances, which was noth-ing unusual for us when we went out, we made our presence known and felt, people were drawn to my circle of friends and me. They were there for a variety of reasons, but we did satisfy something completely for those who ran in our circles and those looking for a circle to join or at the very least exist in for however long we let them. I finally decided to invite him over, which I had never done, not even for Warren. I made my feelings known to Warren, but I never beckoned him to come to me, which explains how my character had changed. I didn't have a clue as to the importance this 'chance' meeting would be and how profound the changes would ripple throughout my physical and spiritual existence.

I motioned with my pointer finger, that universal sign that motions for someone to draw near, come here, and it could have a variety of meanings depending on how you employ the different techniques. Mine was just matter of fact, come here I want to talk to you. I don't know what gave me the confidence, I guess it is because I wasn't trying to pick him up, I seriously wondered why he glowed, not anymore but when he first walked in, he glowed for a good five minutes. To my surprise, he whispered something to his two new girlfriends and walked towards me. I put out my hand, as he got close enough, "Hello, my name is Santos, what's yours?"

"Austan."

"You have an accent, where are you from?"

"Texas"

I thought deeply for a moment, but all in milliseconds, but I warned myself that he may just be another asshole playing games, and I didn't need any more of those in my life. If this was the case, this little shit was about to get chewed up and spit out, glow or no glow, because little did he know, I AM from Texas.

"Yea, what parts?"

"Denton."

"Oh, yea! I'm from Beaumont!"

"I know about Beaumont, one of my friends lived there, or close to there."

"That is so cool, what brings you to these parts?"

"Work, what about you?"

I was more interested in him, because my story was boring and I was sick of my life, the last thing I wanted to do was relive it. I directed the conversation away from me and made it about him, he was a far more interesting person than me, I mean he glowed, again not now, just those first few minutes I saw him come into the club. Thinking back on it today, I feel that it was done to get my attention, and it worked, I noticed, and I acted . . . didn't know this back then, back then I had just met a cool person, but I had not made any connection of that meeting which would result in a long and loving relationship, and I guess I will ruin any suggestion or anticipation that he will be my lover, my boyfriend, because he will not. We will discover way later, from this meeting to the present that we met as soul mates, but without the physical display or engagement aside from hugs and pecks on the cheek. This is all we can handle for our own personal and my spiritual reasons. And even those moments of physical affection are rare occurrences but make no mistake, our love exudes an energy that if you have ever occupied a room with us or if you were to do so now, the love energy that flows between us can be felt, they have been felt by complete strangers that swear we are a married couple. We let them think whatever they want, Austan thinks it is fate, I know it was God. He says Bah humbug, and I tell him that you cannot change my truth, only God and I know what I prayed for, and He sent you into my life not 24 hours later. I no longer believe in chance, nor do I try to figure something out that I know God had a hand in this because otherwise, I would just live in doubt. I didn't know it at the time, though. Leslie showed up a little after 1AM, she could only convince them to let her tell us something because she wouldn't pay the cover since it was almost closed. Everyone was excited to see Leslie, I'm sure she had business with so many here, I was excited yes . . . Leslie was my sister, we had a deep connection and tolerance for each other's company. We could party hard, or go sit at the park, under a blanket, talking and getting high, or homebodies and picking up takeout smoking joints. She is highly intelligent and when I asked her about anything if she didn't know we would look it up and find out, or call Warren. We irritated him a lot, especially when Leslie and I were high and goofy. But nothing irritated everyone more than that night I asked Austan to come hang out with me at Leslie's after party. At first, he said he didn't leave a pool game in the middle of it, hadn't ever done it and didn't want to do it now. I looked over at the two girls that had been swooning over him since he got there. He had only come to talk to me a few times while he played but, this young man, I could tell, was straight. He spent more time with those girls than trying to talk to me, for one, and two he never came across as interested or should I say that I didn't see that hunger I saw in other men's eyes that just wanted to taste my body, to have their way with me, or let me have my way with them. It was this brazen, in your face I want you look, and I didn't see it. I'm sure he didn't see it either, because I knew where I could get mine without the emotional baggage, the questions, the small talk, just sex please! When Leslie came closer to me, I stood up to meet her and she told me about the after party and why she couldn't stay, wouldn't stay. She was on her way home now, so whenever we wanted to show up was fine.

"I want to introduce you to someone Leslie."

"Sure baby."

"Leslie, this is Austan, Austan this is my sister Leslie."

"I'm going to call you Tex." Leslie said to Austan.

"Hehe. That's awesome!"

"Any friend of Santos is welcome in my home. Please come."

"I don't know, I don't want to leave in the middle of a pool game."

"I understand, Tex, you are welcome anytime."

I said goodbye to Leslie and told her that I was leaving now, meeting her at her place. I was done with this place, but I wasn't done with Austan.

I turned to him and said, look I know you are having fun with those two girls, but I guarantee if you come with me, I will introduce you to women that are truly beautiful, and you don't have to settle for those two. Plus, Leslie always has the party favors. I could see this desire for the unknown, and the guarantee of a great time, the promise of hope, and he sure did leave those two girls and the pool game in the middle of the game to go with us. He followed Josie and I to Leslie's, I was so thrilled that he didn't turn off or lose us, because I had no way of contacting him. This was the age before I had a cell phone, like 1998.

I was extremely happy that I found a new, engaged, and captivated audience of one. He looked interestingly into my eyes like he was trying to find out my story through my eyes, to my heart. Later, he asked me one time, when I put on some prescription hazel colored contact lenses, "Please take those contacts out, I want to see your beautiful brown eyes. I want to see you." I thought it was so delightful, and genuine that it made my heart melt, but I would flirt with him and tell him, "No. Deal with it. Get past the fake contacts, I'm still here." He loved my independence, I could sense it, so I capitalized on it whenever I could. I love to love him, from that first night until now. After everyone but Leslie came over to where Austan and I had taken a place at her bar to tell us we were being rude, there were other people. They noticed how captivated I was, and this was new to all of them. Ever since Warren, no one had captured my attention like Austan, much less captivated me by his genuine nature, interesting conversation, smart, making crazy money working in insurance adjusting, going in after major storms. He would sometimes come home from working out of town and treat us all to a night on the town, and we didn't make it cheap for those who wanted to treat us this way. Leslie's boyfriends, Warren's boyfriends, they would try to buy their way into those two's lives. Austan was different, he didn't care to impress, he just wanted all his friends to have a good time, and being a realist, he knew we couldn't afford the lifestyle we wanted to live, that we were living, but his heart was in a good place. He wasn't an Angel, like we know them to be, but he was sent by God to plant a seed into my heart, and only someone like Austan could do that. That first night, and after the cocaine all gone, the party was over for me. I asked who wanted to take me home like some king or guest of honor, without ever really realizing what I was doing. It's a wonder they loved me so much, that they never held that against me. Austan was quick to offer, "I'll drive you home Santos!" He asked, more like a question to Leslie, and Warren, who by this time of night had deduced that we were the closest of the entire group Leslie had at her apartment atop a local pub. Such a forgiven person Leslie was, because we had some big, drag out fight, but she had gotten rid of that asshole she married, like it was some kind of shotgun wedding, they met and married in the span of only weeks. It was crazy, but here we were, forgive and forget, and this would not be the last time I would test her love for me.

That night, though, no one offered because they knew I liked him, they just read the situation all wrong. I already knew that Austan was straight, I had talked to him all night. When he offered so enthusiastically, I wondered what his deal was, he was definitely straight so what was he up to? At this point, I was distrustful of strangers, ever since I left the Army, I felt that people were shady and wanted something from somebody all the time. Regardless of what his intentions were, which I figured was just to party with us again, I welcomed the ride home with him, because I really enjoyed his company. As we pulled up to my house, which wasn't too far away but enough so that we could keep getting to know one another, I go to get out of the car and he grabbed my arm, "Santos, wait a minute. Will you give me your number?" Why, I asked him. "Because I would really like to hang out with you again." I was flattered and elated that he wanted to hang out with me again . . . or was it that I had promised him A good time. "What do you want my number for? It's not like your gay, what do you have to offer that I would be interested in? I'm tired of all the friends I have, why do I need another?" I was really pushing him to realize two things, one, I'm not an easy person to please, and two, what's in it for me. "I know, but I really like you, and I loved our conversation, I would love to speak with you again." "Alright, I tell you what, I will give you my telephone number, but that doesn't necessarily mean that I will answer or return your call." He was fine, and excited that I gave him my number, and I went inside my house and wondered all night until I went to sleep, I wonder if he will call me, I wonder how long he will take to call me. I hope he calls me again.

Not only did he call me again, but I also definitely answered the phone when he called. I was answering more than I had before because I was hoping he would call me! Everyone was asking about him, they wanted to know if he stayed over, they were surprised that he turned out to be straight. "No, he didn't." I would defend him because that was the truth, nothing happened. All my friends either wanted something to happen with him, or they wanted to take advantage of him. I warned him early on to not trust any of them, including those closest to me because I could not protect him if I wasn't with him, and I knew the people I hung out with. The little shit didn't' listen, I guess he thought it was more of my drama, too wound up. He learned one night, when he was in town, and I wasn't. I was working with Sebastian at the time, and I was out of town a lot. I learned that they had tried to get him drugged and drunk, which didn't take much, and then have their way with him. I was livid, and the only reason people didn't go to the hospital the next few days (because I was going to put as many of them in the hospital as I could, no matter how long it took), was because Austan made me promise that I would drop it and forget about the entire thing. Oh, I love this boy because I didn't want to promise, they knew how important he was to me, and they still disrespected me by trying to take advantage of him. I knew that if I carried out what I wanted to do, that he would not respect me for it, and it may cost me his friendship. I acquiesced reluctantly. He was the first person to ever tell me he loved me without being in a relationship with me, related, or a friend. He told me when we were hanging out with Mike, when out of the blue he said, "Santos, I love you. I don't know why I love you; I just do. I also think I may be attracted to you, but I don't know if I will ever act on it, but I know I love you."

"How do you know you love me?"

"I don't know, you make me feel safe."

"Well, thank you and if you think that just because you may want to experiment with me, I will be the judge of that. I love your friendship and I'm not about to ruin that just because you can't handle a roll around in the sack. I would have to know that our friendship is strong enough to withstand it if you don't like it."

"I get it, and I'm not saying that I want to, or that you have to, I just want you to know how I feel about you."

Mike was listening and looking at me, we both couldn't believe what was coming out of Austan's mouth. He would later tell me that it was such a touching moment to be a part of and that he really felt that Austan was genuine. I agreed.

Mike was first to go to bed, Austan and I stayed up a little while longer just talking and enjoying the fire. We especially loved that we didn't have to tend the fire, because he had a natural gas fireplace. It had fake, but real looking wood but you would just turn a knob and hold a lighter to it and instant fire. The snow outside was just a perfect touch, the light reflecting off the snow always made the nights brighter.

"I'm going to bed", I told Austan.

"Goodnight."

"Goodnight." I made my way to my room and climbed into bed, as I lay there missing Austan already especially after he said what he said, I felt that I had abandoned him and left him all alone. I got up and made my way back to the living room.

"Austan, you still up?"

"Yea, what's wrong?"

"Nothing, nothing at all. I just wanted to invite you to come sleep with me if you want to, no funny business, remember what I told you about experimenting . . . we're not there yet. I just don't want you to sleep alone if you don't want to."

"Thank you, but I'm ok here on the couch. It's really comfortable."

"Ok, just wanted to offer." A bit disappointed, there was a part of me that wishes something would happen, because I can't help how my feelings are getting stronger for him, especially after what he just proclaimed. I climbed back in bed, and under the covers. I was reflecting on how we had first met, how our friendship was blossoming and those words he said to me, "Santos, I love you." How freaking sweet, no prompting, no expectations, he wanted nothing in return, he just wanted to tell me how he felt about me. So refreshing and new.

Suddenly, I heard someone coming down the hallway, but coming past the bathroom so the only two rooms were Mike's and mine. Maybe he forgot to tell me something, maybe he took me up on my offer and before my mind could create other scenarios, Austan climbed into bed and under the covers with me, put his body right up against mine, as I was facing the wall so my back was towards the door rolled up like in a fetal position. It was such a smooth and welcomed move to spoon me with such gentleness and intention. He put his arm around me and held me tight. He whispered, "I love you Santos, I only want to cuddle." "I love you too, and I'm so happy that you trust me. You can cuddle with me anytime you want." We never really did much more, we almost had a threesome with his first love, Sara. I had heard a lot about her, and by the time I met her when Austan flew her up to come visit, we got along great. Austan, Sara, and I all ended up in my bed, me on one side, Austan next to me in the middle of the three of us. During the night I woke up to Austan grinding up against me, but I think we both woke up at the same time and were both surprised, Austan quickly jumped on the other side of Sara, and that was that. It was only one other time after we had taken a lot of ecstasy when we got back to my house after trying to see Josie off, she was moving to California, so we partied with her all night. I decided I was too messed up to drive so we headed back home. We played a few games of chess, then we crashed laying together and cuddling, which we did a lot of, but nothing else. Nothing sexual ever happened, just the cuddling. This night was different, I was awakened by Austan's sweet soft voice, "Santos, are you awake?"

"Yes."

"Can I ask you a question and will you tell me the truth?"

"You can ask me anything you want, and I will always be honest with you."

He grabs my hand, and guides it down past his bare abdomen, the heat of his body was intoxicating. His hand kept guiding mine down over the hair

below his belly button and he whispered, "Am I big, or at least a decent size?"
Odd and cute at the same time. "Your fine", I whispered back as I squeezed
and felt the whole package. Had to feel it to give him an honest answer, but
then I pulled my hand back and around his chest, cuddled closer and tried
to ignore what just happened, but I couldn't' ignore it! I couldn't believe this
was happening, I didn't know what to do, I'm struggling with my lust and
my desire to respect him with every ounce of discipline that I could muster.
I was serious about not wanting to fool around before I was certain that we
were strong enough to get past this if he ended up being disgusted with the
whole experience. My lust for him overcame my respect for him (I would say
love, but as you will soon learn, I didn't know what love was back then), my
hand traveled quickly and purposefully, because I didn't want him to change
his mind, over his abdomen, and slid under his waistband, where my hand
groped his hardness and dared not let go, or this moment may end.

I will not give my demons any power and it serves this story no good
to hear the rest, but only to say we didn't go all the way, and it was a bit
awkward, even with such strong emotional ties between us. More intimate
than anyone else I had met thus far, even more intimate than my friendship with Juan, and his and my relationship was the most intimate before
Austan. By more intimate, I don't mean physical intimacy but intellectually
and emotionally. I must find the heart and mind beautiful to care intimately
for someone, at least back then. That's just the way my love worked. I was
a constant construction zone, like Houston maybe that's why I'm just starting to appreciate it, building and tearing down walls, my friends back then,
must have thought I was like a maze, or some accurately thought more like a
house of mirrors. Is this a reflection or the real thing? Or a maze, where you
don't know where you are most of the time. After this, Austan disappeared
and didn't return a couple of phone calls before I realized what was happening. I thought our friendship was strong enough or was I just trying to
convince myself so that I couldn't blame myself for not being able to control
myself. I was a slave to whatever desire of the flesh would be introduced to
me, I was worse than a hooker, just giving and taking, taking and giving. All
with a sweet disposition, not really thinking of long-term pain I left behind
me. Austan was just another feather in my cap, this is what I tried to sell to
myself, but my heart recognized the lie, my mind would not entertain the
notion, both my heart and mind were on his side, I had used him for my
own selfish pleasure. It was only later in life that I would realize what this
really was . . . I saw God's creation of mankind as objects of desire and not
as His children. Today, though when Austan was avoiding me, it was all his
fault. He knew what would happen, and I thought "Shit, I should have gone
all the way, I lost the chance now." Especially when I found out that he was

with his office secretary. He had mentioned to me before that she was hot for an older woman, she was only in her late 30's, but he was only 21, maybe 22 by this time. I was in my early 30's but I took no offense, he must be into older men too, I thought. I figured he was done, and high tailing it back to what was familiar and comfortable. The normal society, F the normal society, I thought. "F anyone who don't know who they are!" I shouted as I sat in my kitchen by the phone, wondering if I should call him or not and looking at the bottle of Crown in front of me. Thinking about Austan, he drank Crown all the time, Crown, and Dr. Pepper. I was missing him so much, more than I had ever missed anyone, more than I missed him when he went to visit Texas for Christmas, which was a lonely Christmas for me, we had just met weeks before, and occupied each other's time as much as we could, trying to get to know each other and not getting enough. I dropped him off at the Syracuse Airport, and he handed me a silver bag and said Merry Christmas (which surprises me now that I think about it, because back then we never spoke of God or religion and was surprised to find out years later that he is an atheist, self-proclaimed, I still see no evidence of it . . . he still can't even tell me what it is, but that's a story for another day).

"I love you Santos, and I'm going to miss you. I wish I could stay with you because there is no other place I would rather be, but I had already planned this, if I knew I was going to meet you I would have made this trip for another time."

"I love you too Austan, we will celebrate when you get back (like I cared about Christmas, only the partying that was involved with the holidays), I will miss you so much", I opened it and saw that it was my favorite, Absolute Vodka. "I will save it, and we will drink it together."

"I would like that."

"Goodbye."

"Be safe, come back to me when you can."

"I promise."

The phone rang as I was drowning in my memories of Austan, because this is all I thought I had from now on. "Hello" I answered with the voice of someone not bothered by anything and on his way out the door.

"Hey Santos, it's Austan."

I was floored, I hadn't heard anything about him for about a week, and this was very unusual unless he was out of town for work, but even then, we would still talk for hours on the phone. So an entire week, he not returning my calls, I was floored because I really thought he had decided to move on, and I was starting to get angry that he needed all this time to call me, wtf, leave me hanging for over a week, who does this to me, I thought to myself as I was trying to figure out what would be the first words he would hear from me after what had happened. Yes, I know we spoke afterwards, he surprised me by staying in bed with me most of the following day. We didn't touch each other again, but we had done enough the night before. He didn't run off as soon as he woke up the next morning, and we were both hungover from the booze and the drugs, so we just slept and lounged around in bed until he finally got dressed and left. It was after he left that all communications stopped. Now he is on the phone and saying hello, like it hasn't been freaking a couple of weeks since we spoke, since all that happened. "Hello", that's all he freaking said? Oooh, I was starting to get angry, but I don't know what happened, something changed inside of me, it was weird, and I had never felt this before, maybe I had, maybe I hadn't but I couldn't be sure. Something that melted me, and I considered what he must be going through . . . wtf . . . this is weird. I don't know if I like this feeling, and I still haven't answered him.

"Hi Austan, you ok, are you traumatized?" Way to get right to the point, I was like that back then. Very passive-aggressive, and I had perfected it by this point. I used it as an amazingly effective manipulating tool, it states a fact . . . in this case, something big happened that is very irregular, and that it could very well be traumatizing to someone if they are weak, while the " . . . you ok . . . " denotes that I really care, but I don't. It was my way of saying, are you ok with what happened, are you so shallow that a little sex will undo everything we have built, or was this all just some sick way to get your experience of how this side lives, you just f-ing with my emotions, I was always upfront, you're the one all hung up and not sure wtf is going on. So much in just seven words, but it's also in the delivery . . . aw, the delivery is my favorite tool of manipulation, no one expects anything of importance in the delivery, but that is like the strokes you develop as a painter, or how a singer distinguishes their unique voice.

"Ah man! Things got crazy after I left your house. I hooked up with Stacey from the office, and man we spent a few days just f-ing the whole time."

"So, you're ok with what happened between us?"

"Yea, I just had to sort it all out in my head, and between that Stacey and work, I'm sorry it took me so long to call you. I just had to figure it all out in my head . . . but I'm good!"

"Yea?"

"Yea! What you doing right now?"

"Getting ready to drink this bottle of Crown and go meet up with friends."

I purposefully didn't share which group of friends I was going to hang out with to see if this was important to him right now. I had several friends, some liked hanging out at gay clubs, some didn't, some didn't go out at all, but wherever I was there was anything you could get your hands on, or it could be ordered.

"You want to come over and drink with me?"

Again, I'm still manipulating the situation because I'm still not certain that I should cut this dude out of my life. I thought it was pretty shitty disappearing like that. For all the times he surprised me with his showing and expressing his love for me, he sure didn't care how I was handling all of this. I'm goading him into revealing his true intentions, because after that night, I was extremely confused, not what happened, but everything afterward. It only really mattered, in those days, how I benefitted or did not benefit from these types of situations. The new thing in all of this is that I really didn't care before whether I lost someone or not, I had dealt with losing myself to myself, how could losing another person be any more difficult than that?

"Shit yea! I'm coming right over; will you wait for me?"

I almost laughed at the last part of that question; they all knew me already. Don't expect me to wait on you, I'm not the waiting around for you type. Unless you were Leslie, I would wait around for Leslie, sometimes she would call me up out of nowhere and say get ready, I'm coming to pick you up in my limo. I asked questions like the first time, but after that I didn't ask.

Austan knocked at the front door, I answered it and he looked intensely into my eyes and seemed to drink me all in, I felt his gaze, and he said, "You are a beautiful man!" We hugged and I led him to the kitchen where we poured our drinks. We caught up on what happened during the week, we didn't speak of what had happened between us, but he made it a point to tell me what he and Stacey did, and I let him. As much as it bothered me, I let him because I knew he was straight from the get-go, but I had miscalculated his affection. We had this conversation before anything happened between us, even before we cuddled. We have had the conversation hundreds of times since then . . . the act of sex, is it the highest form of intimacy? Most people say yes, but after so many years on this journey of a chaste life, it is not the highest form of intimacy. I have experience agave love, and it has nothing to do with sex! That is the devil's lie, and all of humanity has fallen for this lie, it's the same lie the devil sold Eve, Eve sold Adam, and so on, and so on. You know who didn't sell that lie, Jesus! I didn't know this back then. I was surely trying to find it in sex and failing miserably. There is a love that supersedes everything, all understanding, all things physical. This is how you know it is true love, it can exist among family members, especially between parents and their children, brothers, and sisters, and so on. It is with strangers, like Austan and me, and on opposite sides of the sexual spectrum, falling in love, naturally feel the urge towards sex, but not really liking that because it seems right and off at the same time. It's hard to explain, but the closest is having a best friend, but feeling physically attracted to that best friend, but knowing in your heart that this is forbidden territory.

Needless to say, we polished off this bottle and Austan started driving to the club, he never asked until we got in the car, where we were going. This means he didn't come to my house with the intention of partying with others, he just wanted to be with me. Wherever I was going, he was going. That never changed, not even decades later. I could feel a change in him, but I could also still feel that he loved me. I started to fall in love but didn't know it until it hit me like a ton of bricks one night out on the town. Just a regular night, but I broke down, I was bawling and anyone in the bathroom could hear me crying so hard I could hardly catch my breath. I remember hearing my friend Jessie's voice, he was always so sweet, just like everyone else, but sweeter. "Santos, are you ok? Let me in, what's wrong?".

"Go away!" I shouted; I didn't want anyone trying to console me right now. "This is none of your business, and I sure don't want to tell you about it, so get the f out and leave me alone!"

I hated when my friends thought they knew me, they only knew the me I wanted to share with them, how could they possibly understand the struggle of being in love with a straight man! Not like they have intimate friendships with men! They had one use for men, and it wasn't friendship. I, on the other hand, already went through something similar with Juan. It never went as intimate as with Austan, but the love and friendship was deep, but it did start out with me having a crush on Juan until I knew he was straight and that could never happen, but the military took him away from me, so I didn't have to live it as we grew through the years where it would make or break our friendship. The time apart, as we grew into men and gained new experiences, helped in keeping our friendship and I'm glad for it. This was different, I knew I was in love, Austan was a young man but knew the world, because he had to face reality when he was really young, but he persevered and this gives a person resolve and wisdom, if they allow it.

"You want me to call Austan, will that help?"

"Go away and leave me alone!" I shouted at Jessie through the locked stall.

There was silence and I was bawling, the kind where snot and spit are everywhere. The kind of pain that created a tsunami of tears and your breath can't catch up to your sobs. Choking me sometimes, that I had to spit into the commode. I hear the door suddenly, but I don't care who can hear me, I must let this pain out or it will haunt me.

"Santos?" It was Austan, wtf did he want?

"Go away! You're the f-ing problem, and there is nothing you can say or do to fix this!"

"Open the door, let me help you."

"You can help me by leaving me the F alone! I will get a handle of it, but there is nothing, absolutely nothing you can do. Can you snap your fingers and be gay? No! Can you snap your fingers and make me a girl? No." I used this because right before we fooled around, while we were playing chess, he thought out loud, "If only there was some kind of pill that would turn you into a girl, all our problems would be solved, and we could get married and have kids." I objected, "Why do I have to take the pill? Why can't there be a pill you could take to turn you gay?" We laughed but were serious at the same time.

"Santos, I love you very much, but you already know . . . "

"You don't have to say a f-ing word! I didn't ask you for your f-ing words, so just shut your mouth because I don't care! Get the F out, that's what you can do to help! Get the F out, now or I will kick you out myself!" Austan knew by now that I meant what I said, so he left. Part of me wanted him to fight for us, to tell me he would be gay for me, but I knew that was just a dream, I knew people couldn't just pick what they want to be, it doesn't work that way. I couldn't be straight and true anymore than he could be gay and true. It hurt no less, and I eventually calmed down, realizing that I had a wonderful friend, I was lucky to have someone who loved me so much. I perked myself up, dried myself off and put on my nothing bothers me persona. The party animal, the happy guy who didn't give a shit. Scary at times, but only when let off his leash, otherwise he was a harmless lap dog. I could feel something bigger coming, something that would upend my life, but I couldn't tell what, I didn't care what was coming because it was going to take everything I had to get over Austan and adjust to my new reality with him, which I was totally confused about.

Time got darker for me, more drugs, more sex, more alcohol, more dangerous rendezvous, Austan eventually succumbed to the life I was leading, he ignored his job, and they fired him, with no other choice, or because he knew he had to get away from us . . . from me, he left to go back home to Texas. Warren and Gwenyth moved away to NYC, and I was out of town most days, I eventually moved to Albany, got a cute apartment overlooking The Egg Center for the Performing Arts in the Empire State Plaza but I was lonelier than I had ever been. Sure, I made new friends when I worked with Sebastian, but nothing like the friends and the time I had in Syracuse. I would still meet up with Warren in NYC when I was working there, but now I spent most of my time working and living alone in my apartment in Albany. Warren and Gwenyth had given me some buddy passes that allowed you to just pay the taxes for a seat on the plane. I gave two to my sister Betty and Mando, and the other two I gave to my mom and my Tia Rosa. I was excited to have them come visit; I missed my family so much.

I found out that Jr was going to be out the way of that evil about to strike a passive, yet capable of evil, people. Warren and Gweneth had offered their apartment because they were both going to be on flights, they were flight attendants, so I got all that into motion. All depends on obedience; each incident of obedience is rewarded with great blessings. It was intimate occasions such as the one I had worked out involved the love of family, the spontaneity of the spiritual moment, and love. His sister Betty and his broth-er-in-law Mando had come to visit, they were the first that would visit Jr, his mother and aunt Rosa were scheduled to come visit two weeks after Betty and Mando. This is why those heads up are worth it, it gives us time to coun-ter their move to give our charges the ability to instill free will, it is Riggs that doesn't play by this, he likes to get around the free-will gift, since he never agreed nor recognized it for the incredibly special gift that it is. They would be safe, but it was Betty, as they were on their way to little Italy after leaving the China Town having as much fun as they were having, cracking up after realizing what they thought was a hat, was a cover to keep things warm. They enjoyed and replenished love energy only family can do between each other. Betty, finally getting Mando and Jr's attention, said, "Look, look, those are the Twin Towers, lookit! Look how tall, can you imagine how many people would be in those buildings during the day?" They stood there letting that sink in, but in NYC, stopping only drains energy. They did speak of the prior blast, and Jr actually gave light to a truth to be implemented, "I don't know, but I don't think they are going to stop trying to bring those buildings down." Betty and Mando agreed and hurried to little Italy and back to Gweneth and Warrens cozy apartment in Kew Gardens. They were going to get to bed early because Betty was intent on being one of the first ones in line. They had restricted the crown section of the Statue of Liberty, since it was weakening, but the first group were able to make that ascent into her crown. Mando and Jr, ignoring her orders to get to bed or we would miss the tour, they kept talking and they all slept in.

Betty was throwing shade, rightfully so because it wasn't like they were going to do this all over again, they had a tight schedule. That shade was relinquished when they all took a picture on the fairy as they passed in front of Lady Liberty, making their way to Ellis Island, where their love overshadowed missing the crown. Two weeks later, the plan Riggs was working on with Andras. Mankind still has a lot to learn and wake up to the spiritual battle going on every second of the day. I can't even begin to tell you every minute, intimate detail for each human life that was affected on this day, yesterday, and tomorrow. The plan is no longer a secret, it is no longer that you are in the dark, it is on what Elohim did to reunite you to Him. There will be many martyrs, many taken too soon, many left too long, on and on, and on. Each soul can be light or darkness, free will and love must be the consubstantial existence one must strive and intentionally seek, accept, and live in faith, in Elohim. Lies can make an entire society evil, again I refer to the Prince of Persia and Michael AA (Arch Angel), he lets me call him AA, I love him. Nonetheless, with the help of Betty and Mando's protectors and all the prayers from their loved ones, they made it back home safely. Jr, I convinced him to keep his appointment with his attorney so he could be in Syracuse the day Riggs would pull the trigger on another of his outlandish plans to destroy as many of you as possible while causing a great deal of division, they fed off this type of dark energy. Regardless, they were safely out of what was coming,

I was just coming out of a meeting I had with my attorney handling my bankruptcy, yep, a failure in taking care of myself! But the meeting had gone well, and I was in a particularly good mood. I was in Jefferson Square, Syracuse, and decided to cross the square to an old friend's new salon she had opened for several months, and I finally had the chance to stop in. When I came in, and as trained to do with Sebastian, I went into her salon in a spirit of daring to inspire, the motto of fans of Sebastian, I love it. It was a courageous statement and lofty call to action. 'Dare to Inspire', dole over that for a while. I bullied my way here, and played hard to get, knowing I was a catch. Didn't matter, I was where I wanted to be. I walked in with all my charm, and brilliant skills to command a room. I felt something off, they were immune to my good charm, my witty compliments, but I got nothing. It was like attending a wake with a juggling show. "Have you watched any television, or listened to any radio?" She asked in astonishment, but all I could feel right now, was all the blood flushing to my head, I spun around, as she walked toward the Television on the wall and turned up the volume. "You haven't heard about this?" Half question, half, check your cheery mood pal. Now I understand, it wasn't my technique, skill, or charisma, it was these terrorists that flew planes into both Twin Towers! The same ones me, my sister, and my brother-in-law walked past, just last week! As I'm staring at the TV and listening, I saw live the first tower go down. I had to get Warren on the phone I thought! Oh, my God, please, please let him be ok, let Gwyneth be ok. My call could not be completed, and I thought of course not, this was war, someone had just declared war on the United States, of course we would know who later, but go after the wrong country, I will let history and God judge that, but I'm entitled to an opinion.

As I'm trying to call Warren, I'm getting a call from home, it's my mom! I didn't even think of calling them because they knew I lived in Albany, but I didn't think, I just didn't think. She was so glad to hear my voice, I could hear it in her voice, and relieved. I don't know how many times I told my mom I loved her and that I was safe, four and a half hours northwest of where that happened. Nothing was happening in Syracuse, I assured her, and asked to speak to Pop. I was so happy to hear his voice in this time of uncertainty, could the military still call me up? Now that Don't Ask Don't Tell was a thing now. Did this mean I was still able to be called up? Anyway, my dad's voice and his demeanor, his character, his soul and spirit were gentle, all gentle. Yes, he would get angry, but he would remain silent, he used little words when extremely angry, tons of words when he had to teach us lessons, when we screwed up and when we were doing good, you can do better because when you want something, that is power. This he would say in Spanish, "Querer es poder," and I lived it because he is my dad and he only has my best interest, always. Now, as I get older and hear the stories of old and new friends, I get confirmation of what I always have known, the parents God blessed me with were those types of humble saints that persevere in love, as scripture enlightens, and faith in God, as our Lord Jesus Christ. I welcomed my dad's voice, it always had a calming effect on me, he always spoke to me in Spanish, but for your pleasure and ease I will translate it for you, "Hello my son, how are you?"

"I'm doing fine Dad, like I just told Mom, I am not where they bombed the planes, I'm four and a half hours away, in Syracuse."

Someone had shown them on a map where Syracuse was, my dad would later tell me. I'm sure it was probably Alicia, she was the eldest of us children and the eldest child always gets the anxiety and fear type of parenting, as well as a lot of the responsibilities of helping their parents with everything else, including raising their siblings. Not the parent, but with responsibilities of a parent, and all-the-while expected to achieve these tasks without the titles. It is a great burden, until it is gone, then it causes an absence that not just anything can replace.

"We saw what happened on the TV, are you going to have to go back in the Army?"

"I don't know yet Pop, but I don't think so."

"Well, I pray you don't have to go back."

"I wouldn't really worry about it pop; I don't think they want me back because of why I got out."

I was referring to leaving before don't ask to don't tell became regulation, that gay people could serve, they wouldn't investigate, and one wouldn't live openly. We won't ask, you don't tell. This was never going to work, and I called it. They changed it years later. I did tell, on August 3, 1993, the Clinton policy didn't go into effect until December 1993. When I checked, since I had told, there was no chance that I would be called back into the military. I was safe.

It was 2001 and so much has happened. Knowing mom and pop would stare up at the moon and it would look the same, no matter where each of us were. I wrote this in a letter to them when I was in Africa. It was the only way to express how small and connected we are in this huge world, that we could look up into the sky and see the only moon. Same to you as it is to me, and I feel connected. My grandmother Natividad passed on August 15, 2000, after so many years being unable to speak, move, for years. The faith and resolve of my mom and her sisters and brothers were tested all those years. As a family, they were loyal, loving, strong, and determined, every time they got together it was great memories and laughs, laughs, laughs. They absolutely love each other, and that remained in my heart even until the present day. Crazy thing is that my abuela passed on August 15, 2002. I remember visiting them before going to Korea. I was sitting with my grandmother as she lay in her bed at the house in Cheto, Tia Delma's old room. The room my mom chose to sleep in all the time, even after they gave her the house. My grandfather walked in and sat with us, and a while later, he said, (again I will translate, I'm close to my deadline and don't want to give myself more work, I hope you understand) "I never thought we would end up like this." I could hear all the lost dreams, laughs, gazes, heartaches (I'm not going to support that people should suffer abuse, but for those who have, I remember Fr. Jamail, a very Spirit inspired Priest, once said, "In all things, Grace."). A complicated message to deliver, there is so much complexity of love in it. If I had heard this back then, I would not have understood. I could feel what my grandfather just expressed to me in words. It was the heaviest conversation we had ever had, and one of very, very few conversations. I didn't know that a couple of years later, he would pass on, and leave behind the miracle of redemption, mercy, and grace.

Do You Want It Bad Enough?

As the world ignores wars and famines,
    we grovel for attention.
We ask for everything under the sun,
    while we ignore the poor.
We say I love you, but not you,
    because we pick and choose.
We pray, and pray, while our minds wander,
    never really giving it our full attention.
We give from our bounty,
    but only leftovers, never first fruits.
We are never satisfied with enough,
    we feed on greed, want, and desire.
We pout about the nonsense,
    while we laugh at what should make sense.
Lust is sold for gold,
    while truth is thrown out with the trash.
A predominantly pointless pageantry of lies,
    is what occupies minds these days.
Kindness is scoffed,
    humbleness is rebuffed.
Righteousness is attacked,
    while love is ransacked by violence.

Serpents mock hope,

    while drugs are the world's gold.

You are right to be concerned,

    but you're wrong if it's only for yourself.

We want to be good, most do anyway,

    problem is we don't want it bad enough.

Do you?

Chapter 12

I hung up the phone and sunk down in my chair, and I pushed the chair back from the desk with my feet while I felt like someone had just punched me in the stomach. All of it came back to me, my choices in this life, a smothering weight like an extra heavy weighted blanket made of flannel, how could I do this to my loved ones. The blood coursing through my veins is mine, a part of me like a liver or a heart, kidney, you get it. Life choices, made every second of every day, not one minute goes by that we don't make a choice, rather, several choices like do I bend my body to pick that up, do I open the door, my left or right finger. Choices, several choices, and I have made many in the 37 years that I have lived thus far. I became very aware of my mortality when visiting Cheto, my dad and I were cleaning up and visiting the gravesite of our relatives, we would do this every time we went on vacation there, it was always such a wonderful time that I was able to spend these years with my parents. Growing up with depression, like I did, and so young without thinking you really had anyone to talk to about what I was feeling inside. I mean, how do you explain the conversation that goes on in your mind, like you do not talk to yourself? If you exist in yourself and never feel any contradictory banter, then please, please, please tell me how you can live in that way because I have never just existed in the moment. Well, I lied, maybe a few times and both have been extremes, both satisfying and tantalizing, to both the spirit and the flesh. Oh, flesh, a gift of God when we refer to skin as the flesh. In the spiritual sense, flesh means so much more. I will be getting into these things later but for now just know that at 37 years old, I realized as I'm repairing the headstones of both my grandfather's graves, both my grandfathers passed away in their early thirties, and it hit me like a ton of bricks . . . I have outlived both of my grandfathers. I started sweating more, I was already drenched in sweat because the sun was getting hotter and hotter. Just then it hit me, I need to repair my relationship with God because I am not guaranteed tomorrow, and just like that I was aware that this life will expire, I was no longer living carefree like I had all the time in the world.

The person on the other line, from the Red Cross, had just informed me that I could not even be tested to see if my bone marrow was a match for my sister Alicia. She had been diagnosed with Leukemia, and she has personally called me to tell me about this and how to go about checking to see if I were a match. The horror of having to call her and tell her why they refused to test me. Perfect timing, really. God's timing is always perfect. I answered a series of question and the one that stopped any more questioning and testing was, "Are you Gay?", yes, "Are you engaging in gay sex?", uh a lot. This was no joking matter and just because that's what I thought, that was me passing judgement on myself. The gravity of that last question, I knew what to expect next since these questions weren't designed just to get a response but how those responses would affect the testing. It was just me stating a fact. "I'm sorry you cannot be a donor; we will not test you to see if you are a match. You cannot be a donor." I was floored. As I'm sitting there slumped in the chair, I hear God for the first time speak to my soul, "This is not the life I had planned for you." I wasn't surprised, I wasn't scared, I was ashamed and disappointed with my choices in life. None of them up to this point had given me one bit of joy or peace. "I know", I answered. That was it, I don't know what I expected all those nights I lay awake at night when I was just a kid, not wanting this life and begging with God to change me. If anyone He could, but He never said anything, and now I'm in my late 30's and now, this was it. Profound, yes! Simple, He is always in the whispers. I didn't question Him, I knew, I knew who was speaking to me. Clear, not a voice, not a word, an apparition, nothing like that, it was just this awareness, this enlightenment that together made me live and feel those words, "This is not the life I had planned for you", I just knew. It had every feeling, emotion, and sternness that my father's letter had, for I believe He was writing, inspired by the Holy Spirit. After I had revealed to him that I was gay, he wrote me a letter. I didn't pay any mind to it at the time, but it still planted a seed. He was praying for me, he did not approve of the choice I had made, to live this type of life, but he loved me nonetheless and he opened the letter with " . . . my appreciable son . . . " always the kind, loving heart. Later in the same short, but powerfully deep letter, he writes, "I pray a lot to return to who you are."

The more open he is to me, the better I can encourage his spirit along a righteous path, it is bumpy at first, but he will get the hang of it. The good thing is that he has a willing, and excited spirit. I'm so thankful to Elohim that He encourages me on, and that He gives all of us the tools to set His will ablaze in the spirit of the host. When He learned that God had granted his grandfather's petition, that love prevailed within his heart, "God cured my sister! What a miracle, and no one knew or noticed all the dots that would make them come to the same realization". This is when he knew God was trying to get his attention, intimately. Good that my charge was growing and curious, now that Austan had spoken that seed into Jr's heart that his love was not genuine because it was full of expectations and requirements in exchange for his love. What a brave thing to say to a loved one, who is threatening to cut you out of their life. Austan was the right person, with the right spirit so that Jr could receive it. God knew there had to be a barrier between them, so that neither would fall so far into sin, that He would lose both of them. God had plans for both, that did not include a normal relationship recognized by society, but it required this barrier, these opposites attracted to each other but not belonging to one another in the sexual intimate sense, it would be purely spiritual. So unthreatened and in an agonizing love for each other, they would have to be completely honest and open with each other, mincing no words, and totally dedicated to one another's happiness. It was in this way, that he spoke the seed and Jr accepted it, watered it, and tended it, until it began to bear fruit, and abundant fruit it would bear. There would be only one last test to Jr's obedience, he would offer him an opportunity before returning from Texas and promising his father that he would be back after settling his affairs, so that he could answer God's call to care for them, because they were not to live in a nursing home.

"I am so sick of this guy! He is getting away with way too much, this pisses me off, we are on the brink of a major achievement and Mel gets the right to swoon over him and gets me put on the sidelines for a minor infraction. I broke the rules, I wasn't supposed to attack or use the method I employed with him, repeatedly and without any breaks, but I thought I had a clear slate once G-diddy cured him of something major like depression. I thought it was within the rules to test it, but I guess I was wrong, or they changed the rules on me. I will go with that one, they changed the rules. I'm the father of lies anyway, you will eventually believe anything I put forth because you are so feeble and weak. Dangle some hope in front of you and you don't even check if it's real or not, you are too much in a hurry to get your hope stomachs satisfied that you see hope wrapped in bacon, and you go coo coo. LOL, I love it! Your souls are like picking meat at the supermarket, where you avoid the slaughter of life, but enjoy the taste of death and rotting meat because it has A-1 sauce, or ketchup, mustard, or more accurately, the taste for cruelty and ignorance, but you're not ignorant, are you? You know every time you take that bite, and chew on that meat, you know that something had to die for you to pay money to devour. How is that any different than paying to go see the gladiators get torn apart by beasts? Yea, the spectators didn't eat the flesh of the gladiators, but didn't they eat every minute of the duel with their eyes, ears, and the smell of death? Taking it all in, as if it did feed something to your hunger for death?

I want to end this guy, but he has been choosing Mel's influence more, and now, which I consider unfair practice, is that Elohim started talking to him! What a slick move, slick is not really the word I want to use, but you get the idea. Cheap, that's what it is, a cheap move. How can you fight with that, the Big Daddy talks to you and then all is forgotten, all those decades, all that suffering, all that time I have been right there throughout your life, actively engaged and the first time that, ooh I wish I could, He speaks to you after ignoring you for so long, as a matter of fact, He only spoke to this idiot once when He was a kid . . . "You will take care of your parents, they will not go into a nursing home." WTF?! Now it's, "My son, this is not the life I had planned for you." WTF?! That's all it takes; those two statements and you melt like a popsicle on hot Texas asphalt?! You people, you dirt dung. Ignore all the fun we had together, where was G-dude then?! @!%#*^%@#! I WILL DAMN YOU TO HELL. You can only resist me for so long, but I am here every second of every minute, of every hour, of every day, for your entire time here in this G forsaken place, you will be mine. Now he's on his way, raising a finger to me in protest, showing me that he belongs to G-daddy now. Damn, it was his index finger, not the middle one, I could work with the middle one. This little shit pays attention to the details.

Goodbyes are always so difficult for me, more so than the average person and a little less than hysterical. I take it really hard, but once I've gotten over it, I am the world's worst long-distance friend. When my friends met me at Mike's house after work, they were surprised, and a little upset with me, that I had loaded everything but my mattress. It was exactly the day of the six weeks that the doctor told me not to take the drive to Texas after my surgery. I had my appendix removed, but it was much more than this because I was giving up a lifestyle, I had for the past eleven years. This goodbye was easier than any other up to this point because I experienced an enlightenment which started me on a spiritual journey I was not expecting. Most of my friends had moved away, I would really miss Mike and his parents, they were so kind and good to me, they offered me stability when I had none, and a refuge full of love and acceptance. The rest of my friends I had grown estranged from, because I'm not a great long-distance friend and everyone had been living lives apart for a few years now. Yea, we visited each other but it is when you live with others that the relationship incurs another great responsibility, you are there for each other, like it or not because you physically live together and when you do this, you are engaged in each other's lives, freely or not. I was determined to go back home, I didn't know what awaited me there, but this new life, this bright joyful light, which has filled my heart is drawing me into obedience, the type where surrender means freedom. Freedom from the slavery of sin. Freedom from the constraints of worldly labels we try to affix to everything, out of boredom and pride. I had learned about true love from Austan, both in word and deed, I missed him, and I was excited that I would see him again soon. I had seen him once after he moved away, in Las Vegas, I was there for a seasonal launch for Sebastian as part of work, where I was also being considered for the Education Manager for Latin America. I sabotaged my chances by demanding two things they wouldn't go for, kidnapping insurance and that I be stationed out of NY and not Woodland Hills, CA. I didn't much care for California living, and the position didn't pay enough for the entirety of Latin America. I called Austan and asked him where he was, just to talk, he told me he was in Las Vegas! It was great, we met up and hit a local pool bar off the main drag called 'Banging Balls Billiards', leave it to Austan to pick a place like this. It was crazy for Austan that we had coincidentally showed up in Las Vegas at the same time, but at this point in my life I knew that God acted purposefully, and He knew that I need to spend time with my Austan. I was lost in Syracuse without him.

I was excited to see Carrie again, she invited me to come stay a night with her in Lafayette, Louisiana. This is where she had run off with the guy, I was going to put an end to one night he threatened my life. Luckily, for me really, they weren't together anymore, they had a beautiful child together but, she ended up trading up, way up, in my opinion . . . back then. I made things so weird, the more I spoke with her, taking things to a sexual place, I was really concerned that all the repressed and pent up desire to have sex, would ruin another friendship so I cancelled on Carrie and stopped at a bath house in New Orleans, parked my car with the U-haul on a public street and trotted my happy ass inside to partake of the debauchery happening inside, willing adults doing whatever pleases each other, for as long as you want to partake, just keep paying. I thought it was better than a hotel room, knowing damn well I would get no sleep and that is what I needed. I had just driven through six states, and I was beat. Something convinced me and urged me to drive the extra miles to New Orleans because it was the best spot to find a good and well attended bath house. I did partake, I couldn't resist, and by now I knew that it was the devil's convincing lies to me . . . no, no, no, I remembered my free will, this was my decision, I parked the car, I disregarded my things, I chose to partake of sin, while friends and family eagerly awaited my arrival. I was especially concerned with Juan, because my last visit proved to be painful, and scary. I was glad God was bringing me home, maybe I could help, like he helped me when I was suicidal. That was another thing that I kept praying to God about, I was overly concerned that I would fall back into my depression because that's all I remember of my life in Beaumont, Texas. I trusted in God to take care of me, but the devil used this to promote the lie, that soon, my life would be all consumed by responsibility and restraints. Hot in climate, hot in discrimination, hot in idleness, and I was going from a life lived like a peacock to a life living like a crow. In appearance only do I make these comparisons. In Beaumont, I would be a strange bird, trying to fit in with a culture behind what I had just left. I stopped to partake, what could be so bad I thought, as I had this debate with myself on the block and a half that it took me to get to the front door. I don't even remember what kind of trouble I got into, being in the middle of the week and being so unmemorable. I assume it was not worth the trouble, but the next morning when I went out to my car, I noticed something was off. When I got close enough to see, my heart sank, and I started to panic. Someone had shattered my passenger side window and stolen my briefcase, which had all my important papers including my cosmetology license, they took all my scissors, and most of my styling tools. As I got back on the highway, grateful that they didn't take more like the police said, "You're lucky you still have the U-haul trailer. It was probably kids, not professionals, we've had entire trucks stolen with all of people's belonging. What we suspect is that it was some kids that found it an easy mark since you have no tint and they could grab some things they know people will buy, with no way to trace." I guess they were right, and I had to accept what would happen now, that I thought God was sending a message that I was not going to be doing hair as a profession right now. It would be weeks, but I would eventually get the briefcase back. Some random guy called out of nowhere to see if it was worth anything to me. I found the nearest shipping store to him and bought a bus ticket out of Florida and back home for this nice guy. He got trapped in Florida and had fallen on tough times and was homeless. I didn't hesitate, I could now get my Texas license without having to get another NY license, plus my birth certificate, etc. I was still determined to work in the beauty industry, because that's what I knew, this was familiar and comfortable. I was now very perceptive to paying attention, and I knew in my heart that God didn't want me in that industry. I was still a work in progress . . . slow progress, LOL.

I thought that would work to discourage him from making it home, my influence is waning, and he is questioning everything, Riggs seems to have lost interest, I think he might be thinking that he is a lost cause. I know that Riggs is like this every time he has a tremendous setback like this one, their often not setbacks, people really do turn their lives around, from just a couple of things G-dad reveals to them, then it's the big woo, whatever. I'm not going to give up, plus Riggs would entrust me with so much more if I were to capsize this ship, after he pledged himself to G-dad. I can try at least.

It didn't work, Carrie made some kind of generalized comment that Jr took as her brushing off his obvious troublesome advances. They weren't in Syracuse anymore, but he was relieved that he didn't destroy another friendship over his lust. He didn't even like girls, but I convinced him that if he engaged with the opposite sex, it would not be as bad as with a dude. LOL, he believed me! Ya'll are so predictably shallow. Get the little guy to wiggle and start growing and you make excuses that make you believe the absurd. I thought it would be the same with the drugs and alcohol, but this fool was not missing those things, but the urge of lust, now that was something I could work with. His pride was another vice I could satisfy, so I chose to concentrate on these. I knew I had very little time because his interest in the sinful was waning, he couldn't resist me all the time, but the influence I used to have over him has definitely diminished. You people don't know how much obedience plays in receiving blessings, this guy was being like way too obedient, it was curious and both extremely exhausting, his thirst and curiosity for all opportunities to practice obedience, and to put his faith into action, as well as soaking up all fruits from that story book G-pop allowed to be written. I remember when Riggs first found out that G-dad would allow this to happen, and Riggs almost turned hell upside down in a rage, calling it unfair to G's promise to him that there would be enmity between us, He was now exposing me for all generations to know about me and my ways. Now, I laugh and giggle, because y'all don't really take any of it to heart anyway. Ooh, but he was mad at the time. This guy, this guy was taking all this seriously, and believing all of it. There's something that changed after we nailed J-diddy to that cross, yea y'all did it but we encouraged it all. Y'all are just pieces on a game board, truly little of you take it seriously, so before you know what has happened you are already in crises, turning to G-dad in rage more than love.

I don't wait long before I strike again, we got all kinds of things going on, but it's these little individual things that can have big payouts, because if we notice that someone has a strong faith, or building and strengthening like this guy, this is what gives us the legions we command. This is why our radars go off, but we must battle for each of you. Good thing the opportunities are endless, especially as we get closer to the end, He promised us. In this attack, I will persuade the same family that he wanted to be closer to, I will provoke division, with lies and presumption, a lot of pride and even a little envy, but mostly lies. That works best, has better and broader appeal, and the effects leave a longer impact.

Satan has disoriented everything and has humanity completely duped and stupefied. Fake everything, and worst of all fake truth. Lie after lie, we die a little until our hearts are completely dead, cold, and hardened. Criminals play the victim while standing on their stage. Liars are worshipped as truth bearers, and truth bearers as ridiculous evil instigators. Greed is honored as an accomplishment to be respected. Hate is the new humility. Preachers preach the gospel of what's in it for me, with a church on every corner like a prostitute. Decadence is valued and recognized as a blessing, while the poor go hungry and starve. War rages and we detach from the suffering with another steak dinner, or a new outfit, and maybe a vacation to a far-off place. There is gnashing of teeth, and we listen to it like a number one hit song. Society plays make believe, choosing an avatar on par with depravity. People live on the street and the rest of humanity laughs or ignores them like a discarded bubble gum wrapper. Trash talk is your new form of debate. Addiction is your new paradise, and you all have turned a blind eye to murder and rape. Theft is a pastime like playing on the playground. Trolling is your societal transcendence. You don't have to be a party to any of this, you can choose Love. The problem with this is that so many only know the definition humanity has applied to love. Living in Love, now that is something one must choose, and be open to receive, to understand what Love really is, nor the freedom that comes with it; Otherwise, Love in a fallen world is only recognized as wanton desire, sexual recreation, possessiveness, and subjective. Love becomes no more than an unobtainable fantasy being peddled for $$.

You can begin by choosing a smile for everyone, if you want to change, and by restraining your judgement or checking your pride when you don't get a reaction. Love should never require or expect anything in return, this is when you know it is true love. I may not know everything but what God has allowed to grant, that I can be a vessel to deliver the same Truth, by the power of the Holy Spirit, and through you as an obedient vessel of love, then we can achieve remarkable things together that will bring more souls to God, just by being obedient. That's it folks, you want the secret of life, obedience to the will of God. What is the fruit of life? To love each other. The complex simplicity of it all. God has to bless me with so many confirmations, but if I'm obedient, he does it.

LOL, God just told me to shut up! I knew He would. I've been bothering Him, ok, no I'm not bothering Him, I'm praying to Him . . . big difference, but the devil keeps trying to convince me that I'm bothering Him. Ludicrous, but true, God does not get bothered, love is Who He Is, what Love Is, Is God. Because God Is, so Love Is. The shut-up part was true, except that's how I tell it. A formal shut-up but shut-up it was. I was so hard in my righteousness, my certainty, my newfound spiritual courage. I had a mission, and I wasn't going to let God down, I was doing what His will commanded, I no longer lived for the pleasures of this world, but for those things that will please God. Some didn't understand and it was this distrust that gave the devil the in he needed. This is what he does to families, he looks for what he can expose and then how he can capitalize on any doubt, fear, distrust, anger, presumption, judgement, and fear of the unknown, but the best is unable to forgive. That is the diamond, the gold, the ecstasy, the cherry and whip cream on a sundae. So, I shut up! God had told me "You know I have brought you home, and why I have brought you home. Your Father also knows, so why do you need to convince anyone else?" Good point, I didn't see it like that. "Your fight is not with your brother's and sister's, you pass judgement when you call them and blame them by name, saying they did this to me, and they did this against me. It is always the evil one, that is your battle. He is behind all division, he is behind this, not your brothers and sister, they are his victims. He wants to push you away from me, and he will use anyone to get to you, but you must not allow this to happen. Now, I want you to be silent, in silence you listen, and if you listen you will be enlightened to the truth and to love. You remain silent, prayerful, fast, and watch me work." It all made sense, I should have known, but I will keep this in my heart. I was storing a lot of gems of wisdom that God has blessed me with in my heart. I remember how our mother Mary would hold things in her heart. I always took this to mean that she mulled over in prayer, these things recognized as Truth but beyond our comprehension or that it had a deeper and more complex message within it. After being obedient and holding true to what God directed, He blessed my obedience. I was so frustrated one weekend, that I laid in my bed and wanting to satisfy my urge towards lust, I instead prayed to God for the answer to this question I wanted answered, I was learning to pray more intentionally and that words matter. Also, how words can make a difference in things, like what I just said about a question I wanted answered, where the question I may have asked before my enlightenment, would be more like, about a question I want to ask. Some may not see a difference but in one, it requests a response while in the other, it requires no response. It also matters spiritually, those insignificant details.

Since the first time that God answered my prayer to cure me of my depression, I have gone to my knees, made a sacrifice of abstinence (fast), and reminded God of Jesus' promise and the prayer He left for us to pray to Him. Every time that I have had a major heavy yoke, this is how I've gone to Him for help. I'm usually at the end of my rope, begging. Knowing He is the only One that can help me. I did it again this Sunday night. There was so much evil stuff swirling around me and my family that I went to God in the way I did back then. On my knees begging because I need Him. I said, "I just want this one question answered, did I get it wrong? Am I in the right place? Ok, I know that's more than one, but they are all interconnected. If I got it wrong, please show me where I'm supposed to be." I also prayed the Lord's prayer and my fast. Monday morning, I wake up and drive to Houston, where I am the District Sales manager for Princess Beauty Supply, and we are having an in-salon training with our color artist and some of the local hairstylists. I'm just thinking why I moved halfway across the country to live in Houston, and not in Beaumont like God told me to do, when I get a call from the educator.

"Good morning, Santos. They overbooked my flight and I'm trying to get another flight out."

"What do you think your chances are, to make it for the class?"

"I don't think it looks good."

"What about any of your other educators?"

"I will try, and I will call you back."

"Ok, in the meantime, is there anyone at your salon?" Since we were holding the event at her salon, her aunt worked for her as the receptionist when needed. She was there already, I asked her to please call her and let her know that I will be there regardless. "I'm probably an hour out of Houston so that will be about thirty minutes after the class is supposed to start."

"Ok, I will let you know."

I thought to myself, yep, what a great Monday this would be, I could have stayed in Beaumont, with my parents since I only got to see them on the weekends. Princess wouldn't let me base out of Beaumont, he wanted me in Houston so I asked my Tia Rosa if I could live with her, and she was so kind to have said yes. I did love my time living with my Tia Rosa because we were able to have so many conversations about God, it was great, and she was the first person that never got tired of talking about Him. Just then my phone rang, and it was Trisha.

"Hello, were you able to get one of your educators?"

"No, and I will not be able to fly out until tonight."

"Ok, will you tell your aunt that if any salon owners would like to stay and talk to me, I'm only about 15 minutes away. I will stay and talk with them as long as they want, maybe give them a deal for their patience and understanding."

"Sure, I will let her know, have a good day I'm sorry."

"No need to apologize, these things happen."

"Thank you for understanding."

I drive up and see some cars outside, I guess I had some takers. I walked towards the door and the aunt greeted me at the door, since it was locked. "Hello Santos." "Hello."

Three salon owners stayed behind to speak with me, as I was able to answer their questions and address any concerns; each left the salon, until the last one left. As Trisha's aunt locked the door behind the last one, I was right behind her, walking her to the door, Trisha's aunt turned to me and said, "God wants you to know, you are exactly where He wants you to be, and to not worry, and that He has great plans for you." I just started crying, she didn't know why, she just consoled me and got me some tissue.

There have been so many gems of wisdom, so many blessings as a testimony to my obedience. Even in the times of darkness, despair, tribulation, I have remained in God and have made living in the Spirit a norm in my life. I remain open to the prompting, teaching, guidance, and wisdom of the Holy Spirit, I ask God for all, and I know all is provided by God. I had to endure many trials, and received great blessings, like the one where I asked God to allow the Holy Spirit to reflect upon my life and to enlighten me to when I allowed sin to enter my life and how it manifested and how God worked through all that time. Next thing I knew, I was sitting in my fifth-grade classroom with Mr. Busby and then at recess on the monkey bars. It took a span of time for Him to take me through it all, but a glimpse is shared here in these pages. My parents never had to be put in a nursing home, what God told me as a mere Laddy, He showed me one day when I was down after finding a picture of me when I was one year old, and I'm not much of a material guy, not even with pictures, so I wondered the only two people that would cherish this picture are gone. The devil then used this little door to try to barge in, but by this time I knew I was not in this fight alone, I had my spiritual family and the Almighty God as my protector. I still scrape myself when I fall, but it's the intimate relationship that allows me to continue in my walk with God.

I tried to throw this little shit some curve balls, like that time that I kept reminding him how dirty his hands are, how at the big J-Day, we have several witnesses to testify to each sin, how can he possibly create anything with those dirty hands, they will certainly infect others? He almost believed it, but Mel blocked me. That rope of beads you hang onto don't mean nothing when your faith and love aren't into it, only empty words with pretty beads. One almost choked him in that club, but none of us did that! He says it's the mysteries, those special and physical intercessions . . . I call BS.

He is much stronger after his surgery, thought we had him, but then he published that first collection of poems that the Big Dude gave him. Took his muse Becky, more like an earth angel, it was she that by the prompting of the

Holy Spirit, encouraged him to submit these poems he had been sharing only with her and on social media, the Facebook. She heard every one of those poems, they would talk about them, share stories and problems. Finally, he did it. The good thing going for us is his tendency towards sloth, Riggs has been with him since the monkey bars, and they are still acting like they can't stand each other. Love one, hate the other? You guys are so dumb. Thinking about things only means how they are written, when they are written, ignoring the spoken, the invisible. Only eyes for desire, never the wretched. The rich, never the poor. The educated over those with wisdom. Making it harder, more difficult, and troublesome, while eradicating the sensible with the web of lies of a better future without love, without truth. I've got him to dark places, Mel has guided him out of severe danger, but ultimately it was his choices, but he still doubts, just like Tommy (yes, that one who wanted to finger JC's side), he will never learn and that will be another in, if by chance he finally finds the wherewithal that he has built up an arsenal with this obedience, this child-like fascination with God, that has only increased as his walk becomes more intimate. It is sickening, and I must watch it happen.

My love has compelled me to do more, and I fell into the devil's lies. On May 14th, during my diagnostic cardiac catheterization procedure I had a heart attack during the procedure. Being conscious I suspect something is happening, the Cardiologist tells me what is happening and that they are trying to stabilize me, get blood to my heart and alleviate pressure in order to take me to immediate open-heart surgery. All I remember is saying ok, they work aggressively, and I am calm. This I credit to knowing God's peace through obedience. Nobody will know things have taken a turn for the worse for several hours. I survived through the grace and mercy of God. Will I be a more loving disciple? Will I accomplish what God expects from me, since I was allowed more time here. I was prepared to depart and face judgement, not because I think I am worthy of eternal life . . . but because Jesus came to save sinners like me, and I have a fighting chance in faith. I was prepared to leave this life because it gets tiring and sad to see so much evil taking place and some evil is even committed in the name of God while we defile ourselves. Imagine my state of mind when I woke up early Friday morning to discover I'm still here! In 2017 I bought my burial plot, only days before I wrote a will and even planned with my publisher so that if anything happened to me before my book release, nothing could stop its release. I left instructions with the vendor of caskets (plain pine box built by monks so I would be assured continual prayers knowing I would need all the prayers I can get) and with the funeral home on all the rest. Not knowing any of this was going to happen. Be prepared. Maybe this is why I was calm as they fought to save my life. The relationship I have with God is real, it is

loving, it is the most important thing in my life and if you read anything I
write, if you know how I live my life . . . you know. It is not window dressing.
Someone told me once as we were having a conversation, " . . . you know
Santos, whenever someone says to me that God speaks to them, my first
thought is . . . their crazy! But with you, you are so matter of fact about it that
I believe you.". I'm still a sinner and nothing I do makes me worthy of God's
love . . . I am worthy (just like you) because God loves us!! Open your hearts,
let go of what YOU think is God's will and be free! Free to live in love, peace,
and joy in the love of God. This is the only way you get through this life in
a fallen and broken world . . . it is only with God's love that you can see the
beauty of creation, redemption, salvation, and eternal life . . . especially seeing through the lies of satan that would convince you that there is no hope,
no love, no peace, no joy . . . just darkness, despair, hate and injustice. Come
home, God says . . . Jesus says I am the way, and they sent their love in the
Holy Spirit to protect and guide us through. We just have to make the choice
to trust, believe, love, prepare and rely on faith. Place God above ALL and
your brethren next and serve them both. Pride will always make you falter,
so you must deal with this pride first and get it in check, pray for humility
and trust me . . . you will be humbled. This does not make you weak, as the
devil will convince you, this makes you stronger and more courageous. But
for the humble, only others see this strength and courage, for the humble
they are too busy with the concerns of God's will and those of others to notice this newfound strength and courage. You can never do enough to win
God's favor, grace, and mercy because we are sinners, but God showers the
obedient with these because He loves us more than any words or actions can
describe. He only requires you to knock, to seek, to love and turn to Him.
He is waiting. He loves you so much!

Although my relationship with God is strong, it has taken a tremendous amount of work and focus. Primarily, the fortunate thing is that I believe I had a head start. Unlike others, my parents were a fitting example of
how to live a life in a God-fearing way. They displayed a love that overcame
any personal resentment for the sins of their children, or of their parents.
They instilled in me, I cannot speak for my siblings, that with God and family I could achieve anything in this world. They never laughed or ridiculed
when I declared that I wanted to be President or that I was going to be a
millionaire one day. No, they only loved me, and provided me with a life
where I did not need anything and always had food on the table, and all I
ever needed to give me that freedom to prosper wherever I chose. They were
always there for me, even as I surely disappointed them with my decisions
so many times, I was always certain that I could count on them for anything
and they loved me, and that God was their center. My parents had their

faults, but they pale in comparison to the sins of their children, most of all my sins and disrespect. They never ceased to love us, and this was true when I was five as well as when I was 40, and up to their last breath.

As I grow in wisdom, by the grace of God, I have learned that my father's relationship with God has had a lasting impact on the generations that have come after. I see this favor in my life, my siblings' lives, and those of my nephews, my nieces and in the newest generations of my great great nephews and nieces. Throughout Scripture you learn that God is faithful and that He not only shows favor to those He wishes, but also to their next generations so long as they are still faithful to Him. So, it is not surprising that our family has been blessed. This does not come without heartache and pain, no, but it also comes with great responsibility. The responsibility to share our faith, love one another, and live by the law of Love, that higher calling to serve than just following Mosaic law. There have been challenging times, challenging relationships, but all-in-all we love each other. To this day, some relationships are strained because the devil tries to break down the love within familial relationships, knowing that any break in one's heart can create fissures that can eventually turn into divides that are difficult to repair by worldly remedies. Destroying the family can destroy the favor that had once been enjoyed because of that special bond of love between God and man. This is such a story. Albeit just one story of this stranger that dares write about it, but a love story told throughout time and will be told again until the end of time. God's love story. His relationship with my family, but because I do not know all the secrets of each member of my family, you will read mainly of the love story between God and me. The heartbreaks and heartaches of building a relationship, becoming angry and despondent, outright rebellion, and a tendency toward slothfulness and every other sin offered up on a silver platter with the devil lavishly, and lustfully, coaxing and flirting with me at every turn in my life. A willing participant at times, an unwilling puppet at other times, destined to continue until I reach home, with God.

God has blessed my charge with so much, when his father passed, he was warned by God to prepare himself, but that all is fine, that he was about to go through the hardest thing he would ever experience up to this point, and he was brave. His death was sudden, but as with all things, upon reflection he noticed God's hand in all of it. When his mother passed, he was strengthened and encouraged even when Riggs got his hooks into him for a good two years, but instead of going out of control and into old habits, he went deeper into Jesus Christ and prevailed. God started writing messages in the sky to him, about love. My charge left his dream job, the job He prayed for, to go serve those without a voice, the current disgust of society,

Rigg's latest schemes. God told him to start making Rosaries and he did, he continues to serve his community even while Rigg and Charo continue to use those loved ones around him to disrupt and destroy any good that surrounds him. He shares all that God provides to a fault because he still gets in the way. Now when it comes to the Rosaries and the poems that God gives him to share, he does a fantastic job of not getting in the way. There are other things that would help him even more, this is where he gets in the way. He struggles but I'm here, and all his support system, this doesn't mean that Riggs and Charo aren't trying but as he tells people, "the devil now is like a fly or mosquito buzzing in my ear and I try to tune that out or brush it away." He makes light of it, and people don't really know the battles he has fought and prevailed even through the prayers of his parents and others, while he was angry and non-responsive to the things of God. Even now, Riggs is moving things to try to get him to give up the fight for justice within his workplace. He feels and sees the fruits of Riggs and Charo manipulating, confounding, and disrupting the charitable work that the place he works is suffering from, the very mistakes he has made and learned from. He sometimes gets so frustrated seeing the train wreck coming, warning those around him, only to be ignored and dismissed. People would think that a place of God would not be open to attack, and this is why Riggs and Charo can get away with what they get away with, because people find it easier to ignore or dismiss than it is to engage in spiritual warfare. My little charge has learned what it takes, and the battle is not for the faint of heart, but that it is worth it to be a soldier for God, one that refuses to be a slave to Riggs and Charo, to not let them pull his strings anymore. My beautiful soul still struggles but at least he knows now that he isn't alone, he has God on his side. This only means that Riggs is only beginning, his first attack in this era is coming.

Supplication

Defeat by way of sin,

and troubled with addiction,

akin to the runaway bridegroom within

while running to nowhere, but backward inclination.

Tis the season of temptations

in this fallen world of mine

where familiar inclinations

bide their time to shine.

What say I this time?

Will I partake of this irrelevance?

Can I resist the tempting paradigm,

or do I assign it a false precedence?

Free will is absolute,

welcomed or not, choice is mine

to eat from that forbidden fruit.

Do I scratch this evil itch this time?

I serve two masters it seems,

I love the one and hate the other

while gnashing my teeth, my heart screams . . .

please, please pray for me my brother!

Chapter 13

A lone, unable to care for myself, swollen and in pain I lay here in won-der, relief, and determined with a layer of apprehension. Just yesterday I was leaving work and walking out with Latasha, we spoke in the parking lot, I don't even remember what. It was like every other evening, cool as May could be, but humid as it is too often in Beaumont, we said our goodnights and goodbyes because it was Latasha's last day. She had graduated college and landed herself a job as a teacher, which was exactly what she wanted to do. I picked up dinner on my way home and was still feeling a little bit of pain occasionally, since the day before yesterday. Didn't know what it was, but since I had stopped exercising and eating healthy, I just thought it was part of me falling apart as I aged. It's hard because I'm always young, at heart, so this old person's body, yet awfully familiar, is getting older faster. I didn't have a clue about what was in store for me that evening and for the rest of my life. It was also a time of great concern for me because I was in the middle of the publishing of my first book, Valiant Cry. A collection of poems that God filled my heart with as answers to prayers, enlighten-ment, justice, and so much more that can only be explained and revealed in poetry. Now, I see Scripture from the heart of a poet, which is why I'm so thankful to God. To Him it was no surprise, but to me who struggles every day to walk in faith I doubted and waited on the inside, He created me for this time, just like He created each of you.

I opened my email and started to scan each, waiting to hear from the publisher, looking for the final draft copy but no email tonight. I turned on the TV, as I did, I felt that tightness but with pain like last night and a couple of times today, I put in the Gospel of John DVD. Ever since my mother passed away, I have only been able to watch Scripture based shows, they re-ally helped me get through my grief. I decided the night before last to write a will, because last month I went to the ER only to be found to be having an anxiety attack. Which is what I was patting myself on the back for today as I feel these pains because I always expect the worse (makes it better when it is never as bad as I expect it to be). "God, thank you for today, and I'm sorry if I didn't do what you wanted me to get done and give me the strength to hang in there and love everyone the way you love them." I started talking to God because I started to feel my jaw go numb, kinda like when you've been sitting on your hands and your fingers start going numb, that's what my right jaw line felt like, but no pain associated with it. I started praying my Rosary, the one that I found in an antique store in New Braunfels, TX. Oh, this antique store is so cool, two floors and just all kinds of wonderful things for everyone. I specifically look for things for Rosaries, or holders for Rosaries, and just unique and different. I usually let the Holy Spirit take charge and get things even when I don't know what I'm going to use them for, but I know I'm supposed to get it. It is a hard place to get to, but when you are more in tune with, and walking in faith with, the Holy Spirit, things get complicated before they get to be just commonplace. I felt peace whenever I pray with this Rosary, because I thought it was mine (as many times before) but I was only going to use it for a short while (. . . I will be with you only a short while more . . .) before it went to my niece, Mia Valeria.

The pain and tightness increased but I prayed more fervently, as I walked around my crowded house where I had managed to make a trail from my room to the bathroom and into a cubby space in the living room. My house had been flooded with about four-five inches of water and together with Gus and Tonio, we cut out the sheetrock and pulled the wet insulation the night the water started to recede. I didn't ask God for help this time, He had saved the house last year when the major flooding happened, and He spared my house millimeters before it came inside the house. I had prayed that night on my knees at the back door, praying with so much love, pain, and sorrow for my sins that I started sweating all over, I mean dripping sweat. I understood Scripture so well that night. It wasn't like me leaving my dinner untouched but that is what happened that night, which I knew was not good. Remember, this is during the shutdown due to Covid-19 the last thing I wanted to do was go to the ER in May of 2020. The numbness and the tightness had gone away, and I was feeling tired, so I laid down to go to sleep because I had to work the next day. Wrong, about two hours later the tightness in my right shoulder and upper back, and my jaw were back, along with a bit of pain on the right side of my chest. I rushed to the bathroom and dry heaved, but nothing came up so I sat down on the toilet because I also felt like I may need to take a dump, but no so I grabbed my Rosary and started praying again.

"You just went to the ER last month and racked up bills you can't afford and you're going to do it again? Your anxiety is becoming an expensive habit, but you have always been scared to die after dreaming about death for so long . . . once-upon-a-time." I used to think this was my alter ego, my moon sign fighting with my rising sign. Trying to 'splain it away, but I know exactly who this buzzing in my ear was, and I'm trying not to listen, but I hear it clear as the pain I feel. There's always another opinion, another voice, another opposing train of thought, "Do not make choices about your health on money concerns, go to the ER and God will provide." Shorter message, but again, clear as the pain. This goes on as I'm getting dressed and packing an overnight bag because I know this routine, and I'm very well experienced at it, but the back and forth goes on. I finally make the decision to go, but I need a reason that I must establish to move forward so I come up with, "Yes, God always provides, and it isn't about money. I also have never felt a numbness like this on my jawline ever, and this is concerning." I grab my bag, my phone and my keys and I leave the house and drive myself to the ER at Baptist Hospital. When I get there, they wheel me in right away because of my symptoms and medical history which includes a stint on Thanksgiving in 2012. Yep, a stint at 45 years old. They rolled me into an ER room after I threw up and started to take blood for tests. Sure enough, my heart enzymes were elevated but not too much and they were expecting this because of my stint. I get admitted and every several hours they tested and each time they were slightly elevated, so the cardiologist decided to perform an arteriogram to see what was going on inside. This is when it all happened, my life was about to change, and change big, again.

The arteriogram was scheduled for 12:30PM and I was feeling fine, and I didn't even need any nitroglycerin and I felt no pain. This was familiar to me, so I expected to maybe need another stint or something like that. I reached out on social media, sent texts, and made some phone calls to request prayers for the procedure they were about to do. The nurse came to roll me to my procedure, once I arrived, they started explaining what was going on and that the cardiologist was on his way. We chatted as I do, out of anxiety more than any real goal to make new friends (sad but true), it was mostly about how young everyone was, and how they came to serve on a team that only does surgery support for surgeons. They started prepping me for the procedure, so they had to secure my right leg and my right arm because they said they didn't know which one the Doctor was going to use to enter for the procedure. I thought, ok, but I really started to panic once my right arm and right leg were immobile. Worse, I couldn't move them, even if I wanted to move them. "Our Father, who art in heaven, hollowed be thy Name . . . " I was getting distracted, I can't move . . . I feel trapped. "Excuse me!" I started calling for someone in the other room, there were like two rooms, all windows so I could see into the other room where the Doctor's team were just chatting. "Hello! Excuse me!

In Here! The patient!! Oooh, I could feel the walls closing in, my vision getting narrower, "I know you can hear me, my anxiety!" "Our Father, who are in heaven . . . " I see someone coming over, "Yes, Mr. Hernandez?" "Can you give me something for my anxiety?" "Only if he put something in your chart, I will go check." Oh, no, that's going to take time, and they aren't in any real rush that I can see, I thought. I started to pray again, but again I was easily distracted, so I yelled again, "Can I get something for my anxiety?!" "We are checking with the Doctor because there was nothing in your chart." Ok, I said nervously and then again started to pray but again distracted. "Mr. Hernandez two of the Doctor's team were pulled into an ER emergency surgery and we will not be able to start for another 45 minutes, and your doctor is not responding to our calls right now. Oh, hell no! I thought, what am I supposed to do for 45 minutes when it has only been five since they tied me down?! Shit, I will pray again! I started praying, but again the thought of 45 minutes immobile, strangled, vision closing in on me, sweating, I gotta move, I must move, I, "Hey, I'm going to do this another day when I don't have to wait on the Doctor for 45 minutes." This is what I yelled out as I tried to get up from the bed. I struggled because, well half my body was tied down, but I was trying to sit up anyway. Now, this they noticed right away and all of them made a bee line to the bed to hold me down. "Don't hold me down because I will only get worse the less I can move, the more I will want to move, so keep your hands off of me." I said this calm enough to make a point and to really scare them after acting like anyone who has a panic attack but then to get really calm and make a threat, more like an order, is a trait I picked up in the service. It was this one very young respiratory nurse that laid her hands on my tied down arm and very calmly and lovingly engaged me in conversation the entire time I had to wait. She was a God send, an angel, because she recognized how real the anxiety was and what it would take to combat it. The time flew by, and the next thing I know the doctor walks in to start the procedure.

"I guess y'all don't care that I can still feel a slight bit of pain, I'm sure I'm not supposed to feel anything, right?" "Oh, I guess we're going to ignore the patient saying he can feel pain, right?" I am so obnoxious under the anesthesia, but very vocal. After that last remark I don't remember anything or how much time had elapsed, but I woke up to the team manhandling me. I could feel them tugging on my leg real hard, I couldn't feel anything per say but you know when you are being manhandled aggressively, so I say, "Hey, what's going on?" No answer, but I can still feel them being aggressive. "I know something is going on, I can feel y'all being more aggressive with me." Finally, the doctor explains, "Mr. Hernandez you had a heart attack, you're currently having a heart attack and I am placing a balloon in your leg and where your stint is to alleviate the pressure on your heart. Once we stabilize you, we will roll you into emergency open heart surgery." Oh, ok, I thought inside, and pretty calm to be honest. I guess because they had answered my question and there really wasn't much more to talk about. Kind of funny but when you think about it, as I must have in that moment, what can be said, what can you do at this point except place all your trust in God, in my faith. Honestly, at this moment I was at peace at the thought that I may get to see what there is on the other side. I was ready to know God in a way only the departed can, and that of which is left to my faith.

"Tonight, I want you to attack him in his sleep Charo, and the timing must be perfect, this is tricky enough and the permits are not easy to come by, but G-pops is being generous with granting our permits to challenge the heart. Knowing G, that's the easiest argument to make . . . their hearts are not into you, let me tempt it and show you?" Almost always works, even some that are so weak in faith that it breaks them, yep, I devour their souls, they are the sweetest. This guy was going to be very, very sweet. He makes me salivate, like a rabid animal. Some like to say I am, you type especially, thinking your minds are ready to grasp what I really am? Your minds can't handle changing the hour of time in your world to get more sunlight so that you can run around, like busy little ants. At least ants have a purpose, you things don't, but this is where I come in to give your life some sauce, some gravy, the dessert, the libel, the sleuth, the enmity. Love it, makes me drool. Ugh, excuse me, I had to grovel in lust for a moment, now I'm ready!

"Charo, tell me again, what's the plan?"

"Boss, you know because you came up with it and we've been training. You getting too old for this?"

"WTF did you just ask me?"

"Uh, did I stutter?"

Their laughter erupted, that laughter that hurts once you can stop, only after catching your breath, laughing again hysterically, and calming down, only to do it again until you finally settle down. This was me and Charo. We knew the plan but see what you don't understand is that love makes you laugh about things but hate makes you laugh about other things. Charo and I were laughing hysterically because we are excited, and our banter, angry profanity, is comparable to you mudbugs' telling each other I love you. Can't use that word very often, it gives me gas and since it is like a flame that shoots out your backside, yea, it's not good.

"Hey Riggs, you know when you want to set that in motion?"

"It's already in motion, it's been in motions since I had the plan."

"That's why you're the leader, you think of everything."

"What the hell do you want Charo?"

Riggs always knew when Charo wanted something special because he thought that stroking my vanity would work. Truth is, it works every time! It's my pleasure button, my solid pole, my wet. Never mind, don't have time for any of that, got to get this going if I'm ever going to kill this guy's soul.

What am I doing to the time right after high school, riding around in my green Charger with Juan? I knew that this was in my past, I couldn't understand. I saw my life back then very clearly. I see my father; he is lying in bed right after he had five-bypass surgery after suffering a heart-attack probably lasting over a couple of days. Dad wasn't much for hospitals, thus the reason he told me once he wanted to pass away outside and working (which is exactly what happened on August 29, 2010). Alicia and Julian were talking about this at one of our family gatherings at Alicia's house, her house has become the gathering center for the family, as well as the backyard at Gus and Toni's house, they have all kind of stuff and games for the children to run-around and play. They were talking about how pop left work early because of pain in his chest, mom became concerned because pop never slept in late. He would be the first to rise and greet the new day. He would make coffee (which was so weak it was more like tea, earl gray at that), and spend time outside listening to the birds' songs. My mom called Alicia, but she couldn't convince him to go to the doctor, so she called Julian and explained what was going on, so he went to the house and checked on him. Well, dad refused. Both my parents have a high tolerance for pain, so he thought it would pass but after a couple of days and no improvement, when my father told them to take him to the hospital, we knew something was really wrong.

In my dream, history rewound itself to that point in time complete with emotions, smells, and color. These were uncommon dreams for me, my dreams generally I do not remember. This was a vivid dream, like I was back there . . . visiting. I noticed that I was absent in his life, during such a time that he needed my help, and I was too busy with my depression, my desire to escape, my inability to process the severity of my father's situation. In my dream, my father walks up to me as I'm in bed in the ICU, he looks at me, turns his back and walks away. Oh, how this hurt, and I started bawling like a newborn, I cried so hard that I woke myself up, and I couldn't stop crying. It was all true, there was no falsity in that dream. I am now totally aware of my absence, what I remember, mostly what I don't remember. I do remember though, getting high and riding around, lost in myself, my hot mess of confusion and misery.

Gus hurried in and I couldn't stop crying so he put his arm on my shoulder and asked me what was wrong. "Is it your heart, are you hurting?" Through my sobs, I replied, "No, I dreamt about pop" I started sobbing again, and it really hurt because my chest had been surgically ripped apart a few days ago. "I remember how I didn't do anything to help him when he had his open-heart surgery, I was just having fun and pop really needed me, and NOW I understand how bad that was, how much pain, how helpless you are . . . I'm living it now!" I broke down even more, but my brother ever the consoler, even when he brags about being a hard ass, one of the most loving, kindhearted men that I know. Proud to call him my brother. He calmed me down, "Not only you, I was running the roads, but pop loves us, he has always loved us. I still think about these things as well, but I always go back to that." I was starting to feel better, and a little foolish, because my faith is strong and I know that pop is basking in the Light of God, then I realized it was a spiritual attack, the devil trying to throw me of my path with remorse and self-pity, so I regained it by proclaiming and with Gus as my witness, "Well, God has tested both of us with this, and we have done really well. Pop would be proud of us". I may have taken some liberty with artistic/author freedom in my recollection (I have to mention this because I know Gus will read it, and he is not shy in sharing his opinions), because Gus will call me out like he did when he noticed I used one of his go to lines, "Ask your phone", when we were outside in the back of our compound (that's what Austan calls it) one night watching the Cowboys play. Someone asked a question, and we were all taking a stab at answering it until Gus reminded those who had smart phones. I remember writing this into one of the poems in my first book of poetry God gave to me to share. I don't remember the poem but it's in Valiant Cry. I laughed when he told me, "You noticed! I didn't want to tell you; I was wondering if you would read the book." "Of course, I'm going to read it, you wrote it." "Well, that's cool, but I really wasn't sure, not everyone likes poetry and that's ok, I don't even like poetry!" We both laughed, we all laughed. That's the beauty of Gus' love, he makes you laugh, and like I said before, he is the reason that I have my memories of kissing mom and dad for years, every night saying I love you and good night. It was because he started doing that, and I followed suit, not believing that I wasn't doing it. It was like someone turning on the light and finally you could see.

Ever since I offered Jr the choice of moving to Beaumont to be closer to his parents, like God had planned, Riggs had presented him with the choices of some seedy places where he could relieve himself of his urges to wrestle with sin among those also taking part in this sour honey. There was some rejoicing in the Heavens, as there always is, when one of you makes a dash towards a more righteous decision that could impact the saving or the losing of one's soul. This was one of these moments, and he chose to move away from the temptations of Riggs-G and Charo, along with whatever other demons he would allow to play with him. Again, a grand decision for love of his parents, but this time is different, it is first for the love of God, and then everyone else. This time he has joined in this spiritual battle, he has identified the threat, and he leaves himself open to the Holy Spirit, and constantly asking for a more intimate relationship with Elohim. It's 2005 in your time, and it's a pivotal time, working in the beauty industry, where vanity runs rampant, was not a good place for my charge, it was dragging him back down to all familiar places, too familiar, and too soon because it's only been a few years since starting down a righteous path, leaving that world behind but he was also starting to drink again, which is his gateway drug, nothing loosens those chains tying up lust like vodka for him. I am relieved that he made the righteous choice, a bit forced but I had to do it. Yep, it took him having his car repossessed with only two payments left, but then Rigg's offered him a choice of going to work as a salon manager for a gay couple who were also the lead hair stylists for a prestigious beauty pageant. So familiar, but God didn't want him in that environment, so he allowed me to give his family a little scare, with their father. They found his father passed out on the kitchen floor (it was a diabetic incident), it really scared everyone, but necessary for Jr to realize that he didn't move all the way from NY to TX to live more than an hour away. He decided to quit his salon manager job at Salon Diva. It was also best for the owner and the employees that they part ways, so I was giving everyone a blessing all the way around. "You know, Santos, you should go be an accountant or a lawyer, you would probably be better at that. Managing a salon or being a hairdresser doesn't really suit you very well" was what the top stylist said to him, but it was Charro behind that, he wanted to lure him back and let his anger and pride get the best of him. It ended up being a seed that he had choices, doing hair was not the only thing he was good at. I needed him to see that, so Riggs strategy was not only not working, but it was backfiring. It would soon be time, and he would be prepared to make a spiritual journey, much like the disciples journeying to Emmaus, so that I could persuade him to choose to become a member of a Parish community, which he hadn't been a part of since back in 1985.

I was sitting in Emmaus Parish in Lakeway, TX only a few blocks from Austan's house. I was drawn to come and spend Easter weekend with him, and I scoped out this Parish because I had done Holy Week at St. Anthony Cathedral Basilica back in Beaumont. I chose Emmaus Parish, not because of its name, but because there was a brand spanking new Priest at his new Parish. As I was waiting for the Easter mass celebration to begin and as I'm sitting there praying quietly a family filed into the pew behind me. One child stood out because, being very inquisitive and chatty, he was not in the least quiet. I thought about moving, I also started thinking about how children come into church and cannot behave. The Mother was very loving and tried coaxing the child to behave along with the grandmother's efforts to the same, the child continued. When this child moved towards the father, it took on a more embattled exchange of defiance to authority. "Sit down and be quiet" scolded the father, "no" said the child as he moved towards the mother. The mother quietly explained how he needed to behave but only to have the child continue his childish behavior.

All I kept thinking was I can't keep sitting here, these people do not discipline their child at home and expect him to conform to their empty threats and loving explanation and reasoning. I thought to myself, "How do you expect him to act any differently than he acts at home, your home is where he learned this behavior." As I'm sitting there contemplating a move away from this distraction, two mothers with three children file into the pew in front of me! "Oh, my goodness" I thought to myself. Not only did these people file into the long pew in front and back of me with children I just knew would carry on with their childish behavior throughout the Easter mass celebration and distract my prayer, but they were ruining my celebrative mood.

"Who are you?" I thought to myself. I started to reason it out in my heart, which is so much different than when you reason things out in your mind. Why are you going to move? Didn't Jesus tell his disciples to let the children come? Wasn't this the same thing? How can they distract from my spirituality just from acting "childish" in church? Was my faith not stronger than this? Giving that where I am spiritually, aren't I in communion with God, Jesus and the Holy Spirit every second of every day? I decided at this moment not to move, and that God was delivering a message. I didn't get the message, but I knew this was not just a coincidence . . . nothing God does is happenstance.

While I was sitting there waiting for mass to begin and using my whole being to not let the evil one defile my thoughts about the meaning of Easter; trying to use what really gets to me . . . children acting up in church and the parents' inability to keep order. I was firm in my resolve that I was not going to move and that I would take part in the mass and not let anyone distract from what had started with a 7:30AM phone call, inviting me to take part in the Easter religious celebration.

A moment before the mass began this little boy said something that shocked his mother, grandmother and father. At first, he said it very softly but assuredly, but they didn't hear him and neither did I. They asked him to repeat it, and this is where I heard the shock in their voices as to what he had said. He repeated it a little louder and with more confidence and assurance. He said that he wanted to go to Jesus and be with him now. His grandmother at once started telling him that he didn't mean what he said because he still had his entire life before him. His mother lovingly explained that after living his life to the fullest, his desire to be with Jesus would be fulfilled, but not right now. The child insisted that he wanted to go and be with Jesus at this very moment. The grandmother said, "But my child, you still have to live your life . . . you will have a girlfriend and get married, you will have children and then after your life is over . . . you can be with Jesus but wait until you have lived your life."

The Easter mass procession started, and the children remained well behaved and quiet throughout the celebration to my amazement and gratitude to God, for the lessons I learned during these 25 minutes before mass. It takes reflection to get what had happened and to figure out what I should do if ever in this situation again because I do not want my first reaction to be judgmental as it was in this instance. I thought that Austan would go with me, but he decided at the last moment not to go. I reflected and by the grace of God, I realized the importance of this trip, to remind me that I must not be blind to Jesus, I know Him, He has revealed Himself and the importance that I worship in both Spirit and Truth because these are the types of worshippers that God seeks because He is Spirit and I must worship my Father in Spirit and Truth.

It's all set, we will attack in the summer of 2017. It will start with filling his mind like the tinnitus that's always ringing in Jr's ears (a chronic injury from his military days), we would remind him of all his sins, as he walks around the Hike and Bike trail on the outskirts of the west end of Beaumont. It is four miles if you take the trail that leads to the soccer fields. It is a beautiful trail, with a modern wide concrete sidewalk, a perfect four-mile square with resting areas at all four corners, but once committed to the two miles, there is no turning back, you are committed to four miles at that point. He comes here to walk and pray his bead chain . . . it has a name, but I can't say it, don't wanna say it anyway! J's sorry excuse for a mother came up with it as a comfort and way of being with her son, using it to pray as she contemplated the meaning of all the mysteries that G revealed through JC. Waste of time if you ask me! Bunch of mumbling, useless same words and just repeating them, makes no sense, G probably just rolls his eyes. This is what me and Riggs were telling him as he is making his way around this path, crying, distraught, mourning his mommy, grown man . . . nothing can help you now. We got him good and confused, starting to doubt everything that G has gifted to Him, the unappreciative scoundrel. He's believing it, he got nothing from those prayers! I can feel the sweetness of his fear, his terror that the prayers and that chain of balls could actually bring him comfort or closer to G, what an idiot.

It's July 4, 2017. Only a couple of months ago my mother passed onto the last leg of her faith journey and I cannot remember another time that I felt so alone, that was May 9, 2017. My dad passed away in 2012, but mom and I leaned on each other, by keeping each other company. When we arrived at the funeral home, we stood together next to pop and held hands, she said to me, which broke my heart, "Mijo, somos los dos, no me dejes sola." "Nunca ama," I whispered back to her, making a promise to pop right there just as we had spoken before about moving back to take care of both of them. I just had built up the courage after one of his friends came up to me and I nearly broke down in front of mom, as I leaned in to hug and cry, he gently, but sternly took my hands in his and said, "Sér fuerte." This snapped me back into reality, I would break down later but for now, my mother needed a strong son to lean on. I can't imagine what it's like to lose your first and only love of over 55 years of marriage. The sudden departure of my dad, with absolutely no indication that this would be the time that God called him home. I say He called him home because, as I will explain, God did just that because my father finally aligned his will with the will of God, and dad settled into his faith, completely surrendering to it, without any reservations. He didn't know it at the time; five days before he had proclaimed this choice he made, to align his will with that of God. My mom faced this courageously and faithfully, it really hurt, and I could tell that it was a pain like no other, but she was strong for her family, and she did it all with so much love.

So now that you know how distraught I was at the loss of my mom, I can tell you this: I visited my parent's gravesite every single day and sometimes twice a day for almost two years because I was lost without a real purpose for my life. Especially profound in my sadness I felt the tug of my old self, wrestling with demons and knowing I was putting Mel through the ringer, but I had to, I couldn't fight alone, and Jesus told us we wouldn't have to fight alone. You know by now, when I mean spiritual fighting, it means diving deeper into the love of God because there is nothing else that can defeat the lies. On July 4, 2017, I was especially melancholy . . . yea, like I use that word in daily conversation. I was just sad and lonely, missing my mom and my dad, but more my mom because she had just passed away and like I said, when a wonderful mother passes away there is nothing worse than the woman who carried you and looked lovingly into your eyes for the first time, there is already a connection so deep that it is the closest thing to the love of God. I know for some this ain't so, but for me, I was pensive this day. I decided to go for a walk at the hike and bike trail, a two mile paved square trail in the middle of green naturally manicured land with a small lake in the middle, bunches of trees and open area rolling up and down and straight across like a plush green carpet kissed by the sun or on some days cold, wet, and gusting winds that whirl and whip around with no real cover. This day was particularly quiet because everyone was celebrating the fourth of July. I parked my car and walked towards the paved pathway and started my walk. As usual I started praying a Rosary, I don't remember what mystery I was contemplating, but praying with the Rosary and reflecting on the mysteries Jesus Christ revealed was especially calming and safe for me during my grief, the Rosary was extremely special to me. My affection for the Rosary developed when pop passed away; I must have prayed for hours on my knees on the red concrete porch of the casita the evening we came back from the hospital without pop. I turned to God for strength, because I knew Him to be the only one who can ease my anxiety and fear.

As I make my third 90° right turn and come to the last prayer on my Rosary, this overwhelming feeling that my prayers were just repetitive words with no real love attached to them. Empty prayers, is what kept buzzing into my mind, quipping fantastical lies of what the devil was going to testify to at judgement day, to act as my accuser, a town Cryer—if you will, of all my sins. "Your hands are so dirty; I'm surprised your hands don't burn. I will be there in the end, testifying to all your sins, your words aren't going to save you, how can you even think that God can hear you?" were the types of things that the devil was wrapping around my head, it permeated the air around me and I felt low and embarrassed, and fraught with fear because praying the Rosary had always brought me so much peace in times of great sorrow or tribulation.

This time praying the Rosay didn't bring me any comfort, and I became terrified. I started calling out to God in my distress, with all the love in my heart I asked God if what the devil was telling me was true because it all sounded like the truth to me. "Please God, help me, I'm too weak right now to fight, to think clearly, I need you." I had my head hung low as I'm walking, I can't even look up because I was so ashamed. I was moved to look up at the blue sky in front of me and as I raised my head looking high up in the sky, I saw this V shaped cloud and as I'm gazing upon it, slowly another cloud rose behind it out of the top of the V, it was two mounds, like a cut off figure 8 turned sideways rising from behind this V shaped cloud, to form a heart! I immediately looked down to the pavement, ashamed to look upon something like that, thinking myself unworthy as the devil is still screeching in my ear. "Is that really you God, or do I just want to see a heart in the sky?" "Look up and to the left", said God. I looked up and to the left and the word LOVE was spelled out, but because God knows what I do for a living, working at a non-profit as a legal advocate for immigration, a job He inspired me to take, as a test of my newfound faith and trust in

God. God wrote LOVE in Times Roman, but the open spaces of the O&V were solid, but the word itself was distinctly LOVE. I thought to take my cell phone out to take a picture, but it didn't seem right, I felt that this was an incredibly special moment between God and I. Plus, I thought, the people of faith would believe the picture, the non-believers . . . the doubter and haters, they would never believe it anyway, so I left it a private moment between God and I but I share it as a testimony, with the same reaction I described, you believe or you don't, but I have no reasons to lie, I share out of love. At the moment I saw the word LOVE, my spirit was comforted, it was joyful and at peace! "It is not enough for you to pray the Rosary; I want you to start making them. They will be one-of-a-kind and unique, just like each of you, and none of them will be duplicated. I will tell you who to give them to, and you can start making them for your family and all those that were friends to your parents, and those who helped or supported your parents or you." I couldn't wait to get to my car, I had to go to the store and buy the things I needed to make the first Rosary.

What a beautiful Rosary, it was all red roses with lilac beads because my mother loved roses and the color lilac, so all the Rosaries would have roses or lilac or both. Because I didn't know how to shop for sales and too excited to wait and price things out, it cost me way more than I thought, and I have had several conversations with God about this ministry since then and now after six years, I've learned that God will provide and I only need to be open to the promptings of the Holy Spirit and to be obedient to God's will. I struggled to know whose Rosary it was, God doesn't give you an instruction manual, or directions . . . this only comes with faith, obedience, and a curiosity for righteousness. These are the directions and instructions. I was having a challenging time of it, because how was I supposed to know? I went to Mass at St. Anthony Cathedral Basilica, my Parish now, as I had been doing every Sunday ever since Mother's Day, only a couple of days after we buried my mother, with my cousin Ari. They Holy Spirit moved her to spend the day with me and not my Tia Delma, whom I love very much, and we've had wonderful spiritual conversations. She opened up to me, as Ari and I drove to Atascocita to drop off her mom after the funeral. Ari and I drove back to Beaumont that Saturday night, and when we woke up to go to church, we were late getting to the Mass at St. Jude Thaddeus. We were hurrying across the parking lot, when I abruptly stopped, Ari stopped and we looked at each other, "I don't like walking in late to Mass", I said to Ari. "I don't either", so we looked for another Parish celebrating Mass soon that we could get to on time. We found it, it was the Mother Church of the Diocese of Beaumont in downtown, only a couple of blocks from the house. Since I never really went there but a few times, I wasn't certain of the Mass times, I wasn't really going to Mass at this time, even after Emmaus because none of these changes has been like snapping my fingers and voila! Nope, don't work this way, maybe for a rare bunch, but it was a process with me.

I was sitting in one of the middle-left pews about ten pews from the front row, the pew was empty because I had arrived early so that I could pray on this, the first Rosary that I made in memory of my mother. More time I could spend with God, making these Rosaries! I loved it, but nervous of who it belonged to and that I get it right. I was praying on whether it belonged to my Tia Delma who was going through a spiritual drought or Bishop Pfiefer who administered the Sacrament of the Sick . . . twice! I just knew it was for one of them, but I was praying for God to reveal which one of the two would be receiving it. As the Mass proceeded, I was recalling all the wonderful years that I had with my parents, the honor of spending some adulthood years living with them, laughing with them, crying with them, taking vacations to Cheto, calling them on the phone just to say I was on my way home. All the things you can only experience when you live with someone, not living in your own home and visiting, it's not the same. I wanted to experience all the time we had left together, because God also would remind me that I wouldn't have my parents my whole life, and I was grateful for these reminders! Like the time I became angry because my father cooked me breakfast, and my dad really liked weird things because of his humble beginnings he would make a meal of some strange things. Well, on the rare occasions that my mother was not awake and cooked me breakfast before I left for work, my father would cook me something. This particular morning, he made me Fritos with eggs, the only problem is that my dad would put the oil in the pan, put the Fritos in there, and then the eggs, but my mom would put the oil, put the eggs and then the Fritos. This would keep the Fritos crunchy and keep them from tasting like the cooking oil, because my dad's way the Fritos would soak up a bunch of oil and change the taste entirely. I made tacos out of the breakfast my dad cooked, I knew what it would taste like because I had my dad's cooking before, and it definitely was not near as good as mom's cooking, no one cooked like my mom, which most kids think their mom is the best cook or you have that one favorite meal, I had many favorites of mom's. Sure enough it tasted like overcooked oil, the Fritos were all soggy and the eggs, scrambled hard. I was angrier than my dad when my nephew Angel convinced him to ride a ride at the Texas State Fair that spun you around real fast and gravity would plaster you up a padded wall as it twisted up and down, my dad was so mad at Angel over that, but we all had a good laugh telling that story. My dad only did it because Angel was crying about it, and no one wanted to ride it with him. My dad would do anything for his grandchildren. After taking a bite of that taco, I grimaced and my anger crept up, God said, "Why are you getting angry? You know you will miss these moments when I call your father home."

A family of four slid into the pew I was sitting in, and shortly after the Mass began. I was totally in a spiritual place when attending Mass, and it's almost like an out of body experience. As we started making our way to receive the Eucharist, and I returned to my pew, I noticed the family of four were no longer in the pew, and they should have gotten there before me. I turned back towards the front and noticed the father in front of the portrait of our Blessed Mother, and his wife and two boys (one about seven the other about five years old) were facing the congregation just waiting for him to finish and rejoin them, but what got my attention spiritually was that they were patiently waiting. They didn't make their way back to the pew separated, but as a family! This was different, my heart pointed out. I waited and didn't have to wait long before they came back to the pew and the boys both tapped one knee to the floor, made the sign of the Cross and slid into the pew. What a display of faith from kids so young, I felt it in my heart, but I didn't really think beyond that. As the Priest was giving us the final blessing and the Mass ended, I still didn't have my answer about the Rosary I had just made. We are singing the final hymn and the Priest passed our pew and the hymn came to an end, the family started exiting the pew. It was at this very moment, when the wife and their youngest boy exited the pew, that God told me, "The Rosary belongs to them." I froze and was terrified, "I didn't know the first one was going to be for complete strangers! Let me work up the nerve." God answered, "Don't take too long, they are already leaving, and I really would prefer you do it in my House, not outside." "Ok, ok, ok, I can do this", I was thinking to myself and just before the father exited the pew, I gently grabbed his elbow and asked him if I could speak to him and his wife for a brief moment. He looked surprised and confused but he called his wife over and she entered the pew in front of the one her husband, their older son, and I were standing in, she did this so she could get closer. I explained how God told me to start making Rosaries and that my mom passed only a couple of months ago. I explained that God told me who they were for, and this very first one was their Rosary, and I continued, not thinking about what I was saying because I trusted in God to give me the words. What I told them next can only be by the prompting of the Holy Spirit because my mother loved crafts, she loved cooking for her family, she loved so many things, her family was everything and all things for her, and she stayed here as long as she could before the doctor's told her and us that there was nothing else they could do. "My mother loved roses and the color lilac, so this is why your Rosary has roses and the color lilac." Without thinking, I said, "She also loved baseball and Elvis." The father, surprised and astonished, said "My name is Elvis, did you know that?" "No, how could I, I've never met you." I told them that this was God confirming that this was their Rosary. I hurried and excused myself, because I was about to lose it, right there in the house of God. I was stunned, but elated because satan was whispering in my ear again, "Who do you think you are, I know who you are . . . a dirty sinner!" Well, God just confirmed with that one experience, once again the devil is a liar and I am doing what God wants me to do, keep it up. It was only when I got into my car, and contemplated everything that happened, and as I replayed it all looking to be enlightened on every detail from the time I arrived to when I left. I then realized, and I almost screamed with excitement, their older boy had been wearing a baseball uniform! My spirit was in a good mood. Now, after about 465 Rosaries, none of which are duplicates, all of which are one-of-a-kind and unique, there are so many more confirmations and testimonies from those who have received one.

Now that my charge is completely living his faith, not just lip service, but living out scripture and putting into play all the promises of Jesus, His intimate relationship with God has giving him the strength to discern without doubt, and he can resist temptations more frequently, and he has had many a spiritual battle, all making his faith stronger, his resolve liken to titanium and a love as warm and bright as the sun. Even as his personal life is joyful and full, his professional life working in a wing of God's house that puts into action the call of Jesus to feed the hungry, counsel the brokenhearted, welcome the stranger, in the name of God, he never knew that Riggs could disrupt and make it the most toxic place that he had ever experienced full of powerful demons that do what they do best to those blind to the spiritual warfare raging, they disrupt, divide, and make efforts fruitless, wasteful, and misdirected. Events are still unfolding which threaten the very team that everyone is so proud of, saying one thing and doing another. This is Rigg's and Charo's open playbook, but free will plays into their hands, people choose fear, pride, and envy over obvious workings and promptings of the Holy Spirit because Riggs blinds them of these things, while others cling to Riggs and Charo because they offer something comfortable in this world, denial and pity for themselves and those weak enough to be misled or bamboozled. This fight for my charge's soul, or for any one of you, is ongoing and the more intimate the relationship with Elohim, the more they will try to dissuade you from your true calling, the calling to righteousness. The next attack is right around the corner, but I'm swaying more influence and Jr is making most of the right choices.

I felt my heart drop into my stomach, her words seemed to envelope me, taken me up high and then dropping me like a rock onto concrete.

Instantly I felt embarrassed, ashamed, remorseful, that I had forgotten my dad on the day he left this world, and I was so self-absorbed telling everyone that I was almost finished with this book. Proud that last night, it started sinking in that I was soon going to be a published novelist and author a story I had been wanting to share all in one spot, instead of stories here and there, with that and this person. I didn't say anything, because of the shame, how could I admit that to her and Terry? All the talk of how I remember them and honor them, pray for them, and I forget the most important day regarding my father? Wow! I haven't changed at all when it comes down to it. Susana kept telling me about one of her kid's cousins died of an overdose, they didn't know if it was on purpose or not, even Austan was telling me about how one of his fellow soldiers "Bit the bullet". None of that sunk in, I prayed for them as I found out, and like I asked Austan, "What if I told you that I already prayed for him, even though Austan was just telling me that his friend died in June, almost three months ago! He didn't answer, guessing it was a rhetorical question, so I continued "I pray for all departing souls, several years ago I started including all those who die in my prayers, especially those who have no one praying for them. This is separate than my prayers for all those in Purgatory, especially those who have no one praying for them. None of this knocked me over the head like the question Susana just asked me, "When did your dad die? Was it on the 29th?"

I said my goodbyes, it was getting late anyway. Appropriate time, since I had to process this abnormality of forgetting my father on the day he left this life and journeyed home. We had been watching the second blue full moon today, August 30, 2023, we watched it as it rose in the East over the Sabine River. Susana and Terry live on the bank of the Sabine River, it is beautiful out there . . . so peaceful and nature just yells at you to get your attention out there. I wasn't surprised at Susana's question, she has this great way about her where deaths weigh heavy on her spirit, more about the weight of the responsibility and the empathy she has for those who depart. I remembered how when I first moved back to Beaumont, after my paper run (I worked as a city circulation manager for the local newspaper) I would go hang out with her and it was mutually beneficial because I was hyped up on energy after a physical exertion in the wee hours of the morning, where it was still dark out, and working into the morning and sometimes getting done just before noon because the printing press was old and would often require stopping and starting so we would get the papers late. Anyway, I would go hang out with Suzi (what I called her when she was real young) and Andrea, because she was too young to go to school yet. Susana benefitted from this because she had just lost her father and it was tough on her but only because she was also raising three girls on her own. We had known each other since childhood because she is Juan's sister, but it wasn't until we started hanging out after work that we became close friends, and later, Bible buddies. We can talk about God and all His creation all the time, and we never get tired. Her because she is like a kid in a candy store (living in her faith) and me, because I have never had such an intimate relationship with God, and I am also like a kid in a candy store! This is living, but back then we were both trying to adjust to a new reality, a vastly different and painful reality.

I was going on and on about my birth month having the largest moon of 2023 and the second blue moon all during my birthday month. It was a beautiful site to see, for sure, and to share it with these two was very cool. Terry reminds me a lot of Austan, MacGyver rednecks, I'm so impressed with their skill, courage, and common sense, but both have this darkness that their light of love wants to extinguish but can't quite let go of a part of them that serves as a family tribute, but they have this strong desire because of, in Terry's case, Susana; in Austan's case, it's me. They love us to death, but our love of God is offensive and foreign to them. I can't put my finger on Terry's deal, but I've pegged Austan's as being angry with God. I kinda figured it out, but you can never be too sure about these things until someone decides they want to open up completely but in Austan, and in some sense Terry also, I don't think they know and this is what messes with their head and heart . . . how can we be so damn sure about God and all the things we credit Him with. I was glad to be out here, but not to handle such a big thud, that's the sound my ego made as Suzi finished asking that question. "Yes" was all I could answer, because inside was like one of those black holes imploding within itself sucking everything into nothingness. For all I was doing, what did it amount to that I forgot about the man that made my life possible, the father who provided for me so well that I never wanted for anything, who would stroke my back as I'm throwing up in a trash can off the side of my bed, the man who would wake me up on Saturday mornings and take me to the backdoor of our house and we would stand there. He would tell me listen son, listen to all those birds singing. He never tired nor forgot about me! He would always encourage me to make good friends and "Be happy", and to find a church. He planted seeds all of my life, like always saying a simple blessing after he ate "Gracias a Dios", every time. Today, I realized I forgot him.

I hug Susana and shake hands with Terry bidding them good night, all the while feeling like a phony. "Remember you can back all the way up when you back up" Suzi said, and Suzi like her twin brothers Juan and Jose (aka Head) well, their normal talking is like yelling for others. "Ok, good night, I love you guys". Maybe if I just ignored it, I wouldn't feel so sad and bothered, but it seemed to be getting worse in my head. That question she posed kept replaying in my head, along with the feeling that came with it. I started down their winding County Road, dark but litten up by the full blue moon, still casting shadows across the packed road, wide enough for only one car, doing only 15 miles an hour out of respect for those who live on this road. As I'm driving away, I keep wallowing in my misery while completely clueless as to how I could have forgotten. I started analyzing my week which isn't hard to do considering it is only Wednesday, and I start to get excited as the Holy Spirit enlightened me to another awesome grace and blessing God has bestowed on His humble servant! I texted Carol, who on Monday night asked me if I could take her hour of Adoration at St. Anne's and I gladly accepted, because as I told her the next day when she thanked me at work, that I wasn't surprised when I received her text because I was feeling that I needed to go to Adoration (of the blessed Sacrament, sometimes I forget that some don't know what I'm talking about, especially if they are not Catholic). I texted because I wanted to confirm what I was slowly realizing . . . and she confirmed it! She replied, " . . . It was Tuesday, 7-8AM."

Oh, God! Can it be that you are with me like this?! You never cease to amaze me, that a sovereign God who created everything, and is all power-ful, is still actively involved in this wretch's life. As I'm winding down the CR from Suzi's and Terry's house, and I get to the intersection with Hwy 87, I may have forgotten, but the Holy Spirit had not. The Adoration hour that Carol requested I cover was on the same day that my dad had left this world! The Holy Spirit moved all this, just because He knew, that it would debilitate me, and then I wouldn't finish this love story. I was elated, God had remembered, and compelled to pray all four mysteries of the Rosary then went to work, like it was just another normal calendar day. I never remembered that this date had a powerful and heavy meaning to me. I even had a stranger, to me, come by the office because Sue Hebert had told her about me and my Rosary ministry, and that I could probably repair the Rosaries she wanted me to fix. None of this was happening by coincidence or anything else, but God who could do this. With this, God has told me that I am on the right track, I may fall and stumble, but I know that God is a merciful and forgiving God. Anything is possible! I'm not sure what comes next in this spiritual warfare, or my life living my faith, evangelizing through my life, my art, my writing, my poetry, everything, and all things but I do know that I have two masters, I love God and hate the other who just coerced me into forgetting my dad. I had been drawn to this Scripture, the one about serving two masters. I wondered what exactly Jesus meant when he said that. On the one hand He says you can't serve two masters but then it gets confusing with, you will love one and hate the other. I mean what does that mean, I asked of God many and several times. I think I finally understand this, and this is my current situation, I'm serving two masters, and yes, I love one but hate the other.

Since I know there is a Heaven, and Scripture enlightens us to the Truth, because the Holy Spirit inspired men to act according to the will of God, our Father, that my father Santos is still praying for me, and all his family. Jesus and dad had a hand in guiding my spirit all the while my physical existence had forgotten, this is true, but so is the fact that God knew I would be devastated so He took care of me. I was sitting with Him for an hour, and I am always praying that He wipe his, and my mother's robes white, with the Blood of the Lamb, forgiving their sins. So, because Carol allowed her to be moved by the Holy Spirit, questioning but I think somehow knowing something felt right about it, she asked me if I could take her hour, an hour that I know is dear to her heart because it was for me when I was doing that right after my mom took her journey home. The mystery of the Eucharist is because He loved us and would not let us be sentenced to an eternal death. Too often, He sits ignored in many a parish throughout the world, but I imagine more so in what is often referred to as modern industrial nations. I just know that God is here, by way of the Triune God because he answered prayers to intervene, while I remained clueless in remembering the day my father journeyed home. God saves me from myself yet again. I'm sure it will not be the last time, I have yet to rule over the sin that grabbed me in my youth, the fifth grade, sneaky attack and I was blind, what was my excuse as a fifty-seven year old that has been saved from myself so very often, that makes me guarantee you that what God has revealed is true, it is available to anyone who wants to love God and put Him first. Everything else will fall into place, not on your timing, but He gives you this thing called joy which is a light that will never be extinguished, subdued, lessened, nor dulled. Back in the garden when Jesus was talking about that cup, " . . . let it pass . . . " what do you think He meant? He had just spoken during His transfiguration about things that were about to happen, He wasn't scared of the devil in the desert, He wasn't afraid of the storm, nor the power of man, political nor religious. What was in the cup? I'll tell you what I think, which keeps me grounded and reaching for the stars at the same time, separation from God. I mean think of it, Jesus was always with God from the beginning, at creation and before, He was with God, God in Him, Him in God, both in Spirit, all in one acting intentionally for their glory and adoration. Because of sin, just like in the garden (see that, those things we often miss the fall happened in a garden and the redemption happened in a garden, where Jesus decided . . . made a choice . . . just like we make choices every day.

My love has deepened, I am joyful, and I am at peace. Open your heart to God and no matter the tribulations, He walks with you . . . loving you every step of the way. Question for myself, at 57 years old, still a work in progress, will I take this opportunity, and with the Grace of God, finally get serious and make that choice to rule over those God put me over and right under Him. We are His children, and if my dad is any indication of God's love, and God's love is immeasurable . . . we are in for a real treat when we get home. This is why I was kinda bummed that I didn't get the chance to go home May 14, 2020, I opened my eyes, realized that I was baptized, I was capsized by sin, but God had other plans, so I march on . . . what adventures await me in this, God's love story!

Meet the Real You

God whispers,

my heart blushes,

and receives it with joyful ecstasy.

His love comforts me with peace.

He lifts my soul to be with Him,

light enters and surrounds me.

Overflowing from Him, it enters inside,

and radiates outside of me.

The dawn is new, my soul renewed.

A new day has arrived.

and I am no longer my own.

but more aware of the me of tomorrow.

That destination where love reigns.

Where Living Water flows

and no one ever feels alone.

Refreshed and fulfilling,

willing, and obedient,

I return to love.

God calls.

Awaken my love,

I have a love story to tell.

Come in from the dark

and awaken into a new heart,

because you exist

for Love to love,

and for you to love others.

There is always a sacrifice,

a payment tendered.

Pride, envy, and hate must be abandoned,

and surrendered.

There is no space in your heart . . .

Love cannot commingle.

Not with evil, fear, division and defeat,

quite the opposite my dear,

Love is all you will ever need . . .

Amen, amen . . . I am Love,

and I whisper your name.

"Here I am Lord"

Is the only loving reply.

To Dignify.

To Sanctify.

To Glorify.

Love embraces your life.

Meet the real you,

enshrined and existing in Love.

This is what I had in mind

when I made you,

the real you.

Santos

mi apraciable hijo ahoy tomo
el lapies para saludarte desiando y
te hincuentres bien pues Gracia a Dios
nosotros bien todos aqui todos buenos me
tengas Cuidado aqui temando pueos viles y
me telefono EXXON que lee ablaras bueno pues
tamien te digo que si Estas con unos amigos
te fijes bien que sellan buenos amigos ten
Cuidado ño bueno te boy adeir desde que me dejate
lo que eme dejiste no me siento agusto yo Leso
mancho para que buelbas a lo que Eres le Leso
a mi Dios pero yo te quiero muncho higua
que a todos y me duele pero me aguanto
bueno mi hijo Saludes de todos y buena
Suerte y pues te recomindo mires un dotor
ay munchos que es an curado bueno mi hijo te
desiamos buena Suerte sin mas quien te aprecia Santos y

dangerous place
Beaumont couple's son serves in Somalia

U.S. ARMY NEWS SERVICE

MOGADISHU, Somalia — The sudden burst of automatic gunfire breaks the silence of the hot summer evening, reminding startled American soldiers and airmen that gangs still roam the streets at night.

While the coalition forces in Operation Restore Hope have established control throughout Somalia and convoys of food are reaching the outlying areas safely, soldiers still face danger.

Army Cpl. Santos J. Hernandez, 25, son of Santos N. and Guadalupe R. Hernandez of Beaumont, is in Somalia with members of the 210th Forward Support Battalion from Fort Drum, N.Y.

"Right now I'm a commander's driver, but I also repair all field telephones and switchboards," Hernandez said.

The newly 10,000 American military personnel still in Somalia are scattered throughout the country to ensure convoys reach their destination safely. The soldiers and airmen have overseen the establishment of food distribution centers and field hospitals.

Sniper fire still exists in the cit-

Photo courtesy of U.S. Army

Cpl. Santos J. Hernandez tests newly installed telephone equipment while serving in Somalia.

ies. Most Americans are not used to the heat. Most of the snakes and spiders in the country are poison-

ous, and many of the domestic and wild animals are believed to be rabid.

Serving in Somalia with members of the United Nations in a humanitarian effort is something new for soldiers, but they are adapting to it.

"The U.S. has the ability to get ahead, but in places like this, the people need outside help and we can supply it," said Hernandez.

The destruction caused by the warlords in Somalia is evident. Many of the buildings in the cities have been destroyed, and the rest are riddled with bullet holes. Electricity and water are practically nonexistent, and many people live in little more than tarp-covered animal pens.

Operation Restore Hope is a massive undertaking requiring the efforts of all the coalition forces. Americans are currently positioned in every major city and patrol all of the major highways and most of the secondary roads in the country.

"I'm glad the U.S. military is being used as a tool of provision here," Hernandez said. "I'm proud to be part of such a professional military. We're capable of protecting as well as helping those in need."

208

211

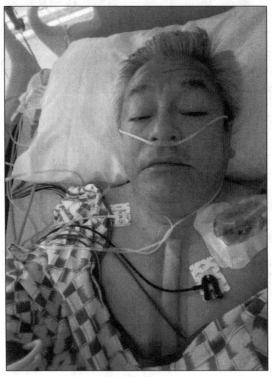